THOSE WERE THE DAYS

Also by Phaedra Greenwood

Beside the Rio Hondo
North with the Spring
Drinking from the Stream

Also by Jim Levy

Corazón (and Merkle)
Cooler Than October Sunlight
The Poems of Caius Herennius Felix
Joy to Come
The Fifth Season
Rowdy's Boy
Mar Egeo
Monet's Eyes
Seen from a Distance

Also by Phaedra Greenwood

Beside the Rio Hondo
North with the Spring
Drinking from the Stream

Also by Jim Levy

Corazón (and Merkle)
Cooler Than October Sunlight
The Poems of Caius Herennius Felix
Joy to Come
The Fifth Season
Rowdy's Boy
Mar Egeo
Monet's Eyes
Seen from a Distance

THOSE WERE THE DAYS

LIFE AND LOVE IN 1970S NEW MEXICO

Phaedra Greenwood and Jim Levy

Atalaya Press

Copyright © 2019 by Phaedra Greenwood and Jim Levy
All rights reserved. No part of this publication may be reproduced, distributed, or transmitted in any form or by any means, including photocopying, recording, or other electronic or mechanical methods, without the prior written permission of the authors, except in the case of brief quotations embodied in critical reviews and certain other non-commercial uses permitted by copyright law.

Atalaya Press
Printed in the United States of America

ISBN: 978-1-7337940-0-8

For Alexander and Sara

ACKNOWLEDGEMENTS

Thanks to Christina Haas for formatting the book and to those who read drafts of it and made many valuable suggestions: Michelle Potter, Bonnie Korman, Bob Bishop, and Linda Fair.

Those Were the Days was a popular song sung by Mary Hopkin. It hit number two on the Billboard 100.

Authors' Note

Those Were The Days was originally a 500 page manuscript written for our children. Relying on letters, journals and scrapbooks, we described how we met, how they came about and the first ten years of their lives in a small Hispanic village. When we finished, we realized that our story was a common one in the 1970s. Two people under the influence of hippie values and excesses, living on the fringe of society, find each other, learn the meaning of love and commitment, buy property, raise their children, and are absorbed into mainstream America.

We have changed the names of some of the people who might wish to be anonymous. Other than that, it's all true, and anyone who lived in those days in northern New Mexico can testify to that.

                Phaedra Greenwood and Jim Levy
                Arroyo Hondo, New Mexico
                March 2019

Contents

Stormy Weather 1
To Cross the Great Water 61
Home Sweet Home 137
Stepping Up 239
Epilogue 319

Stormy Weather

Phaedra

In 1972 when Jim and I were still writing love letters to each other – though we lived in the same house – I wrote: "I think we would be great collaborating on a book. I've worked out a special formula. I start at the end and you start at the beginning and we'll work our way towards the middle. Just don't kill any of the characters. Toss in all our scraps. Then throw the whole thing down the stairs and rearrange it according to which steps the scenes land on. God! If you ever get your hands on my stuff, I'd better start burning."

Well, I didn't burn those first spiral notebooks that I scribbled in to save my sanity. And Jim was keeping a journal, too. So here it is, after all these years, our mutual memoir, letters and journal entries in alternating voices about the first ten years of our relationship, how we met and eventually married. Of course it's about our nuclear family, but it also serves as a window into hippie life in Taos during those wild and roughshod days, for we were surrounded and influenced by the communes. Young people threw out the rules and set out to reinvent themselves; disillusioned radicals and rebels strove to transform society into something more healthy and sustainable. Many tried to return to the land to grow lettuce and raise goats and chickens. (Even in the high mountain desert!) To share the goods, the children and each other. But they discovered that free love wasn't free. The end results were comical . . . and sometimes tragic.

By 1968 when I "dropped out" I wasn't young and idealistic anymore. I was twenty-seven and had been married three times. The first husband was my high school sweetheart and that lasted a year because he drank. I left him for an ex-con who was bisexual and after two years with him, I headed for what I thought was higher ground and I married a poet who cheated on me. It's called serial monogamy.

I had always thought I would have children but fortunately I hadn't had any yet. After taking LSD, I read a mountain of books on mysticism and Tom Wolfe's *The Electric Kool-Aid Acid Test*. I worked a year as a medical secretary at Yale-New Haven Hospital and saved half my income, which amounted to about $1500. I bought my first car, a VW bug, and drove across country to Oregon to tell Ken Kesey that I liked *Sometimes a Great Notion* and to ask him if he had had any out-of-the-body experiences. Two weeks later I found myself bouncing along in a rag-tag caravan of buses as part of the "Please Force" to help supervise the crowd at the Woodstock festival. A week after that we were hired to do another festival at Dallas. Then on to New Mexico where I landed at the Hog Farm commune twenty-five miles from Taos. When I first set foot on the plaza in Taos, heard people speaking Spanish, and saw the big blue mountain hovering over the town, I knew I was home.

Thanks to the living conditions at the commune, I ended up in Holy Cross Hospital with Hepatitis B, pneumonia, malnutrition and dysentery. Over my first winter in Taos, living with friends, I slowly recovered. I was broke, on food stamps, but sitting over the heating grate working on a novel called *Off the Bus*, about my immersion in the hippie world while I was at Woodstock. I suffered from the illusion that the book would *sell and I would get back the nest egg I had blown on the Pranksters and the Hog Farm. At the time, it made karmic sense.*

Over the next year I struggled to find my niche in the community. There were no jobs in the paper; the unemployment office had nothing to offer. A woman at Taos Pueblo said, "In Taos you have to offer a product or a service." I did some copywriting for a friend. I started making bead rings and selling them at Seven Rays Gallery, but that wasn't enough to keep me going. I accepted an offer to be night watchman at the Taos Municipal Airport. I lived out there in a trailer for a couple of months, without pay. I could have applied at Holy Cross Hospital and returned to medical typing, but I couldn't bring myself to do it. I was a writer. That's how I wanted to make my living. I submitted a piece of "automatic writing" to an alternative rag called The Fountain of Light. They not only published it, but the editor paid me fifteen dollars and asked for a piece for the next issue. I was elated. Not that I could live on $15 a month, but it was a start.

Jim
We – my wife Deirdre and I and her two children Evelyn age eight and Edward, whom everyone called Ewar, age five – came to Taos from Mexico in a VW van in May 1969 with a white rat named Fortunata smuggled over the border rolled in a sleeping bag. We had been living for a year in Ajijic on Lake Chapala, where the scene was crazy. The scene in Taos was crazy too. It didn't take us long to realize that hippies were not welcome. There were subtle signs on pickup trucks: *Destroy the Hippies.* A sign in a café

window said: *Keep America Beautiful. Take a Hippie to a Carwash.* The week we arrived, *The Taos News* reported that the Town Council had cancelled Fiestas because of the possibility of "an influx of undesirables" and the Taos Municipal Education Association had passed a resolution that declared "the hippie's presence among our people poses a real and verifiable danger to the moral health and beliefs of our youth, because of their known excesses in drug addiction, sexual and obscene behavior, personal filth and general exhibitionism."

It didn't occur to us that they were speaking about us.

My best friend, Harvey Mudd, who had moved to Taos in 1966 and bought land, loaned us an old adobe in Arroyo Hondo. It was small, with three rooms, about 800 square feet. Harvey said it was built around 1910 and the foundation was just stones fit together. The village was poor; the roads were dirt and had no names – the few that had names had no signs. Although Deirdre and I had Bachelor degrees and teaching credentials from Berkeley, we didn't mind living without indoor plumbing or a phone – in fact we thought it was glamorous. We planted a garden of squash, peas, beans, and corn. We learned about the acequia that ran behind our back door and the skunks that lived under the house. We wore overalls and wielded our shovels in imitation of the old mayordomo who walked the ditches every day of the year.

Like our counter-culture neighbors, Deirdre and I "returned" to the land – a hypothetical return because my family was Jewish from Los Angeles via Newark and Germany and Deirdre's was Catholic from New Jersey via

Ireland. My father was a Freudian psychoanalyst and her father was middle management for a large corporation. We had lots of pets. Fortunata the white rat was joined by three ducks, two ducklings, seven De Kalb hens, nine chicks, a monster of a rooster who terrorized the hens and us, three dogs, two cats, a horse and a pig. We bought the pig from Manuel Ortiz – the runt of the litter weighing in at five pounds. Manuel didn't expect her to survive and asked five dollars for her.

Deirdre and Jim

Our plan was to fatten her up and have her for Christmas. On a steady diet of mash, which we gave her, and dog food, which she took without asking, she grew into an immense animal, all sweetness and appetite. We named her Mariposa and had to put latches on the kitchen cabinets because she liked to burst into the house like a butterfly and rip open bags of rice and flour.

Chambers of Commerce called northern New Mexico

the Land of Enchantment where three cultures lived in harmony. Hardly; it was four cultures, for in the early '60s, hippies started to arrive, living in hovels and communes. The locals were obsessed with them, despised and envied them. The men thought that hippie guys were having sex day and night with hippie chicks which is funny given how stoned and passive most hippies were. Sex came way down the list, after dope, peyote, wine, venison, rice and beans, firewood, food stamps, and more wine.

It was estimated that Taos County had over fifteen communes. In Arroyo Hondo alone, there were three: New Buffalo was thriving in lower Hondo, and Michael Duncan had opened his land in upper Hondo to all comers who were forming Morningstar and Reality Construction Company. Within the county limits, there were also the Hog Farm near Rodarte, the Family in Ranchos de Taos, and Lama Foundation north of San Cristobal – each had an individual identity, a core of like-minded people mingling with drifters who shuttled from one to another.

Phaedra
Before I quite knew what was happening, Roget had me by the arm and was hurrying me out the back door into his car. I was fuming.

"Why do I have to go to this meeting?"

He smiled. "Because you're our only reporter and we feel you should hear what this guy has to say."

It was true, The Fountain of Light was at a turning point. The editor had run off to Hawaii, leaving his notice in green ink scrawled on the toilet seat.

*I'm going to where the grass is greener
'cause staying here is making me meaner.*

Some funds were missing. Or not. No one seemed to know for sure. The publisher had offered me the editor's job, but I wasn't sure I had the skills. Plus I couldn't imagine being the boss, especially over men.

Roget was the graphic designer on the paper, a monthly counter-culture magazine. He contributed beautiful black and white photos of people and landscapes, and graceful pen-and-ink drawings. He had fled from the draft in France, come to the United States four years ago. He spoke fluent English with a charming accent. When he philosophized, no one could understand exactly what he was saying, but everyone inevitably liked him. He was consistently animated, ironic and kind. To me he had the air of an alien observing the customs of the natives.

"Why is my opinion so important?" I said, half to myself. "I was supposed to work on my novel today. Who is this guy, anyway?"

Roget didn't turn his head. The tips of his ears protruded through his thin brown hair.

"He seems pretty together. He's a writer."

"A writer? Have you seen any of his stuff?"

A calm smile. "Some of his poetry is pretty good."

"Humph!" Did I feel competitive, or what?

"Besides, he's lived around here since he was a kid. He knows the people and he might have some ideas to help us make the paper do what we want it to — serve the whole community, instead of being another hip underground publication."

"I think we're already serving the whole community. Of-

fering an alternative. Love instead of hate." One of my first stories had been about Taos Pueblo's struggle to regain control over Blue Lake. I had also covered a story about Earth People's Park, a plan to create a huge commune in Taos for Woodstock refugees so we could continue the celebration.

I shrugged. "Well, if he's really all you say . . . a writer? What's his name?"

Jim

In the spring of 1970, I gave a friend an essay entitled "Call and Answer" to read and she gave it to the graphic designer of a hippie newspaper called *The Fountain of Light*. He invited me to coffee to discuss publishing the essay.

Roget Thomas and I talked for hours. He said that his name was pronounced Row-jhay and that he had left France at eighteen to escape the draft, had flown to Canada, then snuck into the U.S. and ended up in Taos.

Roget was twenty-five, a thin wiry man with pointed ears and lively eyes. He spoke English well, but I had trouble understanding his train of thought, which was abstractly speculative. We talked about *The Fountain of Light* and he asked me to make a few remarks to the staff on how the paper could be improved.

Phaedra

The office of the paper was in the General Store, a building that served as a dry goods store for hippies. We met in a room the size of a cell set up with light boards around the walls; there were no chairs. When Roget and I arrived three people were already there: the treasurer, the bookkeeper, and Cyril who was the patriarch of a Taos commune called The Family.

A few minutes later a man wafted in the door as if propelled by a strong wind. He was about six feet tall with a dark mane of hair, around thirty years old. Smiling and handsome, but in the narrow confines of the room he was too much. Invisible hackles rose along my spine and up the back of my neck.

The rest of us stood leaning against the walls but he sat down on the rug, arms slung loose around his knees. Much to my surprise everyone except me sat down on the floor too. Roget introduced him as Jim Levy, who then proceeded to make a number of suggestions about the paper.

I challenged him. "Have you ever worked on a paper before?"

He looked up at me, a slight smile on his lips. "No," he said in a thoughtful tone. "But I'm a writer."

I bristled. "What do you write?"

He made an off-hand gesture. "Novels, short stories, poetry."

"Have you had anything published?"

He let out an easy laugh. "No. One novel kicked around with an agent in New York for a year, but nothing came of it."

My curiosity was piqued. "What was it about?"

"Oh, a man in prison. . ." He went on, but I had stopped listening. Would my hippie novel "kick around in New York for a year" and then be returned? (Later, that's exactly what happened).

Cyril, who was on the Board of the paper, said that if Levy was so clever, why didn't he run the paper.

At the last staff meeting we had been praying for an editor to come along.

"I'll do it without a salary," Levy said after only a moment of hesitation. "For a month. On one condition – that I have sole control over what goes into it. If you don't like what I put into the next issue, I'll resign and you can get somebody else."

The room was silent. He shot questioning glances at us and waited while we looked at each other. Roget cleared his throat.

Levy stood up and stood over Roget by about a foot. "I don't have to have an answer right now. You can talk it over and let me know."

The treasurer lifted an eyebrow. "Yes. That might be best. But I for one think your offer is interesting. The cost of putting out the paper is seven hundred a month and the paper is in the red. I think it's just a matter of time before our backing runs out."

Levy paused at the door and turned to me with a smile.

"My friends and I like to get together, have coffee and talk about writing. Would you like to join us sometime?"

I drew myself up like a cat eyeing a dog. "I don't talk about writing. I write."

He shrugged and was gone.

A few minutes after he departed, I turned to Roget. Call it curiosity, but it was more than that. In a muffled voice I said, "Is he married?"

"Yes," Roget said in a casual way.

Later, when the staff talked it over, the consensus was that we shouldn't look a gift horse in the mouth. In spite of my hostility – an emotion I could in no way justify or explain even to myself – I, too, voted to hire this guy.

Jim
When I went to the office of the paper, the staff was waiting for me. I banged in, realizing too late how small the room was. I saw a black man, a good-looking blond woman, a good-looking dark-haired woman, Roget and some other people. There were no chairs, so I sat on the carpeted floor with my back against the wall. Then everyone else sat down on the floor except the dark- haired woman, who leaned against the wall. I said that I thought the paper could be improved. As the only alternative newspaper in Taos County, it didn't have to limit itself to hippie material; it could tackle all sorts of things: the political scene, the prevalent violence, poetry, stories, history of northern New Mexico, and so forth.

They were open to this idea, and it turned out, the editor had taken off without warning and they were looking for a new one.

Black man (who seemed to be the leader): "If you think we're doing such a bad job, why don't you run it?"

"I could do that."

The leader explained that there was no money to pay me. This didn't bother me; most people did without much money. Gas was fifty-five cents, sliced bread twenty-five cents, postage stamps six cents. My wife and I were working as part-time teachers at the local hippie school and that was enough. I said I'd take on the newspaper for free, but I wanted full control. He and the dark-haired woman didn't like that proposal at all. We compromised: I would have control, but the Board could veto my decisions.

The leader turned out to be Cyril, the head of a commune called The Family, which he ran like a Roman emperor. The good-looking blond was Cassandra, his lead wife. The dark-haired woman, who obviously didn't like me, was Phaedra, the paper's only reporter. Roget and I started to work on the next issue, overhauling the paper. He abandoned the psychedelic designs with great relief and used his unique eye to create brilliant layouts. We loaded the paper with political and literary material, including accounts of hippies being beaten up, raped, shot at, and in one case, murdered. Soon the paper was reaching a much wider audience. It turned out there was no functioning Board, and I never heard from the staff again.

I avoided the office for a while and focused on my novel about Woodstock. I had been in the thick of it with the Merry Pranksters, and Woodstock was becoming a household word, so I thought the book would be a sure sell. Then I'd have enough money to live on.

One day, having coffee with Roget, he gave me a long look and said, "Jim says you hate him. Is that true?"

"That's what he said?"

"Yes."

"We got off to a bad start. He stopped paying me fifteen dollars a story because everyone else was volunteering their time. But no, I don't hate him."

In the next issue of The Fountain of Light *I published a story about the Hog Farm and Levy published a long prose poem, "Call and Answer," with some fine and sensual descriptions of nature. When I stopped by the office he was busy at his desk. He barely gave me a nod as I handed him my article for* the paper. "By the way," I said, "that was a really nice piece – well written." He looked up, startled, but said nothing. Later he told me I was the only one who responded to it. Call and answer.

The Fountain of Light kept the community apprised of the on-going violence. Two young hippies were camped near the Rio Grande and in the middle of the night, men surrounded them with guns and made them dig their own graves. In the end, they were given a choice: to leave Taos County or to die.

One of the more blatant incidents was when five or six very drunk middle-aged men came out of a bar one afternoon in Arroyo Seco and beat up several Anglos, one of whom wasn't even a hippie. The men were not impressionable youths but the owner of a local clothing store, the assistant manager of Safeway, and several other upstanding citizens. After their labors, they hung around (they were *very* drunk) and offered to demonstrate their prowess to the police. Charged with assault and battery, they were fined five dollars each by the magistrate judge.

The incident was reported in the *Santa Fe New Mexican* but that edition of the paper didn't get distributed in Taos. The driver said that his car had broken down in Española and he had spent the night there. When asked why he didn't distribute the papers the next day, he said that he figured people wouldn't want to read "old news."

The Fountain of Light reported the story in detail, including the names of the perps and the judge who had fined them. For our efforts, the windows of the paper's office were shot out. We put a rifleman on the roof to fire back, but we all agreed that was too much. We started publishing the paper from my house in Arroyo Hondo. I carried a loaded .38 Smith and Wesson under the seat of my car, afraid that I would be ambushed on the dirt road leading to our house.

Over the next six months, Jim and I ran into each other now and then. One night I was at the Taos Inn with a friend and we joined Jim and his wife Deirdre at a table. She turned out to be an attractive woman with an animated round Irish face and a nervous laugh. Jim got up and strolled to the jukebox. I followed and we checked out the songs, stole glances at each other and spoke in guarded tones.

"You're wrong; I don't hate you," I said.

"I don't hate you either."

"That's good to know."

We picked out a few songs and he dropped in some quarters.

A month later I ran into Jim and Deirdre at Lama Foundation north of Taos. It was a commune that opened itself up to the public for lectures, Hindu-like satsangs and Sufi dancing. Baba Ram Dass was a star who came through a few times a year and gave talks and published Be Here Now, *which became a hippie bible.*

Jim and I escaped the dancing and went to the communal kitchen.

"Deirdre loves these things and I tolerate them for her sake," he said.

"I love to dance, but not in a crowd."

There was a loaf of sliced bread on a table and he poked

at it. He picked up the heel and started to eat it.
"No one will notice," he said.
"It's the best part."
He handed it to me and I took a bite.
"You know what this means," I said. "One of us is going to die in a foreign country."

Two public meetings were held to address the violence in Taos as part of the White House Conference on Children and Youth. One would suppose that the meetings would focus on the wide-spread vandalism, beatings, and rapes, but the hot topic was the proposed abolition of food stamps. Many hippies got food stamps and there was a movement afoot to close the food stamp office and thus get rid of the hippies. (It wouldn't have worked; hippies generally took what was available but didn't depend on welfare. They were a resourceful bunch). About two hundred people showed up to each meeting, and the discussions soon evolved into impassioned diatribes, angry exchanges, and, ironically, threats of violence.

Only one concrete idea came from the public meetings: a Human Relations Council. I volunteered to be the unpaid executive director. It was an appropriate role for me, because I was caught between the Anglo families from my past, who assumed I despised the hippies as much as they did, and my hippie neighbors, who assumed I was one of them. No matter that I had no training in mediation or community organizing; no matter that I didn't speak Spanish or that no one else had volunteered and that I was the only person on the "Council."

My second fall in Taos, I waltzed around in the beautiful autumn weather, admiring the gold of the aspens on the mountainsides. Under a deep blue sky, Taos Valley glowed with lazy shafts of sunlight through the yellow leaves of the cottonwoods that lined the streets. But towards the end of October, I woke up to a cold rain. The leaves had all turned brown. I panicked at the sight of snow on the mountains. No not yet! I needed boots and a sleeping bag. Money to get through the winter. I decided to go to Albuquerque, find employment, buy some gear and return to Taos with two hundred dollars in my pocket and find a place of my own. Time to get moving!

When I heard that trouble was brewing I rushed off to try to dispel the tension. Unfortunately I always arrived too late, just like the cops. A guy named Chuck got beaten up in Celso's lounge in the middle of the day. Some of the guys from Reality commune (of all the motleys in Taos, they were the least in touch with reality) went to Celso's and sent in a decoy. Sure enough, he was threatened, and when he ran out, he was followed by half a dozen young drinkers who promptly got their heads played on by hippies with axe handles.

    I knew all the combatants and convened a meeting the next day. We met in the parking lot of Celso's and I suggested some reasons why we could all get along. I mean, we were all poor, struggling to make a living, we all liked alcohol and dope. Why couldn't we just be neighborly? Everyone agreed, and that was that. It had no effect at all. The fights continued. I gave up and the Human Relations "Council" dissolved into thin air.

I didn't find a job in Albuquerque so I hitchhiked to Michigan with thirty-five dollars in my pocket to visit my brother and try to find work, but there were fewer jobs in Mt. Pleasant than in New Mexico. I returned to Taos. Wandering around like this wasn't foreign to me. My father was the son of a famous journalist for The Detroit News but he had a problem holding down a job, so we lived like gypsies, fleeing from town to town, towing a trailer behind an old Pontiac, pursuing my father's dream of writing the Great American Novel. By the time he was fifty, he had had forty-two jobs and I had attended nine different schools.

The people who owned and ran the Da Nahazli school were oblivious to internal tensions between teachers and parents, but Kelly McMillan, a haughty beauty, and I feasted on them. During breaks, we stood in the courtyard of the school and gossiped about her husband Robert, who was a case worker at Social Services, about her friend Donna, and about a middle-age housewife who had found God through a combination of LSD and a young man self-named Destiny. One day, in a particularly unpleasant mood, Kelly turned her sharp eye on Deirdre, whom she described as an East Coast princess who craved affection. With a gush of shame, I enjoyed this assessment and didn't contradict it.

"And me, how would you describe me?" I asked, daring her.

"You're a hedonist who disguises his lusts with a veneer of intellectualism."

"Do you really mean that?"

"More or less."

"I'm flattered."

The contest was on.

When I got back to Taos in the fall of 1970, I landed on a friend named Julie and her five kids. They were happy to see me, but after two nights with kids and dogs crawling over my head, I started prowling the neighborhood for my own place. Half a mile down the road next door to John Nichols, the author, I found an empty adobe toolshed. I talked to Mr. Sanchez, who agreed to rent it to me for ten dollars a month. I had earned a little cash at temp jobs and I thought for sure I would be able to earn ten dollars a month, even in Taos.

I patched up the adobe walls with icy mud from the acequia, punched a hole in the wall for a stovepipe, and Mr. Sanchez helped me install an ancient cast iron woodstove. "It's gonna blast you out when it gets going," he said.

The tool shed was about the size of a cell and dark with only one window. There was just enough room for a table and chair and my mattress on the floor. I nailed up some shelves and attached weather stripping around the door. I picked rosehips and strung them in a garland over the vigas. I spent the last of my money on a cheap little radio, a Mexican rug, two kerosene lanterns and half a cord of piñon. The rug brightened my cell and at night when the lanterns were lit and the stove burning, it was quite cozy. It was November 15th. I was almost broke again, but I thought I was ready for winter.

In December I rented a room above the Apple Tree restaurant in Taos to have a studio where I could write, but I didn't do much writing. I spent my time flirting with

Kelly. I invited her for a walk and we had a cynical conversation about life and literature and our spouses. She was precisely what Deirdre was not: hard, quick, with a lightning-fast mind that caught my ironic sarcasms and shot back with her own. She was beautiful the way models are beautiful, with a striking face and a lean inaccessible body.

It became a routine: once a week, we took a walk. We sat with our backs against Mabel Dodge Luhan's gravestone and needled each other or we went to a hill overlooking Taos and made fun of people we knew.

A friend invited me to meet a sculptor named Ken and we went to his house. It was a modern cinderblock plastered to look like an adobe, with a bay window overlooking the valley. Displayed along the walls in the hall were a series of land-relief forms taken from geological maps of the area, expressed in three dimensions with plaster painted brown, black and white. In the center of each one was a design borrowed from Native American culture made out of nails. They all had an austere professional quality.

And there was Ken waiting for us in the kitchen. He wore a blue shirt, jeans and a red bandana tied loosely around his neck. He was average height, brown eyes and light brown hair just above his shoulders.

We shook hands and he put on the kettle. I sat at the table sipping tea, eavesdropping on the conversation between Ken and my friend. But I perked up when he asked, "Do you know of any children in need who might not get Christmas this year?"

I told him about Julie's children.

He came by my shed the next day to ask me what they might want. "Do the children have warm clothes?" he asked.

I went with him to a local thrift shop where he bought Tommy a winter jacket. It was two sizes too big, "But he'll grow into it," he said.

At first I felt no desire for Kelly. She was a wit, an intellect, a fencing partner, but not a woman or, if a woman, the kind that in her frustration wants to dominate a man. I fell for her mind and I wanted to subdue it. For some reason I declared that we had to make love. She in turn pretended to a passion she didn't feel but said no, there was Deirdre, there was her husband Robert, and there were her kids and my kids.

I pestered her until we set a date on a Saturday morning at her house, when Robert would be in Santa Fe taking a boatbuilding class. I told Deirdre I would be in town playing basketball. Kelly's kids were shuttled off somewhere. She showed me her house, we had coffee in the kitchen, and finally, as if obligated by some adultery manual, we went to bed.

Nothing happened. There was no ignition, no spark.

I said, "Well, the first time is often awkward."

She sat up and looked at me. "Was it awkward?"

On Christmas day Ken arrived at Julie's with a bag of presents: a baseball, matchbox cars for the boys, coloring books and crayons for the girls. We sat on the couch while the children gathered around us. I wore my hair in two pony tails held with leather thongs and my best green leather dress with the patches and beadwork. I think it was that faux Indian garb that got to Ken. "Something chemical," he said later.

Julie leaned in the doorway smoking a cigarette, wearing her favorite white blouse with ruffles down the front and her gold hoop earrings. She had long blond hair and deep brown eyes. Now and then she would punctuate the conversation with orders to the children, "Say thank you. Don't grab. No, that's not for you – put it back. Don't eat all those candies before dinner."

We ate from paper plates perched on our knees: traditional turkey, mashed potatoes and gravy and canned corn. "Are you sure you don't want some more," Julie said. "There's no dessert. I would have made pumpkin pie, but the store was out of pumpkin."

Ken smiled at me. "We're fine."

I wished I had thought to bring a gallon of ice cream for dessert.

A few days later Ken invited me over to make bread. On another day we made candles. When I crashed with a cold he showed up on my doorstep with a bag of oranges. Later he took me for a ride on his Suzuki to the edge of the Rio Grande Gorge. That evening I stayed to dinner. He made spaghetti and offered a bottle of red wine. "Nothing cheaper or more fun than wine and women," he joked. After dinner we danced in the living room to Barbra Streisand singing "Second Hand Rose."

"I think she's so cute," Ken said. "She's my ideal woman."

When the song ended we sank down on the couch. At last he kissed me. Until my shut-off valve clamped down.

He looked into my eyes. "I want to love you. Not just for tonight, for however long it lasts."

I stood up and looked around for my jacket.

He followed me to the hall. "I just want to be good to you, nice to you."

"Not very many people have been nice."

"Well," he said in a soft voice, "maybe it's time for a change."

His fingers probed the palm of my hand. "Don't go," he whispered in my ear. "I want to wake up beside you in the morning."

"No, I have to go home."

He held up one finger to shush me. I nipped it like a coyote. He sprang back.

"If you don't take me home when I ask, I won't come over again."

Ken threw up both hands and went for the car keys. He followed me towards the front door. I glanced back. "I don't go lightly through men's lives," I warned. "I leave footprints in the garden."

He laughed. "That should be the title of your next book."

Kelly and I tried again two weeks later. Same result. There was no "chemistry." I was too weak to break it off. On the contrary, I felt I now owed her something, a sentiment that was against all reason, and to further complicate things, I maintained that I loved her. And she, much to our mutual astonishment, said she loved me. Our wit began to sound stupid, even to us. Instead we started talking seriously of ourselves and our marriages.

"Deirdre and I are so emotionally enmeshed in each other," I said, "it's making us both crazy. Everything I do or say, I worry how it's going to affect her."

"I don't think Robert cares what I say or do."

"Believe me, he cares what you do."

"Yes, of course, but you know what I mean."

"I feel she's sucking the life out of me," I said, unable to stop criticizing Deirdre. It felt good to get it out.

She gave me a look. "At least she's sucking on you."

"Yet, get this, when she went to Lama and spent two nights with the Sufis, I was jealous."

"What? Were they having Tantric sex?"

"No, they were twirling, but she came home happier than I've seen her in months. And I'll tell you, although I don't like it when she's sad, I like it even less when she's jolly."

After a storm, a cold front moved in, a night of brilliant stars. I hadn't chopped enough wood. Piñon is tough and fibrous and doesn't split clean. Half the time I missed the log and knocked it over.

I had been out that day on my bicycle applying for work all over town. It was nine o'clock by the time I got home, and, according to the radio, already twelve below zero. Inside my gloves my fingers were numb. I had about five minutes to get the fire going. Luckily I had laid it before I left for town.

Soon it was snapping and pouring out heat. I fixed a small meal and turned on the radio. Although the stove was going full blast, it didn't seem to be heating the room. I dragged my mattress up to the stove, pulled my knitted hat over my ears and crawled into my sleeping bag. I dozed and kept the radio on for company. On the hour it announced the time and the temperature as it dropped to fifteen below. Twenty. Twenty-five.

The frigid air penetrated every pore of the adobe walls, sank down through the boards in the ceiling and froze the water in the bucket beside the stove. Thirty below. Thirty-five. I ran out of firewood. I was too scared to fall sound asleep, but I must have snoozed for a while. That night broke some sort of record for Taos at forty below.

At first light I struggled out of my sleeping bag and drew a breath of relief as the first rays of sun fell across the floor. I pulled on my boots, flung open the door, seized my axe and started chopping.

Half an hour later Ken pulled up in the driveway. He hopped out of his truck and eased the axe from my hands. "That's no job for a woman."

While I stood panting, he split enough firewood to last another night. His cheeks were red and his eyes were smiling.

"Why don't you come and stay with me until things warm up?"

"Thanks!" I grabbed my crocheted bag and hopped in his truck.

Kelly's husband had met me several times at the school and had even observed one of my classes, which his daughter attended. Now he sensed that something was up.

Kelly said: "He thinks you're a brilliant teacher but also an egoist or rather, to use his word, a narcissist."

Deirdre suspected something too and became more and more distant. When she spent another night at Lama, it occurred to me that she had a lover. It turned out to be worse than that. After she expressed her grief about our marriage to a self-proclaimed guru, he advised her that her husband was "inauthentic."

She and I were in our kitchen and Harvey Mudd was standing by the door going on about coal plants at Four Corners. We were talking over each other and not listening.

"What did you just say?" I asked Deirdre.

"Lahiri Mahasaya says that you are inauthentic."

"He's the guy from Ohio, right?"

"He studied for twenty years with Muktanand Swami."

"Oh, well, then," I sputtered, so enraged I couldn't think of anything else to say.

I wrapped my large hands around her throat, paused, and then drove her slowly to the floor.

Harvey recoiled almost out the door, then started towards us.

It lasted two or three seconds and then I recoiled too, shocked that I felt so murderous. Incredibly, Deirdre didn't strike back at me or call the cops. She looked at me with contempt and went into the bedroom.

I followed her. "Please, please, I am so sorry. Oh God, Deirdre, please, forgive me."

"I forgive you," she said drily.

Yet it had felt good. I had had to do it and it felt good. I think that she, while disgusted with me and beginning to hate me for real, may have felt something similar. For a moment, we had been intimate again, passionate again. But this was the second time I had choked her and I began to understand that there was something seriously disturbed in me.

Why did I choke her? For being so nice? For tying me down? For not loving me enough? For loving me too much? For being a woman? For being in my way? For being so passive? For seeing me as I really am? For not seeing me as I really am?

None of these explained it. Was it shame, guilt, and the wish to end them by ending the marriage, even if that resulted in more shame and guilt?

I stayed at Ken's for ten days. He was working on a plaster model, a sculpture to enter in a contest. The prize was a hefty commission to create an installation for the Taos County courthouse.

To keep me occupied, Ken gave me some leather so I could make a pair of moccasins. We ate soup and salad for dinner and necked in front of the TV until we were both in a sweat. He picked me up and carried me into the bedroom, then disappeared into the bathroom for a long time. I shed my clothes and waited. At last he slid in beside me, modest in his striped pajamas. Taken aback by my nudity, he kissed me on the cheek and told me to go back to sleep.

We got around to making love the following night. He was shy and had no passion for me, but I hoped that time would smooth our way to a laughing familiarity.

The following evening he drank half a bottle of wine while I was fixing dinner. Over fried chicken he mentioned that this was his son's birthday. Robbie was eight. It had been a bitter divorce. His wife had returned all his Christmas pre-

sents for Robbie and hung up the phone when Ken called because he still refused to make child support payments. "Why should I? She's making twice as much as I ever made." He looked at me. "I just love that boy so much." He finished the wine, lay his head on his arms and wept.

A few days later Ken and I tried again, hoping it would get better. "Ah, have you always had this problem?" I asked.

"Well, I was always a slow starter," he said. "I know it's a little late to ask, but what are you using for birth control?"

"I can't get pregnant."

"Did a doctor tell you that?"

I thought about the doctor I saw just before I left New Haven. When I asked him for birth control pills he said with a slice of contempt, "You don't even know if you can get pregnant."

Well, I know for sure you can't, I thought.

I had been on and off the pill since Woodstock. I didn't see much sense taking it when I wasn't involved with anyone. With Ken I was being careless, leaving it to chance. I had been married three times; I was twenty-eight, tired of waiting for everything to be just right.

"Yes," I lied.

Deirdre found an earring on the floor of the VW van and brought it into the kitchen.

"Whose is this?" she asked, her face mottled with anger.

"You got me. Maybe a hitchhiker's?"

"It just appeared out of nowhere?"

"I gave a woman a ride a few days ago."

"You swear to me you aren't having an affair."
"Jesus Deirdre! I am not having an affair."

The next morning was spring-like. For February. I took a short walk on one of those winding back roads in Talpa and wandered into an orchard. Bright sunlight reddened the tips of the apple trees. The pale yellow grasses looked soft. I sat down under an apple tree, lit up a joint and scrawled a few lines on a match cover. Under a vault of blue sky, in the sunny orchard, it came to me like the Angel of Annunciation. I hugged myself inside my green corduroy coat, smug and satisfied, murmuring "With child. I am with child." But I decided not to tell Ken until I was sure.

Ken decided it was a good time to take some art to a gallery in Phoenix that represented his work. He was gone about four days while I housesat for him. He returned with an air of confidence. "I ran into an old girlfriend," he confessed. "Betty and I ended up in bed." With a silly grin, he lifted both palms and shrugged. "I've discovered that I'm capable of loving more than one woman at a time."

You can't even love one, I thought.

Exit stage left, back to my adobe cell. I found a fat padlock on the door. I tromped down the muddy road to see Mr. Sanchez, banged on his door and demanded he let me into my nest.

He raised his eyebrows. "I helped you, didn't I? I helped you put in the stove and replace the glass in the door."

Steam whistled out of my ears. "And I paid for the glass, the stove pipe, the tar, the plastic for the window. I told you that I was free lancing – that I might not have the rent exactly on time, but you'd get your money eventually."

Beneath my bravado, I felt chagrinned.
He came over and took the padlock off the door, but I had to give him one of my lanterns and the rug.
Back to Julie's? She would always put me up and give me a meal. But sleeping on the couch, waking at dawn to the high, excited voices of the children? I was feeling bone weary, strung out. Nevertheless, back to Julie's I went.

I wrote intellectually "witty" letters to Kelly , trying to seduce her mind more successfully than I had her body, while including ardent passages that might ignite something approaching actual passion.

The letters went on for a month, until her husband found one in her purse. For a moment he was ice cold. He said that he had been mistaken, I wasn't a narcissist. Based on my long, wordy, ambivalent letter, I was schizophrenic.

Then he was hot. He said he was going to Arroyo Hondo to tell Deirdre.

Kelly called me at school and said that Robert might be on his way to my house. I jumped into my car and headed home, to tell Deirdre how awful I was, how sorry, to say anything that could make things better.

Genuinely afraid, I strode around the corner of the house. I had no idea what I was going to say, and I had no idea that I was about to say what I did say.

There was Deirdre, in the late winter light, sitting at the outside blue table holding a cup of tea. She looked up, alarmed.

One morning Roget popped in the door and asked me if I'd

like to go out to Arroyo Hondo for a month and take care of Harvey Mudd's house. "It would give you a chance to get some rest."

I had met Harvey the previous summer, when I drove up the dirt road through the quiet village of Arroyo Hondo with Glenda, my first friend in Taos. She said we could pick vegetables from Harvey's and Jim's garden and we picked a bag full of greens, some peas and tomatoes. Afterward, we went inside the big redwood house, sat at the long dining room table and talked to Harvey about an article he was writing for The Fountain of Light called "Towards Understanding Biological Man." I wanted it to be stronger, but he didn't want to scare people to death.

Harvey was our local environmentalist, six foot one and attractive with black curly hair. He was thirty-one and chairman of the New Mexico Citizens for Clean Air and Water. He was also Jim Levy's oldest friend; they had met as fourteen-year-olds at boarding school. He smoked a pipe and tended to tweed jackets with leather patches on the elbows. At the time he was in Santa Fe lobbying the legislature; his partner, Alicia, a woman from Mexico who spoke only a little English, was in the hospital in Santa Fe having their baby.

Roget and his partner Elaine drove me to Harvey's house. The foundation was massive stone and cement. While it was being poured the villagers thought he was fixing to dam the Rio Hondo.

The big living room had a bay window with a classic view of Lobo Peak. Harvey called his home "the Mudd Museum" because it housed his collection of Indian artifacts and Penitentes death fetishes. I was grateful that he trusted me with all this. I was two months pregnant.

As I came around the corner of our house, Deirdre looked up, alarmed by the expression on my face. Years later, she wrote and gave interviews about the moment.
I was out in front of our adobe house drinking a cup of tea. And the car drove up behind the house, I heard the car door slam, and he came around the corner of the house and he just said it. "Things haven't been going well between us. I'm having an affair with somebody else. We need to get a divorce." It was so shocking, even traumatizing, that I had experienced that. It was just a timeless moment.

Her account never varied. This particular one occurred forty-three years later, after she had become a Buddhist nun named Pema Chödrön and had written best-selling books about her approach to life. She was talking on TV with Oprah Winfrey on Oprah's Super Soul Sunday program.

In many interviews and books, Pema said that she threw a stone at me. In fact, we climbed the hill behind the house and sat down in the dirt. We tried to talk; then she stood up, picked up a heavy rock, and raised it over her head. I stood and grabbed her wrist.

"No," I said, "I'm not going to let you hurt me."

It sounded like something out of one of Lawrence's novels.

She slammed the rock down and strode off.

It was lonely at Harvey's but I felt calm. Now and then the caretaker would come around to use the tractor. Or Jim or Deirdre would appear with a basket of laundry, shove it into the washer and take a shower upstairs. While the laundry was drying, one or the other would sit at the long dining room table with me, have a cup of tea or coffee and talk. I was surprised to hear they were breaking up. As Jim put it, they were "throwing furniture at each other."

I didn't tell Jim I was two months pregnant. By a man I didn't love and who didn't love me. But I wanted this baby even though I was homeless, didn't have a car or a job or a clue about how to make a living in Taos. All I really knew how to do was write. If I had had more confidence I might have applied for work at The Taos News, but back then, the editor was not sympathetic to what was commonly called "the hippie invasion." The Taos tourist promoters called Taos "three cultures living together in harmony." Which would never include those dirty, arrogant, drug-ridden, indigent "children of the earth," as some called themselves.

I toyed with giving up, lying down quietly somewhere out of the way, leaving my carcass for someone else to worry about. Yet here I was, eating sour cream and sesame crackers. Moping around, sleeping, staring out the windows in a listless apathy.

My breasts were swollen and sore. When I pressed down on my belly I could feel a soft lump but nothing was stirring yet. Sometimes at night I got a spurt of energy, put on some records and danced in the long living room, danced to my reflection in the bay windows.

Deirdre and I went on living together, going about our days like zombies, she alternating between apathy and anger, while I alternated between feeling unreal and anguish. We pretended I hadn't said anything about an affair and divorce and yet what I had said never left our minds.

Kelly and I met for coffee in town and agreed that we had been foolish.

"We should have waited," she said, which surprised me. I wanted to say, Waited for what?

It was clear we had had different experiences of the affair, but I wasn't about to tell her that although I admired her wit and intelligence, I was not turned on by her.

"I'm leaving Robert," she said.

"You are? Because of us?"

"It's been a long time coming. What about you?"

"I don't know what I'm going to do. I just want to hide my head in a hole."

Jim and I grew close over the month I was housesitting. I related some things about my childhood and my three marriages. He told me about falling in love with Deirdre when she was still married to a wealthy attorney, about moving to Mexico with her and her children, discovering hashish and LSD, having affairs. Neither of us were especially proud of our pasts, but I was pleased how simply and honestly we talked about them.

Of course we talked about writing. His writing. My writing. Maybe he even brought me a few things to read. I wasn't writing much myself, a few notes scribbled on lined paper. One afternoon some Hog Farmers showed up and asked to take baths and showers. I made the mistake of letting them in. They made the mistake of starting up the tractor and nearly drove it off a bridge. They tracked me down wherever I went. And apparently I still didn't know how to say no.

Phaedra explained that she had given herself a new name,

Phaedra Greenwood, after she nearly died in Holy Cross hospital of hepatitis and pneumonia. She was pregnant from a ten-day romance with an artist.

"And the proud father, where is he?"

Her face tightened.

"I just told him a week ago. He's denied the baby is his. He says I had other men but I didn't. And he has a woman in Phoenix and another one in Albuquerque."

I asked her what her "real" name was, but she changed the subject.

We had conversations about literature and writing.

"Meridel Le Sueur is my favorite writer," she said with warmth.

"I don't know her. I don't know who my favorite writer is. It was Lawrence for a long time. When I was twenty-one or so, my mother said that I'd outgrow him. And I said, 'I hope not!' But she was right, I have."

"I think Meridel Le Sueur is the female version of Lawrence. She was a Communist and gave voice to the lower classes. She wrote about women and childbirth. I love her essay *Women of the Breadlines*. She was really into nature. You should read *Salute to Spring*."

Deirdre and I didn't have indoor plumbing, so we occasionally did our laundry at Harvey's house and took showers. One day while waiting for the wash to dry, I was leafing through a *National Geographic* and came across an article about the Niger river. There were pictures of the broad brown river snaking through the desert on its way to the Atlantic. I longed to be that far away. Right then, a plan came to me: book a ticket on a freighter, take it to west Africa and go up the Niger river. It was very specific: I would go to the Niger river to sort things out.

One night I felt the bed trembling. An earthquake! It only lasted about thirty seconds, but it had a profound influence on me. In the morning I noticed that one of the stained glass windows above the library was broken. I felt scared, vulnerable. It happened to be the day Jim lent me his VW van to drive over to Ken's and pick up some things I had left there. I didn't call first; I just pulled up in the driveway. I banged on the door. Ken was in the kitchen having lunch with a young woman. Well, he didn't waste any time. From the glimpse I had of her, she was plain, with her hair in braids. I wasn't seriously jealous, but I tromped around, gratified to see Ken sputtering and flustered. He followed me to the door. "It's just lunch," he said. "Oh sure! Just lunch." I slammed out the door, heaved my clothes in back and took off. By the time I reached Seven Rays Gallery, I was clutching my womb, cramping.

Elaine and Roget were behind the glass counter in the gallery. When they saw my face, Elaine squashed out her cigarette, came around and gave me a hug. Roget peered at me over her shoulder. "You okay?"

"No. I'm not. I'm bleeding!" I wailed.

Elaine took my hand and led me back to a couch in the storage room under the stairs. "Do you want to keep this baby?" she said in a calm voice.

"Yes . . . I don't know. What a world to bring a child into."

The Vietnam war was still raging, it seemed forever.

Elaine motioned to the couch. "Lie down and put your feet up. Take some deep breaths and try to relax. I'll make you some tea."

"Okay . . ." *I lay there for about fifteen minutes, staring up at the low ceiling. I didn't know then that breakthrough bleeding was common in the early trimester. Still, I had aborted once before, with my second husband, and it had started just like this. A few cramps, some minor bleeding. And a teaspoon of fetus in the toilet. I fished it out and took it to a doctor. He wouldn't confirm it, but murmured to the nurse,* "Four weeks."

Yes. I did want this baby. It wasn't being forced on me. I had a choice. I resolved to make more of an effort to calm down, get some rest. Thank god for friends like Elaine and Roget.

I found a book in the library listing freighters that took passengers. After calling some of them, I reached one that had a ship going from New Orleans to Barcelona in June.

"How are you going to pay for this?" Harvey asked.

It was March, a harsh windy day, and we were sitting on the balcony of his house overlooking the ruins of the previous year's garden.

"We have a little savings. I'll leave half with Deirdre and just go. Once I get to Spain I can make some money teaching English."

"I thought you were going to the Niger river."

"I'll get there. I will."

He pulled out his check book and wrote a check for ten thousand dollars.

I didn't protest. We had a peculiar relationship when it came to money. As teens, I had money from summer jobs and gave him some of it. Now he had a lot and I had little. We shared life's adventures so he naturally shared his money. He was a very generous person if he cared for you.

"I'll give half to Deirdre," I said.

"It's for you. You do what you want with it."

Harvey and Alicia came home; my days in Paradise were over.

"Do you have any place to go?" Harvey asked in a kindly tone.

I turned away. "No. But I'll think of something."

I went back up to the Hog Farm for a few days. While I was there I reconnected with two hippies who were caretaking some cabins in Embudo on the Rio Grande. They offered me an empty cabin where I could live rent-free. There was no electricity and no plumbing. We drank out of the Rio Grande. My little cabin was heated by a fireplace that smoked and I was cold. I stuck it out for a couple of months.

Then back to Julie's and her five kids. When nights were warm I grabbed a blanket and slept out in the field where the kids couldn't find me. One day Julie said, "You'd better rustle up some clothes for that baby. I heard there are some in the free box."

So I went by the free box and found some shirts, cloth diapers and rubber pants and washed them out by hand. I carried the dishpan outside and set it on the ground. It was a beautiful spring day, the sun shining through the new cottonwood leaves. As I hung the little shirts on the line it struck me for the first time. I really was going to have this baby. And I was totally unprepared. No man, no home, no savings, no insurance. I felt like a cat looking for a drawer to crawl into.

Then, things changed. I bumped into Deirdre in the alley by the Taos Inn. She was wearing a green-striped dress and her hair in a braid over one shoulder. Her face lit up and she gave me a big hug. "How are you?" she asked.

I took a step back. Both proud and ashamed, I held out my arms to display my swollen belly. "That's how I am."

Her mouth dropped open. "Does the father know about it?"

"Yes. He went into the welfare office and denied that it was his."

"So you're on your own."

"Yes."

"Are you working?"

"Who would hire me?"

She grimaced. "Wow! You're so fearless. I could never do what you're doing."

I laughed. An ironic laugh. "Do I have a choice?"

"Some women would have chosen not to go through it."

She took my arm.

"Listen. Jim is going to Africa and I'm leaving for California for a while. We're going to need a house sitter. Will you be available?"

I was amazed how calm she seemed, smiling and cheerful. I noticed the lines around her eyes, her heart-shaped face, warm, motherly.

"Are you hoping he'll come back to you?" I asked.

"Oh, Phaedra. I never would have left him. He's the man I want."

As for the idea of house sitting, I thought of the dear but

squirming children who had tracked me down as I slept in the field.
  "Yes, I can do it."
  "Good."

This time, it was Deirdre who left. Taking the children with her, she went to my father and stepmother in Los Angeles. It was a perplexing choice. My father was a psychoanalyst who was outwardly genial and inwardly cold, and my stepmother was judgmental and angry. Neither of them had ever shown any genuine interest in Deirdre and the children. Nevertheless, they had two spare bedrooms and a pool.

  I stayed at the house in Arroyo Hondo, feeding the ducks and chickens and all the other animals, watering the plants, planning my trip to Spain and Africa. The ticket from the freighter company came, along with the name of the ship: The Mar Egeo, (the Aegean Sea), due to depart New Orleans June 5, 1971.

  I had trouble sleeping and eating. At times I felt so much guilt about breaking up the family that I sank to my knees and moaned. At other times I felt numb.

Jim came to pick me up at Julie's. I watched out the window while he wrestled with the boys in the backyard and let Willie ride horsie on his back. He helped me load my two cardboard boxes, my old Decca guitar, a manual typewriter and two of my paintings into the van. We drove to Michael's Kitchen for breakfast and talked and talked, completely relaxed. He asked me searching questions about life. All I could do was sing to him, *"We are stardust, we are golden, and we've got to find our way back to the garden."*

"You're so funny," he said.

I got up and bummed a cigarette off a customer.

As we were driving towards Arroyo Hondo, he described his plan to go to Spain and Africa.

"So you're really going," I said. "How long do you think you'll be gone?"

"Two, three years. Maybe forever. I don't know."

I bet you're back by November," I teased. "Send me a postcard with a giraffe on it."

"Wait for me," he said in a deadpan tone. What was he saying? I grinned. He was joking.

"Do I have to be celibate the whole time, or can I mess around a little?"

Deirdre and her kids went to Los Angeles and Jim was in Santa Fe. It was quiet at the end of the valley. The stream sparkled between the big cottonwoods. The mountains gleamed with the last of the snow. I went about the chores slowly, casually, savoring the moment, scattering grain in the chicken yard, collecting the eggs that lay smooth and brown in the yellow straw. Dipping the creamy white pitcher into the stream to water the red geraniums.

Most of the time I enjoyed my solitude. In the afternoon I took a blanket and a book, lay under the trees by the stream and read. It was only in the evening when the birds were flying home two-by-two that I felt melancholy. I sat outside at the round table, played my guitar and watched the sun set.

There were three dogs, two cats, eight chickens and a rat. The rat was Fortunata, that the Levys brought up from Mexi-

co. She lived loose behind the refrigerator. All the chickens in the upper coop got out. After half an hour of chasing them around, scratching my legs and trying to herd them back in by tossing pebbles, I finally gave up and walked away shouting over my shoulder, "Okay for you, stupid chickens!" I sat down on the board bridge for a minute, bathing my scratches in the ditch, and remembered the feed bowl. I went back to the pen to get it, and lo and behold, the "dumb chickens" filed in quietly behind me.

For the first ten days in Hondo I was completely alone. I didn't see or speak to anyone. No car. No telephone. On the eleventh day when the meter man from the gas company knocked at the door, I could barely summon my voice, which sounded faint and cracked.

In Santa Fe I stayed in the casita behind Harvey's house. One afternoon I walked into a little bar off the Plaza and ordered a gin and tonic, and another. By nightfall I could barely walk. I went into more bars in the Monte de Sol area near Harvey's place. When I staggered out, all I could do was register the most basic information. A warm spring night with a gusting breeze. A short street. At the end of it, dancing in the wind, a tree.

Hung over at noon, I went and looked for the short street. There was a street sign at the entrance: Calle Sin Nombre. Well there you have it, on a dead end street without a name, the tree of life.

I stayed drunk for a week, mainly in downtown bars where I was unlikely to run into anyone I knew.

One morning I called Deirdre from Harvey's casita

and told her, trying to sound grim rather than excited that the ticket for the freighter had come.

She was angry and said she never wanted to see me again, ever.

I couldn't think of anything to say.

There was a long silence between us.

"I'm worried about Ewar," she continued in a different tone. "He seems okay but he's having bad dreams and he's wetting his bed."

"I am so sorry. So sorry about all this. About us. About the kids."

"He cries and says in a small voice that he misses you and wants to go home. He misses his friends and the animals. I said that I feel the same way and maybe we'll go home in September or October."

"You know you can. Please, live there if you want. I'll talk to Harvey."

"I told Edward that you might never come back. He said that if there's no Jim, there won't be any stories and Frankenstein and treasure hunts. Don't worry, Evelyn says that if there's no Jim, there'll be Daddy!"

I dreamed a movie star was making love to me. That's how bad it got. Not just horny but lack of touching, feeling isolated. Depressed.

I sat in the armchair by the window, crocheting a blanket for the baby, feeling sorry for myself. I knew how lucky I was to be here, to have food and shelter and a quiet time to rest. I was grateful, yet some hollow place within me remained dismayed. I had no dream for the future. I was not in love anymore.

Harvey showed up, and we went out to dinner at a new flamenco restaurant on the outskirts of Santa Fe. I had stopped drinking so much, but with Harvey, who liked fine whiskeys and wine, I had a margarita and then some wine. After we ate, we continued to drink, and the flamenco show came on. It was the real thing, with a troupe recently come from Spain. I felt desire for the youngest of the dancers. I knew I didn't want her specifically, it was a more general passion, for life, travel, women, God, but especially for women, without the weight of guilt.

As I watched, I found myself thinking about the curl on Phaedra's forehead, I knew that I was falling for her, and, confused, realized that I had fallen for her months ago, when she was housesitting for Harvey. To me, she represented the freedom I wanted for myself. She seemed the wildest freest person I had ever known, but at the same time, there was something dated about her, something 1950s about the way she carried herself. Phaedra, sensual and demure, intuitive and proud, complacent and defiant, who felt the same as I did, that she wanted whatever life had to offer.

Deirdre intuited this. Years later, when I read the journals she had left in the house, I found that she had written that she wanted to be like Phaedra, free, nonpossessive, able to be alone, "Able to take it." She wrote that she realized that a woman like Phaedra would really be much better for me, "an equal with no more games."

I let the yarn fall in my lap, listening to the patter of rain. The large figure of a man in a suede jacket flashed past the win-

dow. I jumped up. My crochet hook bounced to the floor. The wind banged the screen back. Then Jim and I were standing in the kitchen hugging each other.

"I didn't hear you drive up."

"Happy Mother's Day."

"Oh, is it? Thanks."

The word "mother" took on a whole new meaning. Life. It happens. You can believe it or not.

Jim threw down his jacket and sank onto the couch. I put on the kettle.

"Harvey said that it might be too difficult for you, to be here right now."

"I thought it would be, too, seeing the house again, and everything. But it's not nearly as bad as I imagined."

"When does your ship leave?"

"Not until June 5th." His foot began to jiggle. "I thought I might as well wait around here for a few days and try to get some writing done. I'll stay out in the casita, if that's okay with you. I promise not to interfere with your privacy."

I cocked my head. "Well, I wouldn't mind having a man around for a few days to haul my water."

He laughed. "That's what I like about you, you're calculating, but at least you're honest about it."

"I'm pregnant," I said. "Just getting up and down the hill is hard enough. Coffee?"

"Uh, no. Maybe later."

I made some for myself and sat down beside him, tucked my legs up and balanced my cup. "How is Deirdre? Have you seen her?"

His shoulders drooped. "No. She said it was too soon. But I talked to her on the phone. She has to go through all this *with the kids there, while I have the luxury of being alone, free to do nothing but suffer."*

"I'll write her."

"Yes, do." *He smiled and stroked my instep. "It's good to see you, Phaedra. How are you holding up?"*

"Okay. My caseworker is a very interesting man, Robert McMillan."

He sat up, startled. "Oh no! What a bizarre coincidence. He's Kelly's husband."

I drew back. "Really? I'd better be careful what I say to him."

Jim shrugged. "It doesn't matter. What's in the cup?"

"Coffee."

"Where's mine?"

I snorted. "You said maybe later."

"Well, it's later."

I went to see Phaedra in Arroyo Hondo. I knocked on my own front door. She was already at the door and opened it. Without saying a word, we held each other.

"Happy Mother's Day," I said, too loudly.

"Is it? Am I? I guess I am."

We sat on the couch in the living room, which was covered in dog hairs.

"You let the dogs on the couch," I said.

"I do."

"Good. So do I. Deirdre would like to keep me off it; I mean them off it."

"I've been trying to keep them out of my bed," she said, and we both laughed.

"If it's okay with you, I'll hang around a few days, try to get some writing done, help you with the chores."

After dinner I made a fire and we sat on cushions on the floor. I touched her hair.

"It's red in the firelight."

"My mother always called it auburn."

She began to chatter. When she lay back I leaned over and kissed her. She was unresisting, but not responsive.

I stared at the fire. This wasn't going to happen. It was too soon, and Deirdre was too present. But true to old habits, I pushed on.

"Can't we just enjoy the moment?"

What I meant was, you're the wild hippie girl, can't *you* just enjoy the moment?

"I mean, you're free," I added.

"I am, but I'm not so sure about you. You're still full of Deirdre. And I don't want to be just another one of your confessions."

She was right.

"And besides," she added, "you're going to the Niger river."

It was beginning to annoy me, the way everyone said the words Niger river with a hint of sarcasm. Yet I shared their doubts. I was afraid to go off into the world, afraid of what I might learn about myself.

Jim got the pump going and ran a long hose from the acequia into the kitchen sink. I couldn't drink it but I could use it for washing dishes and clothes. After dinner Jim made a fire and we sat on cushions on the floor enjoying the light flickering on adobe walls, the heat on our skin. He touched my hair. "It's red in the firelight."

I began to chatter mindlessly, moving away from him. Feeling like some adolescent virgin. He watched me, smiling, listening, nodding. I lay back with my head on the cushion. He watched the fire in silence for a while. Then he leaned over and kissed me on the mouth. I felt detached, unresisting. He began to unbutton my dress. "Gee, these buttons look familiar."

"They should. Deirdre gave me this dress to be pregnant in." It was the green striped one with pewter-colored buttons all the way down the front.

I sat up, holding back his hand. "Wait."

He sat up too. "Wait for what? Can't you have uncomplicated pleasure, knowing it will be over? After all, you're free."

"Yes. That's how I got pregnant."

A muffled noise.

"And I'm not so sure about you. Your head is still too full of Deirdre. Three in bed is a crowd. I don't want to be the target of her jealousy. Besides, you're leaving for Africa.

He got up, put another log on the fire. His tone was slightly amused. "Well, keep your integrity. I haven't any."

Phaedra and I got stoned and she told me more about her childhood, especially about her father. He wanted to be a writer and wrote a memoir about his childhood, how he nearly drowned when a boy pushed him into a creek, how his mother stripped him and beat him with a trunk strap. As a child, he had a sadistic side, breaking the leg of a baby robin, throwing a rat into a furnace. He loved his mother and hated her and could never please her. Phaedra said there was a history of abuse in her family but didn't go into details.

In turn I told her the few things I knew about my father's childhood in Newark, how at age seven he decided to become a doctor like his father, and how he had been playing with matches in the family barn and started a fire. He pissed on it but the barn burned down and some of the horses didn't escape. It was then his father bought their first car.

So I slept alone and Jim slept out in the casita. It was bad enough that I was living in Deirdre's house, wearing her cast-off clothes, and using her dishes, without sleeping with her husband. I wanted to stop and think it over. I felt confused, almost frightened. Stung by his challenge. But I didn't feel any desire. For a woman, opening herself to a man is also opening herself to life and to death. I thought about Ken, the romantic nonsense, his inability to follow through. My relief. Sex is just something else you do together. There's got to be a lot more to keep the relationship growing.

I returned to Santa Fe but couldn't stay away. Back in Arroyo Hondo, Phaedra and I walked a mile up the canyon towards the Sangre de Cristos. We lay face down in the grass next to the Rio Hondo. After a while, we sat up and tossed twigs into the stream. Then we lay on our backs and watched the clouds. A hawk was soaring high above us. She touched my face lightly.

A storm moved in, with thunder and lightning. We

rushed back to the house and I lit a fire. Outside it started to snow.

Snow in May, we said.

In the midst of this, a car pulled into the driveway. I went out to see who it was. It was two guys from the Hog Farm, looking for Phaedra. There was a big party at the commune that night, to celebrate the full moon in Scorpio, and they had tracked her down to invite her.

To my astonishment, sorrow and anger, she accepted. She packed a few things and took off with them.

He invited me to come for a walk with him back up the canyon. We lay in the grass beside the stream and lost ourselves for an hour tossing pebbles and twigs. Then we rolled over on our backs and watched the clouds for a while. The hawk soaring in the rough spring wind, Jim's warm body next to mine, my head on his arm, the dogs chasing each other madly up and down the path across our legs, making us laugh. It was so simple. So different from anything I had ever imagined. A man. A woman. The hawk, the sky. I felt a shock of recognition.

An afternoon thunderstorm rumbled in. Lightning cracked close by. We hurried home before the rain, breathed again at the sight of the little adobe standing quietly on the hill. He brought in an armload of wood and built a fire while I made the tea.

We sat in the gathering dusk, watching the flames, while outside the rain changed to hail and then to snow. He touched my hand and said "What I'm feeling is love."

I hung my head. He leaned towards me. "I've been in love with you for months," he said. "I fell in love with a cer-

tain curl in your hair." He brushed back my bangs. "Where is it? It's gone. Remember what I told you then?"

"What?"

"That I wouldn't start anything new until it was over with Deirdre."

"Are you sure it's over?"

"Positive. I don't want to live with her again. I've told her so."

"Does she accept that?"

"I think so. She says she doesn't want that old relationship with me anymore either. She says she wants to start over, make a new beginning."

I shook my head. "I don't want to hurt Deirdre."

He lay his hand on my arm. "She told me she loves you. She trusts you. But she knows better than to trust me."

I felt my heart contract. "So much suffering."

He sighed and leaned back. "Deirdre and I identified with joy. We just weren't very good at it. But we were experts at pain. The pain made us feel alive, so it was worth it. Very Lawrencian. But I've learned some lessons. To be complete. To have a good appetite, but not hunger."

I clutched my midriff. "I'm so hungry I could eat the whole world."

"What do you mean?"

Before I could answer, car lights shone in the driveway. A "brother" from the Hog Farm banged on my door to carry me off to the commune for a full-moon-in-Scorpio celebration. Jim looked so disappointed. But I had to go.

So I went and Jim stayed home with the chickens. He was nice about it. "No, you don't have to be back before noon, just before dark."

Again, the experience of the Hog Farm, the drama of sky and earth, fire and drums, chanting, color, intensity, bright faces, costumes, red, blue, white, Earth People, singing around a circle of firelight, lifting our voices to the great blue moon while the fire crackled and blazed and a horse stomped and whinnied by the fence. I stayed over. In the night, just for a moment, I imagined I felt Jim's arm heavy across me.

I returned to Hondo around ten the next morning. Jim and I had breakfast together. He told me he had decided to return to Santa Fe. "I don't want to invade your privacy."

I laughed. "That's silly. I enjoy having you here."

"I'll come back," he said.

I wonder.

In spite of our agreement that it was over, I met Kelly at the Santa Fe library. Each time I saw her again, I felt that little tingle of awe at her beauty, her hollow cheeks and smooth hair, and when she said she wanted to go as far as Galveston with me, or even to New Orleans, I was tempted. It would be a way for me to proclaim my new-found freedom.

She told me about her husband Robert's last visit with Phaedra, to discuss her welfare payments. I couldn't imagine what he felt, sitting in my house. Kelly said he was excited by Phaedra, whom he thinks is available. I knew why he thought that, because she is warm and open, but I also knew he was wrong.

Jim told me that Robert has his eyes on me; and Robert told Kelly that I came running to the door in my nightgown and hugged him. I was in my nightgown but didn't hug him. I just touched his arm as he left. Not a sexual thing, just empathy.

Jim and I talked about how I select what to tell him. He and Deirdre shared all their thoughts and feelings, at least at first. Yes, I did that with my first husband. But after my third husband and his betrayal, I learned to be careful. Not to reveal everything. Trust no one with all my thoughts and feelings.

I got a letter from Deirdre. I read it walking towards Harvey's casita. The letter was hysterical, full of blame and hate for Kelly and for me, full of cries for help. I went into the kitchen, sat down on the floor and cried.

She called in the evening, miserable and frightened. I sat on the bed holding the phone, numb with suffering, my eyes shut. She kept saying she was going insane. She is thinking about signing up for Primal Therapy and asks me to write what I think about it. I sat down and wrote a twenty page treatise, knowing how silly it was for me to advise her, or for her to take my advice, but grateful to be able to help her if she asked. I had the good sense not to send it.

I take a walk back up into the canyon to the spot where we lay to see if there is anything left of us – footprints in the clay? Grass crushed down like the bed of the doe? Nothing. It is as if that moment had never been. I don't dare let myself love him. Yet something in me cries out.

I feel like calling up Deirdre. "May I borrow your pretty husband for one night before he goes? Lie warm and naked in

his arms? After all, you've had him for eight years."
I'm awful. I don't care. It would feel good.
Alicia is going to Santa Fe and I think of sending Jim a note. Just one word. Yes! No! I won't. I will. No, I won't. I want to. I will. No, I'll wait and let what comes to me come. But if he comes back . . . Why have I been fighting so hard? Maybe it really is inevitable. Letting go, and letting it come to me.

As before, Deirdre sensed what was happening. She wrote to Phaedra that she shouldn't hold back because of her. That she loved Phaedra and that made it all right. She knew she couldn't hold onto me or she would never be free. She said if it was going to happen, she would rather it happen now than later because now was the best chance she had of getting through it. She was afraid of not completing the cycle. Again. It was fear, she wrote, that was making her so miserable. She ended by saying she was rushing to the post box on the corner to mail the letter before she lost her nerve.

I was lying on the bed listening to the wind, imagining it was Jim's VW van coming up the hill, picturing him so clearly that I jumped up to look out. Fool! Only the wind. But after a minute, I was so sure I heard it, I jumped up again.
I ran outside. In a moment we were hugging each other.
    Nothing was shattered. Not my illusions, because I hadn't any. We made love on the sheepskin rug in front of the fireplace. No ghosts to haunt me, either of Deirdre or Ken. Whatever consequences are mine. The look of triumph on his face as

he cast off his shirt was worth it in itself. Not hurrying, taking plenty of time. With the music and the firelight. Trying to be careful of the baby and then forgetting all about it. The baby kicked up a storm afterward. I had Jim lay his hand on my belly and feel it kicking. He was as amazed as I am. That's what I really wanted, to have a man love my body as it is now, to share this miracle with me for a little while. He said he had never made love to a pregnant woman before. "I wish it was my child." I wished it too, but because of a lost earring, he's going to Africa.

I was at peace, a new sensation. There was a uncanny, effortless intimacy between us. "Do you realize we could live together?" I said to Phaedra. She just smiled.

We slept apart again, Jim in the casita, me in the house. He came to breakfast smiling. We both wrote all morning, Jim out there, me here. I felt inspired again. We met in the kitchen over the coffee pot, exchanged grins and hurried back to our corners.

After dinner we lay by the fire. Jim rubbed my back with oil. I felt myself resisting, my mind wandering, thinking about my "stop and go" mechanisms, that I'm here and now. This is the man I can let go with. That it was right and good even if we weren't married, even if we hadn't vowed anything to each other.

Baby I wonder what you think of me for all this? Are you glad? You wouldn't be coming into the world if I were a "virtuous" woman. You wouldn't be coming into the world if I were not full of passion and hope. Does it make you glad that your mother has found a lover?

Jim says he is so happy that it hurts. Intensified by knowing it's transient. Maybe he'll come back from Africa knowing who he is and what he wants. By that time I'll have some insight into what is required of a parent. Are we that old cliché, two ships that pass in the night?

"They're screwing all over the landscape," he says, "but they can't actually sleep together!" So last night we slept together on the fold-down couch. He dreams all night he's having a conversation with me that's so real he doesn't realize he's dreaming until he wakes up.

In the morning he turns to me. "Well, that wasn't so bad." I'm laughing. Tonight he's back in the casita and I'm in my own bed. Tomorrow he goes back to Santa Fe.

Today Deirdre called while I was at Harvey's. I talked to her briefly, She wanted to know, "Are you living with Phaedra?" "No." "Are you sleeping with her?" "Yes." "Are you in love with each other?" "Yes." "Is she going with you to Africa?" "No. No way." "Are you still going?" "I have to." A long pause.

I said "I don't want you to hold out false hope. As far as I know, I'll never come back to you. I don't think you should call or write to me anymore."

Well, the honeymoon is over. Now comes the hard part. God, suddenly I feel very tired. I am shaking out rugs and weeping. As soon as Jim returned to Santa Fe, Deirdre called and said she wanted to come home. I can feel what she's feeling. I said, "Of course, come, anytime."

Deirdre says she knew it would happen and she loves me

and it's okay. Poor Deirdre. I know that was really hard to take. She's still traumatized, scared. She went to an analyst and he said he couldn't help her because she knew more than he did. He asked her out to dinner.

Her voice lightened. "Tell Jim not to flip. I'm not going to lay anything on him. Ewar and I just want to be home."

Will I ever see Jim again? Was this morning really goodbye? I wish I could see him one more time before he leaves. But he said he needed some time to contemplate. So do I.

Weird! Deirdre and I will be here together, missing the same man. I'll move my things out into the casita. I realize how much I've enjoyed being alone here. But it's okay. Maybe I can retreat into my writing.

I guess I should at least call Jim and let him know Deirdre is coming home. It's not really very complicated. If I don't try to control it. Just let it go. Jim went off whistling.

Phaedra called and informed me that Deirdre is coming back. I was shocked and angry, for she had told everyone she wasn't ready.

"I'm sorry for you," I said, "I know you want to be alone, but it's her house. There's nothing we can do."

"I understand. It'll be okay."

"I was just lying here thinking about you."

She didn't say anything.

I said: "I won't be content not to see you just because of Deirdre."

The next day I went to see her in Arroyo Hondo. I said "It really hurts to think this might be all we ever have together. That I'm going away for such vague reasons."

"They're not vague to me."

"Unless one of us dies, it's as sure as the sun rising tomorrow."

"What?"

"No, I shouldn't say it. I want to see how you and I turn out."

"It'll keep."

"It's easy to pretend to be confident," I said.

After a pause, I said "Last night I felt that I would come back from Africa to you."

"And I felt that I would wait."

"I don't have to come back. You could get on a plane and join me."

She gave me a long look.

"I wonder," I said, "if any man can live up to you. I do idealize you, not when we're looking into each other's eyes, but other times when you're busy doing something and you don't notice. If, when you get very big and there's no one around to love you, remember how much I loved you."

"I'm not likely to forget."

To Cross the Great Water

*H*e's gone. My heart is weeping. I will get over this. In a day or two. On our last day we went to the pond and he swam while I played in the boat. The clear green water. Making love to his shining wet body. That night we got stoned, took a long walk in the moonlight. He lay on his back in the road laughing while I took a pee. We climbed to the top of the mesa and looked at the mountains all around. We lay in the sagebrush with the dogs sniffing us, watching the stars and wondering.

The fire was still burning when we got home.
He's gone. He took part of me with him.

Dear Harvey,
Bus headed for New Orleans. As we passed Lamy, I realized that Deirdre and Ewar would be coming in on the train in a few hours. It occurred to me, I could get off the bus, greet her joyfully and our lives would return to the way we were.

Near Mineral Wells, I woke and saw from the bus the sun rise out of a cotton field, an orange-pink globe swollen by the atmosphere. The next morning, the boxy ferry left the sullen town of Galveston and entered the Gulf headed for Louisiana. The sun rose and bled in the waves. Sunlight shimmered on the water; seagulls swarmed behind a shrimp boat. The day was still fresh and clear, not yet humid.

I heard a car pull into the driveway. I dressed in a hurry and went out to see who it was. Ken. I hugged him. How could I?

We sat at the outside table in the sunlight. He finally acknowledged that the baby is his. Then he recounted his woes, saying that he had asked Betty to marry him because she is insecure. She is a nurse who lives in Albuquerque. But first he has to tell her about me. "She has to know that while I'm living here I will want to keep seeing you and the baby and be concerned about your welfare." He moved closer, slid an arm around the back of my chair. "I'm perfectly capable of loving more than one woman."

I felt repulsed but didn't want to insult him and push him away. "I think you should assure her that you and I won't be physically involved," I said.

He grimaced, withdrew his arm. He looked tired, older. I was surprised that his haggard appearance evoked no compassion in me. I didn't trust his words. He tried to explain why he said what he did at the welfare office, about not being the father. It hurt me to listen to it, but I listened and nodded. I suggested he bring Betty to meet me and I will assure her I won't be after her husband. He's still living in the same house, only in the garage. Barbara, the owner of the house, came back and locked him out because he was seeing Betty.

Dear Roget,
New Orleans, dawn, I walked to the docks. Five freighters were tied up one after another and I went along them reading their names looking for the Mar Egeo. I walked a long way down the dock, feeling the thick wood beneath my shoes, and back up, and waited until the Basque shipping

office opened. It was filled with clocks and thick ledgers and a Spanish gentleman behind a desk and someone in the corner. The gentleman informed me in gruff English that the ship had been rerouted to pick up more cargo and would arrive in a few days.

I went for a walk this evening with Zoe the dog, then down to Harvey's and Alicia's to do laundry, but mostly just to talk to someone. Petite Alicia, who has the grace and beauty of an Aztec princess, says she can't come out of the bedroom until she has all her makeup on. "Without it, I'm ugly."
  I laughed. "I doubt it."
  She shook her head. "I wish my English was better. Then Harvey and I could have more interesting conversations." She gave me an intent look. "Do you love Jim now?"
  "Yes."
  Measuring with her hands. "A lot or a little?"
  I measured as far as I could reach.
  Harvey came in from his basement photo darkroom. He was wearing a blue shirt with sleeves rolled up. He asked how I was. I said "Okay. I'll get over it." Meaning the pain. "He's such a beautiful man."
  "He loves you, too. He told me so."

Dear Phaedra,
The Mar Egeo, a Basque freighter, left New Orleans at seven in the evening bound for Barcelona. I go up to the highest deck. Shrieks of our whistle. I see the Canal Street ferry slanting across the river towards Algiers. We are headed down the Mississippi. The evening sky is gray with

streaks of red. In one of your letters, you wrote: "Beauty, the everlasting, is in the world." You wrote: "Eyes too full to hold more." Our engines beat and throb. I am so elated. I feel alive as I have not in a long time.

Harvey climbs the hill and knocks on my door to invite me to dinner with him and Alicia at the Taos Inn. I lean forward with joy. He looks at me with concern. "I want Deirdre to come too."

I look away. "Of course. What a great idea."

That afternoon, Harvey and Alicia and I are sitting at the big table in Harvey's dining room waiting for Deirdre to arrive. When she pulls up, she leaps out, all purple legs and manic excitement, hugging me and Harvey. Leaping up and down. I feel her anxiety. She hugs Alicia, hugs me again, touches my hair.

At the Taos Inn the maître d' escorts us to a table by the window, a white linen table cloth and rolled linen napkins. I am careful not to order the most expensive thing on the menu. To ease my nervousness, I light up a cigarette and sit smoking, listening while Harvey and Deirdre talk. She's taken the conversation way back to what happened in Mexico. Jim's affair with a married woman. Deirdre stares at her own freckled hands and says: "I can see why he was attracted to her. She is so free."

Harvey shakes his black tendrils. "I've never seen a woman so trapped. A drug-dealer husband. Seven children. She was stoned all the time. Her life is out of control."

Deirdre eyes him with both hope and desperation. "Jim was thinking of going down to see her, but he was afraid she'd gobble him up."

Harvey and Deirdre continue to bat the conversation back and forth across their divergent viewpoints – hers all love and light. Which inspires in Harvey an occasional "Shit!" and "Fuck!" that warms me to him.

Alicia, stately in a white silk blouse, her black hair falling to her shoulders, fingers her silver ring. What is going on in that complicated mind? Is she hoping for marriage? That is the one thing she never talks about with me.

After dinner we stopped by the Alley Cantina to see the musician Ricky Nelson. Deirdre was much in demand as a dancing partner. Alicia and I watched and giggled. Deirdre was so graceful, and extremely thin. She had lost twenty pounds in California. I saw her beauty, her loveliness shining through.

Deirdre and Ewar have moved into the house and I am in the casita. I didn't ask for all this, but it came to me and I have to deal with it somehow. There are times I'd really like to run away from the whole thing. I want to feel good about my life and myself and what I'm doing. This is a very awkward position for me and I have to make it come out right in my head somehow. I am having this baby alone. That's enough to carry right now. I don't think Jim had any idea how hard this would be for me.

I must be mad. I'm so tired I don't even know it. I can't understand what's happening. Ewar invited two friends over and I invited Julie's boy Tommy. Now the yard is full of squabbling little boys, bragging, threatening, competing. First they shot bows and arrows. Then they smashed ants. Then Ewar and his friends turned on Tommy. Ewar said, "We don't want to play with you. You're not our type." I brought Tommy's brother Randy over to defend him and Ewar and

Tommy began to fight. Deirdre let all this slide by. She let Ewar run over her. Then she took off for an ashram in lower Hondo.

All the boys are in the house shouting at each other, calling names. I can hear it from here. Tommy and Randy come bursting in my door yelling, "Phaedra! They said they're going to beat us up."

I'm on my feet, storming the castle. Yelling, "Enough is enough! If you can't get along you will all have to go home."

Ewar says, "You can't tell me what to do. You don't own this house. I can kick you and George Washington out if I want to."

"Your mom put me in charge," I say. "Nobody is kicking anybody out of the house."

There's a lull. I compromise. I tell Ewar I will take Julie's two boys home if his two friends go home. And he can go play over at their house. I say in a softer tone, "I'm really tired and I need some peace and quiet." So I pack up my two and take them home.

I'm miffed at Deirdre for being so unaware of my needs. Weary of playing guru with her. Being the strong one. I'm human too. All I really know how to do is suffer. And write.

I'm standing up by the ditch in my nightgown watering the pumpkins when Deirdre comes tearing up in the van. Running up to me, trembling. She hands me a letter already torn open. "I couldn't help myself," she says. "It's humiliating."

Stiff with indignation, I say in a bland tone, "I have nothing to hide."

But she's taken the shine off it, the virginity of the envelope, the words. I've been totally invaded. I let it go for the time, take the letter back to the casita, sit down and read it.

It's not what it would have been if it had been mine. There is practically nothing left now of the feeling. The house, the fireplace. Our little ceremonies for each small thing. A ceremony of eating. A ceremony of not eating, of getting up, of going to bed, making love, being apart, being together. It's gone. Entirely. I've written Jim three letters sent airmail to New Orleans. Full of my childish romanticism, poetry, philosophy. Answering his fear, his loneliness, as positively as I can.

His letter is honest. "I love women. Right now you're the lucky one. I love children. On my time, not on theirs." I begin to feel that, too. I don't want to be child-monopolized. This past week I began to have doubts about motherhood, about being taken over. Nonsense, I suppose. I'm not going to let a child take over my life. I'm going to try to maintain some discipline. That's necessary for survival. Mine and his both. Hear that, baby? You come into the world, I learn from you, you learn from me. But I still retain my inner room where not even you can invade me.

Jim writes about realizing that Deirdre's train was coming into Lamy and that he could have met it. He said that he was in shock, as if she was bringing terror with her. He couldn't handle it, couldn't meet her. Indeed, she is bringing the terror of her emptiness, longing for him to be there, to make love to him just once more.

Then Jim writes of being afraid, afraid of this trip, afraid to look inward. I had no idea he was so afraid.

He asks me to write, gives me his dates and addresses.

In the evening I sit on the couch with Deirdre drinking tea. She sits straight but her face is sagging. "I've finally let go," she says in a mournful tone. "I've acknowledged to myself that it's over."

"*Then why did you open the letter?*"
"*I was feeling vulnerable. I'm sorry. I won't do it again.*"
But now I can't trust her, either to pick up my mail or mail letters for me.

Phaedra,
I like writing these letters to you, although I can't mail them until I get to Spain. I am awake at 4 a.m. and go on deck. I have established my spot, my chair, away from the others. We've entered the Atlantic. Up to now, in the protection of the land, the sea has been *liso*, smooth, and so has the ship, but now it's like a merry-go-round horse, dipping and rising.

You think I didn't watch you dancing that night we were so stoned. I didn't want to make you self-conscious. What reminds me is this ship – it moves with an astonishing delicacy. You're a good dancer, which didn't surprise me but I was caught off-guard, I looked up and you were dancing. Without a thought I went outside and looked through the window. I can't tell you how much I loved you while you danced. But I admit it, I was confused. Should I go hug you? Kiss you? No. I wanted you to keep dancing, forever! So I did nothing and watched on the sly. My heart beat. I had impure thoughts, sexual but also possessive. I was proud: "This is my woman."

Tis yet another a day. I am ensconced here in my haven in the casita trying to reassemble my point of view. The last eighteen hours have been very full indeed, but I feel a detachment, an indifference. Not melodrama. Not even numbness. Just vague indifference. It's easy, too easy. Much easier than I expected. A gentle murmuring flow. I feel so pregnant! My mind keeps wandering. I'm only half here.

Phaedra,
It's three bells of the second dog watch. I love writing those words.

To answer a question you once asked me, no I don't see myself romantically. I'm driven, not by fate, but by boredom. Let's be honest, I was sick of the family, which protected me and kept me from the world, sick of people, of books, of talk, of chairs, of feeding the chickens and driving the kids to school.

I move through the world lost but navigating like crazy. "Yes," says Harvey, "navigating by women." He is right; I must find a better way, if I am to return home. And what is home? A familiar bed? A wife? A dog? Every hotel, cabin, floor and field is a home. Look up; there are sun-torn clouds. There is the sun itself, hydrogen fire. These are home, and I am always home.

I set this trip into motion by acts of lust and selfishness in order to be here on this ship. I am on my way and it is going to be a journey.

You wrote: ". . . that we may never know where our travels take us, only the excitement of penetrating deeper into the mystery."

I'm rapidly getting to know Harvey. I must say, I'm impressed by his poetry and stories. He's had a sense of himself as a writer much longer than I have. I try to see what my writing needs to develop. Reading more, building my vocabulary, and beyond that, a soul-expanding honesty I haven't reached yet. Can a woman ever write like a man? Why should I want to? I am reaching into my womanhood for some new interpretation of inner truth. Men like Jim and Harvey excite and confuse me. They are sure of what they know. My mind staggers with unfamiliar words and concepts.

Dear One,
Bauche the steward and I play two-handed canasta and we try to have a conversation but he has no English and I have little Spanish. There is one young seaman who speaks some English, about nineteen years old, beautifully built with dark hair and eyes; we talked about *fútbol* of course. And an old man, still solid and able, wearing an old crumpled railroad hat, who comes and watches us at cards.

I read your letters one last time, in order. They're beautiful, deep, funny. When the time comes, I'll throw them overboard, as we agreed. After meals, if there is anything left on a plate, Adolfo the waiter simply flips the leftover food out a porthole, so maybe I'll just stick your letters under the lettuce and let him dispose of them. Or I will wait for eight bells, midnight, and go on deck and chant incantations and etc.

Dear Phaedra,
Because we agreed not to save each other's letters, I threw yours overboard today. It was ten in the morning, a cool rainy day, the sea dark and restless. I took out my irreplaceable collection of letters, mostly from females, yours,

Deirdre's, cryptic notes from Kelly, my mother's, and read yours again, copied out the wise and beautiful parts, and walked out on deck and flung them into – not the sea unfortunately. The wind picked them up and carried them to the stern, plastering sheets of them on crates, drums, and winches. With visions of the crew roaring with laughter under greasy swinging lamps, I climbed down and picked my way over cables and ropes. It was drizzling and slippery. By the time I got to the stern, the wind had carried away all but a few pages. I kicked them overboard.

Dear Jim,
You ask what happened between me and Deirdre when she came home. It took me two days to figure out how to answer your question. Maybe you've never heard that old Apache saying: "Two women in same wickiup means broken pots."

Early on I consulted the I Ching, the way I do about important things. I got 53: Chien (Gradual Progress) The judgement: Development. The maiden is given in marriage. Good fortune. Perseverance furthers. A line in the fourth place. "The wild goose gradually draws near the tree. Perhaps it will find a flat branch. No blame. A tree is not a suitable place for a wild goose. But if it is clever, it will find a flat branch on which it can get a footing. It is important to be sensible and yielding. This enables the goose to discover a safe place in which life can go on, although she may be surrounded by danger."

Not a stable situation. I thought it would be best to leave and give Deirdre a chance to settle in, to reclaim her territory, so I went up to the Hog Farm for five days and came back to the house as a guest. A much more comfortable position.

How do I see Deirdre you ask. She's a slow-burning star, but she'll probably outlast all us streakers. I think we've all underestimated her. She is intrepid. A little experience under her belt and you may be surprised to see what she's becoming. She's not hollow or shallow. She does her crying and Hare Krishnas alone, in bathtubs, on mountainsides. She's finding that there are other people in the world who love her besides you and Ewar and Evelyn. She's got guts and in many ways I admire her, if you really want to know.

Phaedra, as I am falling asleep, the throb throb of the engines that seem to be saying where are you going, whereare you going, whereareyougoing, and then I am sleeping when a loud explosion wakes me up. Ripping of hull? Ship run aground? The Cuban lady, Chatin, shrieking, racing up and down the passageways. I run onto the deck. Lightning fifty yards off the ship, followed by tremendous thunder banging and cracking.

I fall back to sleep and have a dream, that I wander all night on my horse, back across the sea, through the wet streets of New Orleans, through Beaumont Texas and Mineral Wells New Mexico; I ride up into Arroyo Hondo. I find you asleep in the grass. Asleep?

Dead.

Or not dead. Alive and lusty. Then we are back on the road again, together. It is night and I am behind the wheel. Flat dark land, fences, faces of cattle. I work my way through the gears, first, second, third, fifth, seventh tenth thirtieth. We go through Mineral Wells again and through

Beaumont again, a few motels flash vacancy signs but we don't stop.

Now you are driving. It's dark except for the headlights. We are each in a world of our own.

I look up.

Phaedra, we're driving across the sea!

Rain! Whooopee! The smell of mint and sage and wetness. Delicious!

Ah, the absurdity of it all – life in general – mine in particular. It's coming together though. Roget paid me back fifty so now, with the three hundred Deirdre gave me, I have enough to buy a vehicle. And I've got to get a driver's license. Got hassled at the bank about my check, which brought me down. Got to fix the chicken coop. All that and just feeling physically tired.

I hitched a ride up to the Hog Farm and I hung out with Karen who was a month more pregnant than me. I had heard that she had bad morning sickness and was freaking out, but by the time I saw her she was radiating a mother-to-be glow. We talked baby clothes and exercise and labor until I was bored with it all. Bored and scared. My peace of mind wants an uncluttered, orderly existence. The idea that my life is about to change forever, that I might have to make concessions, might feel tired all the time . . . Oh, bullshit! It's not going to be like that, I told myself. I won't let it be.

When I got back from the Hog Farm, Deirdre came rushing out of the house to greet me. "I didn't mean to drive you away," she said, giving me a big hug. "We can live together. I'm not angry. You don't have to leave."

"It's your house," I said. "I'm just a guest."

"Ewar has gone back to Frisco to spend time with his dad," she said. I breathed a sigh of relief. We walked back to the house, her arm around my shoulder. "It's odd," she said, "My life has just reached the point where I'm about to be alone. My responsibilities are over."

"And mine are just beginning."

She paused and took me in, for a moment saw me clearly. "It's as if our lives are on opposite sides of the coin. And the coin is just turning over." Her tone crested and fell. "It's weird to think that you might be starting out your new life with the same man I just finished with."

When I didn't respond, she said: "I want to find another house nearby. Maybe in Valdez. It's hard to start a new life in this house. The memories."

We fell silent. She touched my shoulder. "I want you to move in with me. We could help each other."

Scrambling for the appropriate response, I took a deep breath. I couldn't imagine the two of us living together now. Writing to, waiting for the same man.

Dear Harvey,
Well I've made it this far, meaning the deck of the Mar Egeo tied up at the dock in Valencia, waiting for customs to summon me. The ship entered the harbor at six this morning, funnels covered with sparkling butterflies. The sun rose red, then orange. Valencia lay pale in the distance and I thought of you wandering Spain in 1961. For me, it is your country and I am only allowed to visit.

I am rambling: ha ha – double meaning. I will write

again from Africa. I appreciate that you are looking in on Phaedra. She is gutsy but still, being alone and pregnant can't be easy. Do you realize that I love her? But we didn't make any promises. I didn't even say that I was returning. It's a dangerous game we are playing, vowing nothing as if by not vowing, we ensure it will happen. I want it to happen but I want this too, this being alone with my thoughts. I'm not sure what she understands or if she'll wait for me. And why should she?

Dear Phaedra,
I got off the ship in Valencia instead of Barcelona. After fourteen days at sea, I stumbled down the ramp and swayed on land. Valencia was a madhouse, cars whizzing, people rushing.

My train ticket was for Cartagena but I was tired and wanted a meal so I got off in Murcia. Dusk in the crowded plaza full of flowers and food stalls. Waiters rushing with Fantas and sherbets and coffee and brandies, the sky full of darting swallows, strings of colored lights. Later I walked the dark streets, ate in a bar – a plate of stuffed eggs, potato salad, for thirty cents, a glass of wine for seven cents. Slept in a narrow dirty room without a light, for seventy cents. At these rates, my $2,500 will last a long, long time.

When I stepped off the train in Algeciras, there was a beautiful young Arab woman. I thought of you in that red and black blouse. She was with an old woman with tattoos over her face.

My plan is to catch a ferry to Tangiers, take the bus to Casablanca and find a freighter or ferry going to west Africa. I have this great desire to be far away in a land where I know no one, among strangers.

Dear Jim,
I helped Deirdre move the rest of her things into her house in Valdez yesterday. Roget came over with a truck. While we were loading up, a violent thunderstorm blew in, black clouds and gusts of wind that hurled the yellow leaves in sheets from the trees, dashing them to the ground. D. was hunched over in the back of the truck trying to hold the tarps down. R. tried to back over some rocks. They both got soaked. Came in for coffee and lunch, laughing. We ate and smoked and talked about writing, security, reality.

The drive to Valdez held us in silence. Cloud-hanging mountains swallowed us up as we drove down the long black tongue of the highway. The house shows the changes she's been through. It is simple, gracious and lovely. She put the kitchen shelves together herself and will be driving in over the most horrendous washed-out road, carrying her wood and water across a narrow footbridge. She's very pleased with her efforts and I'm proud of her. You needn't "try" to love her out of pity. She is to be admired for her courage, her strength, her gentle true spirit. Really, she's one hell of a woman. I'd say she's come through this like a thoroughbred. Roget has really turned on to her in a friendly, admiring way. Even Harvey is beginning to come around, in spite of all his skepticism. I said to D "What's the worst thing that could happen?" She said, "No God."

I've got to get the chicken coop fixed somehow. The roof fell in. I don't feel up to tackling it. I'll fix the windows that were broken when the wind blew like the big bad wolf into my sanctuary. Wind, you are free to come and go as you please,

but you can't invade me.
I've got to see about getting the screens up, too.

Dear Deirdre,
My feelings towards you are passionately deep. All our enthusiasm, all we felt and suffered. And Mexico, the spiritualization of Deirdre Levy. I want to write a history of you, a portrait of you laid bare, like an immense wound.

Our years burrow in my heart like worms, hurting but also letting in light. My heart, a red hot coal crumbling into ash, is . . .

[Unfinished, not sent]

Dear Deirdre
Yesterday I sat with a carafe of red wine in a café on the dock – I am in Algeciras waiting for a ferry to Tangiers – and wrote you an emotional letter, which I had the good sense not to send. I wrote "I love you" and then in the next sentence explained why our marriage is over. Are you sad? Are you triumphant? Causing you to suffer has taught me what it is to suffer. Even flight does not free us from suffering. I am numb. I don't understand what I am doing but I think you know that we had to do something. We had to . . .

[Unfinished, not sent]

No sense in hoping to be with Jim while Deirdre stands between us. She looms bigger than Africa, bigger than half the world. I can't see how it changes. Out of my control. As long as she considers him "hers" and me a threat. She is still Mrs.

James Levy, ring on her finger. I will never be that. Don't even want to be.

Jim said when he told Harvey he loved me, Harvey didn't laugh. "He knows who you are." I don't even know who I am. But I'm glad. Harvey guarantees me the first option on renting the house after Deirdre. But now living here seems senseless. I've got to remember what I'm doing. There is no one I can really confide in. What am I supposed to learn from all this? Got to get back to my aloneness. No use holding on to memories, prolonging the inevitable. He's gone and won't be back for a long time. Maybe never. Dwelling on what we had doesn't make it any easier now. Only pain and discontent with the present. Seems like I've lost a whole week. Not done any writing or sewing or anything. Got to get my thing together before I forget what it is.

Dear Phaedra,
The rumor on Sunday morning was that there was a coup in Morocco and the borders would be sealed. I took my bag and went to the ferry. One more boat was going before they closed the border – so I went.

In Tangiers, a guide found me a room – dark and cheap – then showed me where the hash dens in the medina are. He also offered me young women, young men, I suppose old women and old men too if I wanted them.

I went to a hash den, up a flight of stairs to a large room with men sitting at long tables. In the corner, five musicians squatting in a half circle playing subtle music. There were a few foreigners scattered here and there. I sat with a young Frenchman and some Arab boys of seventeen or so. One of them fascinated me. He had sad gentle eyes, sad slow hands, and a pockmarked face. He gave me a hunk of hash. I offered to pay and he said no. After I smoked some, I put the rest in a match box. The hash and kef are smoked in long two-foot pipes.

Suddenly I realized where I was, in a hash house (the opium was being smoked upstairs), in a room full of stoned Arabs. The boy who'd given me the hash said he was leaving, could I after all give him something. I had no change and gave him the smallest bill I had – saw the look of disgust pass over the Frenchman's face – I'd paid too much. The music went faster and faster, wailing, men clapping, singing shouting – then broke, nearly came to a stop, then started again slower, picking up speed gradually, intricate music, beginning again to wail, matching my inner wailing . . .

We drank hot tea with mint leaves to soothe our throats. I was contemplating the faces around me when an Arab boy of eight or ten swooped in, wiped the table clean and moved on. The match box with my hash was gone, to be sold to another. I had to grin. It is an efficient system.

Dear Jim,
Seems I haven't written or heard from you in quite a while. Roget asks if I've heard from you. When I say no he says, "That's good. That's really good. That means he's let go of this and he's doing what he went there to do."

By tomorrow I should be driving my own little VW Bug. Whoopee! The first big trip I have planned is to the post office to mail this letter. My walking these days is limited from here to Harvey's. Feels like I could drop this kid any time. Probably won't though. Harvey said, "As Jim's agent in the states, I'll pay your medical bills if you'll go to the hospital." I thought that was very generous. But welfare takes care of it. Got to get Ewar's room ready for Alexander.

Roget,
Today I walked through the medina in Rabat and sat in a square drinking tea. Hundreds of men gathered before a TV. The news was showing the fate of the rebellious officers in the coup d'état. We are undergoing the aftermath: tanks in the street, soldiers leveling their rifles at your heart in the most casual manner, buses are stopped and searched. I walked too near the palace and was ordered away by an soldier, who seemed quite angry.

Jim,
You'll be glad to know I can now get to the post office on my own. Deirdre gave me three hundred dollars towards a car. They wanted $450 for it. It had no first gear and needed a clutch plate. Deirdre drove me to Red River to pick it up. It seemed to be in fair condition, black and shiny. I drove back through a violent rain storm and flash flood.

Dear Phaedra,
Bamako, Mali. Me. Here. Oh boy. I caught a plane in Casablanca and for some reason that the airline didn't explain, we stopped here and are being put up in the best hotel in Bamako, the capital of Mali.

   Big trees, green trees, big green trees, and heat like I

have never experienced. I walked down the main street in the heat under the big green trees and wondered what I have gotten into, what do I think I am doing, what *am* I doing? Then reality kicked in, saving reality, blessed reality – I am here. Not Niger; there weren't any planes or boats to Niger and besides, I decided I'd rather be in a country where people speak English, not French. So tomorrow I will be in Ghana. And . . . I will do something in Ghana. . . . I think I am doomed to failure in this endeavor because I am trying to achieve contradictory ends – establish both my reality and my unreality, seek peace while running from it, seek myself while fleeing from myself.

What I want is to drift and in the process to acquire eyes that see in the dark, to be a little mad and to be glass, to be a slow ship in a blue world, to hold still like a deer and move like a deer. To drink, to drink bells, drink lips, drink timetables, drink stars, drink the spaces between electrons. To be the night train. And the day train. The earth and the bird that flies off the earth, the . . .

[Unfinished letter, not sent]

Dear Harvey,
I miss Phaedra. But I don't miss Deirdre. She and I spent some miserable time together in Rabat, me on the bed and she turning in my gut like a tape worm. I ran the gamut, from self-loathing to exaltation. I received a letter from her, written in May from San Francisco, in which she says, "You were very irresponsible to take us on in the first place if you had any idea that you were like what you're like now." Arrghhgh! How could I have known? And what am

I now? And didn't she beg me to save her from her arid marriage? She after all abandoned David to be with me. Oh I have a thousand replies, but no answers to the guilt and pain.

I am in Bamako, Mali, huddled in my hotel room, which is almost clean, trying not to be too frightened. I think of Koestler's idea, that we have to regress in order to progress. The air-conditioner shudders but doesn't blow any cold air. Just walking down the street I sweated like a pig. I stopped to order an ice coffee and forgot the French words and got up and left. My love for Deirdre is so confused with pity, terror and guilt. I tried to be grounded and joyful, to love her on that basis and . . .

[Not sent]

Dear Jim,
Driving back from Red River with no first gear was tricky. It was raining as I set out. By the time I cruised into the canyon the sky was black, etched with lightning above the mountains. The clouds opened up in a deluge. The wipers were beating a tattoo. I could hardly see out the window. Rivers of water flooded the roadsides. The rain changed to hail that bounced off the car, whitening the road and banks of the cliffs as I wound my way through the canyon. There are two times I'm with you: in extreme beauty and in danger. In danger I'm thinking this will make a good story.

Then the avalanches let loose. Muddy water, rocks and gravel spurted out of the hillsides and across the road, torrents of water half way up the tires at eight or nine places along the road. Don't drive into it. This is how people get swept off the road and drowned. But I kept going. As I reached Questa the sun came out, the sky was blue and it was as if it had never happened.

Jim,
Elaine and Roget and I sat on the couch in the living room and Elaine was talking about Edgar Cayce, astrology and California falling into the ocean and Roget was saying I'm not so sure, how can we know and besides who cares? Roget's eyes lit up at the possibility of a stainless steel world without religion or God. And me in the middle. It was comical for it was all that psychic stuff that attracted Roget to Elaine in the first place, that and her unusual looks, tall and slender with stylish glasses and long blond hair. She usually has a cigarette in her long fingers. It didn't hurt that she owns an art gallery near the plaza. I wonder, do we all have a calculating side or is it just me?

I'm going to finish this page and call it a letter.
I miss you. Know how I can tell? I dreamed I was riding a broom handle. It was too skinny. Way pregnant ladies aren't supposed to be horny. I wonder where you are tonight and if you still see the little yellow star and if you think of me sometimes. Sometimes I feel you as close as walking in the door and sometimes not at all. I feel you solid and well – not always happy but well.

Dear Roget,
It's a trip, as they say, to fly into an airport the size of the old Albuquerque airport with the realization that I know not a single person in the city of Accra, in the country of

Ghana, on the continent of Africa. The airplane door opened and I stepped into a blast of moist hot air. The tarmac was squishy under my feet.

I am now in a fort on the coast of Ghana. Getting here was an adventure. I caught a "mammy-truck" in Secondi-Takoradi and it kept breaking down. I had expected to get to Dixcove in daylight and it was getting dark and it broke down again. The driver got out and tinkered with the engine. The other passengers simply got off and walked away. The driver and I looked at each other. It dawned on me that we were not going to get there. I said goodbye and started walking. By now it was dark; I had been advised not to be out in the country at night – cobras, mambas, pit-vipers – but I didn't know what to do. I went off the road and slept in the bush. I lay down on the ground with my glasses, knife and water bottle near my head and listened to the jungle. The sounds were just like in the movies – screaming birds and things croaking and sighing – it was funny. This is called living in the moment. It is becoming a habit. I am not afraid because I am in the world with no chance to escape, nowhere to go and no one to call, surrounded by the universe. Why would it harm me? I am part of it.

What makes me sad is I can't remember his face, his eyes. A falling star, fading fast. What was that all about? I didn't expect to fall in love. Just a few week's pleasantry. It seems so crazy to have it end abruptly, in mid-air. But it had to be that way. It seems so senseless to be having a baby by a man to whom I am nothing, about whom I feel such a sea of indiffer-

ence. I want to run away. My peace is shattered. It's as if the numbness, the daze has worn off and I am really feeling it.

I don't think Jim had any idea how hard this would be for me. I really do wish Deirdre would fall in love again when it's time. That would help.

Dear Harvey,
I caught a ride to Dixcove, right to the door of the fort. A skinny African greeted me, dressed in a loose shirt and shorts, with a long expressive face. His name is Kodjo and he speaks a little English in a wonderful singing rhythm. He showed me a room with a canopied bed and mosquito netting where government officials stay when they visit and offered it to me for five cedis a day. It was dank and dark and I ended up renting this room, in a tower at the top of the fort, for one cedi a day. It has openings in three walls but no glass; and it had no furniture until Kodjo supplied a table, a chair and three cushions for me to sleep on. We settled on an additional fifty pesewas a day for one meal, to be served at sundown.

[A letter from Roget to Jim in his French-inflected English.]
What made me get into that, was the fact that Deirdre came by the other afternoon. Her and Glenda feel so much alike: both of similar inclinations, (which I call the Lama Background). What matters in fact, is that they both spent some time up there, and also that they probably got there for very similar reasons; same thing with the other people who live there now – or the people who have lived there.

The same search for something perfect and illuminated is present in both; they both have – or had – the same attachment for the perfect situation within the most perfect words of wisdom; they both suffer – or have suffered – from noticing here and there that people and situation alike do not –cannot – permanently fit within that frame of vision. They have resented people and situations for not being as holy as they should have been.

Dear Jim,
It's happening so fast I can hardly keep up with it. I'm approaching the horizon of eternity after an eight month voyage on the ocean of life. I can almost see the land. I can smell it. The birds are whirling about my raft as it drifts towards shore. Soon . . . soon I will be landing on the unknown continent called Motherhood, somewhere on the finely marked equator between life and death. It's a very high place, a very lovely prehistoric dawn, where the beginning and the end meet in an eternal circle.

I talked to my father last night, exchanging philosophies of life so similar. Two hours long-distance and worth every penny. When I told him about the baby he said, "Well, this may shock you, but I don't really see why a woman should be denied the experience of having a child just because she doesn't have a husband."

"Really? How do you think Mother will take it?"

"Oh, she won't bat an eye. You're her daughter, and you still would be even if you went to the electric chair. She'll probably be knitting little booties."

Deirdre did such a charming thing – left me a birthday

card and a white pitcher full of red, yellow, white and lavender zinnias and yellow sunflowers with a graceful twirl of morning glories, and a turquoise ring. I've wanted one for years. I really love her.

Dear Phaedra,
Here I am, the wizard of the castle, bearded in the tower, the surf moaning below the fort, waiting for my supper. Vultures are sitting in tall trees and crows are crying overhead. Little gray pigs with big ears are running home along the high walls and sheep and goats are coming into the courtyard. Two canoes are paddling into the cove through the breakers. Cook fires are springing up in the village. In other words, everyone and everything in their place.

Phaedra! Phaedra! I love you. I don't dare say more.

It's nearly dark; my supper has arrived, it's fufu. One of Kodjo's sons brings it. He looks at me shyly and I give him a piece of bread from my stash. Then I light my kerosene lamp.

Your description of you and Deirdre and Roget moving her into the house in Valdez knocked me over. It was all there: the beauty and fierceness of New Mexico, the unspoken intimacy between all of you, the worth of having a home amidst the storms of life, and the picture of the three of you drudging back and forth with her boxes, industrious ants full of wonder, and tired.

Sitting here in its light, I think of the orange firelight that shone on us in Arroyo Hondo. Where do I stand at this point? I can't tell. I feel bad about drifting like this but there's no going back. Is there going forward? One assumes so. I'm not lonely, not afraid, but I am serious. It is time I begin learning about myself.

Arroyo Hondo is my home and I will return there and try to make a go of myself. Like you, I don't want to be married. But I want to be with you, if you still want. Not live together – I need to live alone, I don't know for how long – but I want to be with you, and see you, and love you. Perhaps it's all an illusion based on three weeks of fantasy, but it is the best thing I have had and I want it. I haven't any grand hopes for it – I'm too ironical – but I want it and it is the only thing I want.

A bell rings in the town, loud and tinny. Kodjo makes the rounds of the fort with a lantern, looking for thieves.

In a way, I feel that I am writing this into thin air. I got a letter from you in Rabat, dated June 23, but none since. June 23 was the day the Mar Egeo left New Orleans, a lifetime ago. On the ship I had the sensation that you had died. And maybe you have. My mind goes blank. Or perhaps you've run off with some man who has declared his undying love – "It's about time," you say – in which case I'd have to laugh; it would serve me right. Perhaps you have decided we were romantic fools who invented ourselves out of crepe paper and chaos. But most likely, your letters are taking a long time and I keep missing them.

My letters to Jim are still holding back. I can't let go completely anywhere but in my journal. Keep my bad dreams to myself. When I get away from writing, I really lose perspective. Jim says he can't see himself romantically. Neither can I anymore. I get all bogged down.

Oh, motherhood. What will I feel when I actually hold this child in my arms? When it becomes so much more than baby clothes and a squirming in my belly?

Yesterday I got a long, passionate letter from Jim that made me break down and sob in Deirdre's arms. I offered to let her read it, but she said it would only cause her pain. Her steady blue eyes looked into mine. "When you and Jim get back together again . . . I hope by then I won't be sad and alone."

I trembled inside at the thought, the possibility. I'm tired. Got a rotten headache today. Nobody is coming up my driveway anymore. It's not even my driveway.

Maybe it will be easier when the baby is born. I saw it first as the end of my privacy, a burden and a responsibility. But maybe it will be a blessing to have someone of my own to love and care for. I keep forgetting. It doesn't seem real to me.

I went to see Dr. Shorter. He gave me a quick exam, listened to the baby's heartbeat. He said everything is fine. To come back in a month. "You're no bigger than you should be." But I really feel big to me. I can't get comfortable at night, can't lie on my stomach.

Harvey,

I was getting restless: surprise. So I decided to go out with fishermen, six of them in a long dug-out with an antique motor, at five in the morning. I had understood that it was for a few hours but we went out of the cove, through the waves, and out and out, nearly out of sight of land, maybe ten miles or more. They spread nets on all sides of the dug-out, with the water just a foot away, rising and falling in long waves. And I was sick! I threw up over the side, into the nets. The men smiled, and one of them laughed, not meanly, for they are a kind people. But then cramps came on, which I have had off and on, and diarrhea. They sent me to the back of the boat and I sat on the edge shitting into the sea. They kept moving the boat to get away from my filth.

Dear Jim,
There's been an incredible flow of traffic through here since I last wrote. Starting with two of my pregnant friends from the Hog Farm, Moe and Sesame. They stayed three days, drying out their down sleeping bags. We just lay around comparing bellies, laughing at our group inertness. It was nice to be right in tune with each other, to know this is natural and there's no point in fighting it. Am I ever slowed down! I thought I was getting lazy, but nature apparently knows what she's doing. I keep my little house together, feed the animals, read and write and that's about it.

Tomorrow I will be 29. For my birthday, I guess I'll go to the post office and maybe I will have a letter from you. That would be nice. I looked up Ghana in the atlas. What I'd give to be able to walk on the beach for half an hour.

Deirdre told me she was up at Lama last Sunday, sitting around with Glenda, Ken and Barbara and a couple of other people. Barbara, it turns out, is a school teacher and another of Ken's lovers. My name came up. Barbara asked Deirdre if I was pregnant with Jim's baby. She said, "No, as a matter of fact." Everyone turned to Ken who said yes, it was his. "He said it very casually," Deirdre said.

The next day Ken came into the Seven Rays gallery where I sat mellow and complacent, crocheting. He seemed surprised to see me looking so well, "radiant," he said. He hugged me, kissed me on the neck, dropped down beside me on the couch and talked for forty-five minutes. Mostly about his blow-out with his two women, Betty and Barbara. "I was just trying to love and be kind to as many people as I could," he said, "but I felt like I was standing on the railroad tracks with two trains coming at me head-on."

Having listened patiently to this drama, I decided that it was only fair to mention you. "I've fallen in love, too," I said in a demure tone, without dropping a stitch. But as I said it I was overwhelmed by a déjà vu sensation as if these words were an echo of my mind that was running about five words behind. All recorded on the cosmic tape recorder centuries ago. It felt so weird, I fell silent. Startled, he stared into my eyes. I said, "Jim Levy" and watched his face drop. Then I changed the subject.

Before he left he offered to make a hanging cradle for the baby. I graciously accepted. Roget seemed disappointed when I told him. He was going to make one for me. He was just waiting to see if I had twins. Elaine is planning to give me a cradleboard. That will be nice when I take the baby out into the world.

Jim, I'm so big I can hardly credit it. I'm a whale. The Titanic. I can't really see going on like this for another month. I'm practically immobile. Every move I make has to be carefully planned to conserve energy because when it runs out I'm like a ship gone aground. Is this for real?

Yes, we are a couple of romantic fantasizing fools, but it's nice that we both retain a hard-headed cynical core. It's too easy to fall into the "soul mate" fantasy. When I begin to contemplate actually living with you, I feel frightened by the prospect of a dull, downhill routine, a gradual stifling loss of my inner room, and yours. Leading to an eventual collapse. And me, at the age of thirty-five alone again, bewildered, searching, like Deirdre. No!

Whatever happens, I must not let that happen again. Neither must you. I must be myself and do what I do without fear of losing. I'm going to be callous. I'm not going to worry about your freedom, only my own.

There's no such thing as soul mates. It came in a dream. The narrator said, "Each individual is a separate unique pattern of energy." Then Grandmother came into the dream. She said, "Well, the world is hard on women, but don't you think all this passion is adolescent?" Hmm . . .

I'm vulnerable now because I'm pregnant, but it's no excuse. I chose to carry this alone and I have never lost faith that I can do it. I know I can. Feeling unafraid, beautiful and self-fulfilled. That is what I need to retain. I feel a great sense of relief that you don't want to live with me, that you need to be alone.

Dear Phaedra,
Bored, I decided to go to the beach at Busia. I packed my knife and an orange and took the path across the spit, through the jungle, remembering to walk heavy. That is what Kodjo advised me, to walk heavy so the snakes would feel me coming and get out of the way. Two English girls, volunteer aid workers from Accra, were at the beach, along with the pigs. I sat near their blanket and they made light

conversation. One says she is going swimming. The other one resumes reading *The Manchester Guardian.*

"Don't get caught in the breakers," I advise.

"They're not very big."

To make a long story short, I thought she was drowning and I swam out to rescue her.

"Isn't it beautiful," she shouted.

I realized at that moment that I was sick, and it was probably malaria.

I swam in, staggered through the small rough waves and up the beach. I hurried back to the fort. Five men were clustered around tall drums between the village and the fort, drumming wildly. I got to my room and lay down. It is malaria, I am sure, despite the prevention pills. I dragged them out; the instructions are clear. Take two a week for prevention. If you contract malaria, take six, then take four the next day, then six again, then four again. I have exactly one pill left. I had forgotten to get more when I was in Accra.

I took stock: I am down with malaria in a fort on the Ghana coast. With modern drugs, malaria is not a dangerous disease. On the contrary, it is a trivial event on the coast. I do not have any drugs, however, modern or otherwise.

I descended the stone steps to the courtyard. Kodjo's two wives were sleeping on the ground in the sunlight. I found Kodjo sitting in his darkened room working out his lotto numbers for the week.

"Kodjo,"

Kodjo smiled, leaning his thin face towards me.

"I have malaria."

"You must take the pills," Kodjo said, singing, his head bobbing up and down.

I looked at the lotto sheet and Dr. Lotto's recommendations.

"I have only one pill left."

He bustled among his stacks of possessions.

"I have them," he said, producing a plastic bottle. We went into the courtyard and he emptied an assortment of pills on the lip of the well, pushing them around with his skinny finger as if they were insects.

"Which are for malaria?" I asked.

"These are for cholera. These are for plague. These are for yellow fever. These are for malaria." .

"Chorquinine sulphate pills?"

"I don't know that. The doctors give me."

"You take these for malaria?"

"Oh yes," he sang.

"How often do you take them?"

"Three."

"Three a week?"

"Three a day."

"Three a day?"

"Oh yes."

"How often do your wives take them?" I asked cleverly.

"One."

"One a day?"

"One a week."

"Kodjo. You know the boy Francis?"

"Oh yes."

"Will you send word that I want to see him?"

"I no let him in fort."

"But why not?"

Kodjo's face goes through subtle contortions, which I cannot read.

"Is your eldest son here?"

"He is gone to Takoradi."

Dear Jim,
On August 30, 1971, I went down to the Rio Grande with some friends. I waded out and swam across the cold river and back. Someone teased me, "How can you swim when you're like that?" I said with a grin, "It's easier than walking."

Around 4 a.m. the next morning I began to have cramps, strong and regular. I went down to Harvey's and called Deirdre, because she had offered to drive me to the hospital when the time came. She said she had never seen a baby born, and would it be okay if she watched? I was fine with that. She drove over to pick me up, and Marilyn too. Marilyn is a pregnant hippie neighbor who had built a hut on the island in the canyon. I had invited her to stay with me for a week after my baby was born, in case of an emergency.

Dr. Shorter had urged me to have the baby in the hospital in case anything went awry. I said I would on three conditions: that I not be anesthetized, shaved, or tied down.

I was in the hospital for half a day and nothing. Just a yellow stain on the sheet. I was tense, thinking if I didn't produce something soon, they'd throw me out. Deirdre and Marilyn sat across from each other, quiet and patient, Marilyn embroidering, Deirdre reading and writing. I kept jumping up because I felt as if I had to go to the bathroom and eliminate. Dr. Shorter arrived and gave me a brief exam, which hurt. He said I wasn't dilated enough. It was around one in the afternoon and the labor pains had slowed down. With a sour look he said, "You're having one of those long, northern New Mexico labors. Just putzing around." Like it was my fault. He told the nurse not to let me fall asleep, though it was normally my nap time. He told me to get up and walk around. Which I did. But maybe nature knew what was best. Maybe I needed a rest before the long haul.

I lie on the three cushions and stare at the ceiling. It is pale blue streaked with white. Suddenly anxious, I take off my belt, roll it tight and stick it in my boot. I hide my knife and cash in my boot and put the boot in the duffle bag. Then I throw up.

Later in the afternoon, I listen to the drums, which are mixed with the thumping of a brass band in the village. The gray light shines at the windows. The wind hisses in the sea. I can hear the vultures flap off the palm trees. Somewhere something is clacking. It sounds like the jaw of a wooden puppet. I realize with detachment that it is my teeth clattering.

In the morning, bright light beats at my eyelids. A drowsy exuberance spreads through me.

Francis appears at the door. Kodjo has sent for him after all. I explain the situation, give him money and ask him to go to Takoradi for malaria pills.

Someone came in to ask me what name I wanted on the birth certificate. I had chosen Alexander before he was born. But now I had a choice about his last name? Hmm. I didn't want to use my maiden name. And he couldn't have Ken's last name. So what was left?

Deirdre was a brick. She held my hand, rubbed my back. It was like having a charlie horse in my abdomen. Over and over and over. The contractions were about five minutes apart now. The nurse said not to push. "It's like trying to back a car out of the garage when the door isn't open." (As an adult, Alexander said that he had memories of being squeezed and squeezed and squeezed.) Finally my water broke in a gush of warmth against my aching back. It felt so good.

Only in death could I imagine more pain, though it never occurred to me I might die. But how long could I stand it? I wanted to put on a good show for Marilyn so she would have the confidence to do it. But I never believed there could be so much pain. Pain that becomes the whole focus of your existence. Thank God for Marilyn and Deirdre. I passed a couple of bloody clots and then a gush of bloody liquid. I was a mess.

They wheeled in a young Hispanic girl in labor. She lay in the bed with the sheets up to her chin, her mother standing beside her clutching her hand, her husband pacing the hall. She screamed bloody murder with each pain. She took the anesthetic they offered her. They wheeled her into the delivery room. It was over. "They helped me," she said afterward. "I don't know how. I was out."

I didn't want to be "out" for the most dramatic moment of my life when my baby slipped into the world. I never screamed. Not even once. But I was losing it. When I couldn't take much more, the nurse told me to try to sleep between con-

tractions. Huh? Can you actually do that? I realized that was my only salvation. If I could just plunge into sleep everything would be all right. The question was, did I have enough time between contractions to dive to the bottom? To touch blackness before the next contraction brought me back to the surface? I needed to check in to see if everything was okay between me and Central Control. To have that reassurance from my guides. To leave my body long enough to contact them for help. That was all I had left.

When the next contraction passed, I dove deep and fast, down into the pond, the light fading above me. Almost! Then back up for the next bout. As the next one passed, I dove again. This time I made it. For fifteen or twenty seconds. Down there, time is not. I touched darkness. When I floated back up again it was with a joyous certainty.

The way a train enters a tunnel, I enter my body. My head is being pressed inward. My chest is being crushed by vices. My jaw is quivering and my teeth are clicking. I pull the blanket higher. I can't get warm. Without control I shit my pants.

I wake in a cold sweat. Shadows of clouds wander around the moon-lit floor. A red star glints. I pour water into a glass and drink. It feels like tiny scraps of tin going down.

Is it summer or winter?

They will murder me. I see myself through their eyes, a foreigner who comes to the fort and rents the tower. He is wealthy, possesses a watch, a knife and American boots. I see them creeping like children up the stairs to the parapet, rushing the room, their machetes raised. In their fright, they butcher me.

I want my knife. It is a German knife, of sprung steel. My knife is my best friend. I have a frantic desire for it. It is gone. It is stolen. I balance a glass on the doorknob to warn me when they open the door.

The walls of the room bulge. I realize that I am passing in and out of consciousness. The tall men hovering over the drums are beating funeral drums for me.

I was having a nicotine fit. Marilyn went out in the lobby and came back with a cigarette. I sneaked a few puffs in the bathroom which was strictly forbidden because of the oxygen tanks. Then Marilyn went out to Taos Pueblo and came back with a bottle of greenish liquid, about eight ounces. She said it was peyote tea that had been blessed by Telles Goodmorning. This is what the Indians used to help with labor. I swished it around, then gulped it down.

I squatted in bed, tried Lamaze breathing, which I had read about, and pushed. My hair was a wild tangle, my gown slipped down to my waist so I was half naked. The nurse was shocked. "Lie down. What if someone should drive by and see you?" A half-naked wild hippie giving birth to a fatherless child. "And stop breathing like that," she said. "Just lie down and relax."

Uh-huh.

I lay down, but kept rocking, jiggling, panting. I wanted to know what birth was, to look it in the face undisguised by drugs. But as I labored into the afternoon and evening, everyone was tired of me. Marilyn went home around eleven, but

Deirdre stayed on, faithful to the end. My only friend.

The pain narrowed my focus, blotted out everything else. Even love, even time, even death. It was like some vast force in the cosmos torturing me, testing me, bearing down on me until I was forced to my knees and had to beg for mercy, for release. To admit that I wasn't IT, no matter what Alan Watts said. There was something a hell of a lot more powerful than my puny will.

That relentless life force tunneled down into the depth of me to make sure it had my full attention. The pain was trying to tell me that this is something really big. The biggest! Pulverized, trembling, I broke. I called on my creator.

It didn't help.

My thoughts are like the crashing sea. I pace the room springing from corner to corner. My throat is full of anguish. I stop at the little mirror tacked on the wall and stare at the bearded yellow face. It is a frightening face and I wish it were not mine. I lie down on the cushions and in the midst of this confusion, I wonder, if I die, will my body be transported back to New Mexico or stuck in the cemetery here, to sink into the ground?

Yet I know, with an irrational certainty, that the drumming is not for me and that I am not going to die.

That night, the fever is replaced by another round of chills. The moonlight gilds the jungle with a white sheen. Two cook fires burn in the streets of the town. In the lagoon, a single torch is gliding across the water. The wavering track of light zigzags towards me then widens like a mouth full of teeth.

Maybe the problem was that I couldn't let go. Around two in the morning the nurse came in to give me a shot. "What's in it?" An impatient sigh. "Something to relax you." "I don't want it." She stiffened, frowned. "If you won't take it, then your friend will have to leave."

Deirdre and I exchanged an intense look. I couldn't bear for her to leave when we were so close to the end. So I gave in.

The nurse gave me the shot. I began to feel drowsy. Dr. Shorter and the nurses went out for coffee leaving me with a button to push. Five minutes later, the baby's head came down. I squatted in the bed, pushed the button. After waiting for twenty-two hours, they all had to come running back, don gowns, masks and gloves and wheel me into the delivery room. Deirdre was glued to the observation window.

When I wake in the morning, I am covered in mosquito bites. I scratch them and they bleed. I open the door and the glass falls off the knob and breaks. I find my knife in the duffle bag.

Kodjo comes and sits with me. His older wife appears with a plate of rice and fish. She has long floppy breasts with long smooth nipples. The fish and rice are an improvement over the fufu but I cannot eat.

"You must eat," he says

I'm too sick to eat.

He and his wife confer. She shakes her head.

I take a forkful of rice and sauce and swallow it.

Alexander was born at 2:39 a.m., three weeks early, by my count. How can I describe what I felt when I saw that tiny purple human body wriggling like a fish at the end of a white rope of flesh still attached inside me? One last painful contraction and out came the afterbirth. All that happening voluntarily, like your heart beating. I still don't understand. It's a miracle, such an incredible miracle. Human life. All life. Consciousness. The body, the spirit. Everything! The Creator manifesting itself in the human animal. In a fly. In a cloud. Can you hear me, Creator? Are you there?

Those few moments were the highest high I had ever known. Higher than any acid trip because the pain had so opened my awareness, plummeted me down to the Source.

My baby drew in his first breath, but didn't cry. They lay him on my hips and I touched the bottom of his little foot with one finger. Dr. Shorter touched him first, but I had already touched him in a dream.

They weighed him and inked his footprints on his birth certificate. He weighed six pounds and one ounce and was eighteen inches long. When I saw his birth certificate, I was dismayed to discover that they had used my maiden name and had given my dear baby that name too..

Deirdre was standing in the window, waving, giving me the thumbs up, overjoyed, in tears. They wrapped Alexander in a blanket and took him away, then cleaned me up and wheeled me back into my room. It was such a relief to have the pain stop I would have been high just from that. But when I looked up at the acoustical tiles on the ceiling I noticed flashing colors and feathery frost patterns. "Oh!" I had forgotten all about the peyote tea. I felt serene.

Francis returns from Takoradi and I swallow six pills, two hours later two more, that night two more and still two more. Kodjo suggests I move from the tower into the middle room, the one reserved for government visitors, where there is a bed with mosquito netting.

I do so gratefully, lie down under the canopy, behind the mosquito netting. I am exhausted but cannot sleep.

As the fever recedes, my body is left aching and throbbing. I spend days picking at the bites and scabs, until the sheets are grimy with sweat and blood.

I lie in the dim room inside the netting with books and paper and pen like a pharaoh in his tomb and don't read or write or do anything. I dream of the winters in New Mexico and snow falling on the alfalfa field. When I wake, a wisp of sunlight is curling through a crack in the door. I look past my knees to converse with my feet, comical plates of flesh which I used to walk around on.

In the morning when they brought him to me, I recognized the little boy I had seen in my dreams. Peering into his eyes was like falling down a well into eternity. He was so serious. As if he knew everything. The wisdom of the ages. We just looked at each other and then fell asleep. Dr. Shorter said he was in the posterior position. "I turned him around in the last thirty or forty seconds between the last two pushes." The baby is well. I am well. Got four stitches. So what?

That evening I crept down the hall to see him. He was sleeping on his stomach in a clear plastic bed between two little dark-haired babies. He looked tiny. And he was jaundiced, but I didn't notice that at first. He was completely bald.

When Marilyn came in the next day she said, "You've had a Buddha! He's different from the others. His face looks very placid, serene."

He was muffled in a blanket. I took it off and looked at his toes, slanted like windblown trees, and his bowed legs. I wondered if he would be able to walk okay. If anyone would notice.

I stayed in the hospital for a couple of days.

Twice a day Kodjo comes and sits by my bed. His long brown hands lie on his lap, wrinkled as if they have been in water too long. He is not sympathetic. He comes and sits because he knows that I need contact the way even a sick goat needs contact. I pretend to sleep and I watch him craning his neck and blinking.

One afternoon, there are British voices in the courtyard, a man speaking in a high nasal voice. Soon they are pushing the door to the government room, exploring.

"Here's a bed!" a girl exclaims.

She comes closer; then sees the bearded man behind the netting, perhaps a corpse.

"Richard," she calls to the man.

He comes close, peers through the netting.

"I say, are you alright?"

" . . . just a little malaria . . . trying to sleep . . ."

"Oh, terribly sorry."

I'll say one thing. I'm glad there wasn't a man around for me last night. I wouldn't have wanted him to see me like that. But already I am forgetting the pain. Maybe someday I will do it again. Being pregnant was such a groove. Now he's really here. Little Alexander. Truly, I am blessed. Thank you, god, for a fine healthy child. And being able to lie on my stomach again!

At home, Alexander began his life in a bassinet lined with satin on the floor close to my bed. Now and again I could see his delicate fingers rising above the rim in a ballet pose. I felt very protective of him and didn't want anyone else to get near him, to hold him, not even Marilyn. When he first nursed and the milk "let down" it was like having my foot fall sound asleep – the tingling blood rush when it wakes up, but I soon got used to it.

After ten days of being sick, I woke up feeling better. I took a tour of the parapet, patting the cannons that stuck out to sea, smiling at the orange-faced green lizards that came out of them to look at me. Long languorous waves rolled off the sea. A warm wind rocked the palm trees.

One of Kodjo's wives had taken my clothes and washed them. My shirt and pants lay drying spread-eagled on the court below and looked like a man who had fallen and broken his neck.

I went down to the court and dropped the wooden bucket into the well. When the bucket was full of water, the rope quivered as if there was a live animal at the end of it.

I took my clothes off under the high limestone wall and with a cup, poured cool well water over my hair and face and body. Then I slid the big chunk of green soap from the top down, into every crevice. I rinsed myself with water from the bucket, brushing off the green lather, and stood still while the wind, filled with sun and salt, dried my body.

Back on the parapet, in clean clothes, I greeted the vultures at the top of the tower, the ravens in the palm trees, and I did a quiet dance.

"There," I imagined Kodjo saying, "he is well."

That evening, I saw him at the bottom on the stairway smoking a cigarette in the half-light. I went down and sat next to him. He shut his eyes and drew in a lungful of air, then slowly exhaled into the dusk. He held the cigarette out in front of his face and examined it like a new specimen.

I thanked him for the food, for sitting with me. He smiled. I asked him to thank his wives for me. I went to The Rock of Ages in the morning and bought him a carton of cigarettes.

Dear Jim

I am home and not alone. Little Alexander is with me, and Marilyn. She has moved her few possessions from her hut in the canyon and is staying with me to help with the baby. She's a lazy housekeeper but eager to hold the baby. She peers over my shoulder when I'm nursing, trying to imagine herself in my place. I find it disconcerting.

My baby is so beautiful, it just amazes me. The perfect symmetry of his little head, the clear, deep eyes. Turned up nose, rosy mouth and soft smooth complexion. He's strong and healthy and more aware every day, really into his own survival. I admire his spirit. His red-faced screaming anger and his little reserved half-smile.

He's a good kid. I, for one, don't think he looks like an

old moccasin, which is what Harvey called him.

 I figure in fifteen years or so he'll roll up his sleeping bag, sling his guitar over his shoulder, get on his horse and ride off into the world – and that's what it's all about – to prepare him to do that.

 He won't be real to you till you see him. I wonder how you will feel about him. I feel a small regret that you and I didn't have more than three weeks to be alone together, but that's senseless because there's nothing to be done but go on and make the best of things. I'm a fool I suppose, but when I think of Alex's father I think of you rather than Ken because you are the man closest to my heart.

 Deirdre asked me if Alex cries much. I said no. Neither does he smile much. He is old – I guess OLD moccasin is a good description of his personality. Old, and sad. And wise. Deirdre sees that too. His purpose in the world is something serious and thoughtful. He's very self-possessed, very stout. I feel silly saying nursery rhymes to him . Well, all that is just to say I hope you like him.

 I gave Deirdre your novel, The Egyptian Dish, to read again, thinking she will see. I'm amazed when she's eager to talk about it. "Yes, he's described me so accurately, and our relationship. There are parts where he and I merge, we're so alike." Her round eager face leans towards me. "Yes, he is kind of a Chauvinistic Lawrencian male, but I like that. I have to be able to look up to a man. Even now, if I were to be with a man, it would be like that. When a woman can center in a man, she becomes complete."

 I'm speechless. I can't believe she's actually saying this. Phaedra

Roget,
I take a trip into northern Ghana. On the bus passing Lake Volta: the sun is red. I sleep, and when I wake the full moon is caught in electric wires.

Bolgatanga, six in the morning. I walk out of town. The air is cool, and there is dew on the corn. Huge trees. Glint of a river. Goats tethered in the grass. Men hoeing in the fields. Conical huts in a circle, and I veer away. On the way back, it is already a blistering day, smoke rising out of the town.

Vast market, naked women, vultures walking everywhere, dirt, dogs, flies thick, the smell of shit and urine everywhere.

Record booths line one street and a vendor shouting: "Have you heard your latest records? Souls, high-life and hymns." I am standing in the burning street, James Brown is screaming that It's a Man's World. A naked madman is approaching me. The towering sky above me. Suddenly I am conscious of myself, not in a man's world but in a mad world, without reason or hope.

Mother and Dad came for a short visit. They drove here in Dad's long yellow Buick and stayed at a budget motel in town. They were not enthralled with Taos, although Dad wanted to move here when I was four, to join what he thought was Mabel Dodge Luhan's writing colony. They would have fought like dogs and cats. Grandmother talked him out of it, said the milk and water were bad and the schools terrible. All the same, Mother was disappointed. I remember her showing me a Spanish book for children and teaching me a few words like mesa, with a pen-and-ink drawing of a table.

Mother was quiet, as always, and tried to be positive about the situation in which she found her unmarried daughter. Dad, despite his early acceptance, had nothing good to say. He stood on the hillside in front of the house looking around at the field, the line of blue mountains on the horizon, the river shining through the cottonwoods. He squinted and cast a suspicious glance towards the village a quarter of a mile away. "Why would a rich man like Harvey Mudd build his home in such a poverty-stricken neighborhood?"

I smirked. "There is no wealthy neighborhood in Taos."

When he sat down at our dining room table, from the colonial period with square handmade nails, he said, "A junk dealer wouldn't give you ten cents for this table." Dad was only five foot six, but every time he made one of these remarks, he seemed shorter. I felt embarrassed to be his daughter.

I was nursing Alexander "on demand" which was often. And I did it in front of them, sitting on the banco, a blanket tossed over my shoulder. When I had finished nursing I buttoned my dress, walked over and deposited the baby, his first grandchild, into his arms. Dad gave him a cursory look. "He doesn't know who I am. He doesn't even know I'm here. He's got some filling out to do."

Alexander was only eighteen days old.

In the morning as they were getting ready to leave, Mother patted my arm. "I wish you lived closer," she said. I smiled. "We'll keep in touch."

"I'm glad you have some nice friends."

"Me too!"

While Mom was busy, Dad and I stood in the driveway having one of our deeper conversations. I'm not sure what we *said, but at the end we embraced and he told me he loved me. He gave me fifteen dollars to buy something for the baby. "I'd like to give you more, but this is stretching our budget." With the money, I bought Alexander a colorful Mexican blanket. I would have done better buying diapers.*

Dear Harvey,
I'm in Nairobi, have found two rooms, a suite really, on the fifth floor of a hotel, with windows on two sides. I feel like I'm living in an aviary. I met a girl from Florida, Lucille, at American Express, had coffee, twenty-one years old, naïve, a broad trusting face, a thick braid down her back, we hit if off right away. I liked her eagerness for life. We went to a matinee of *Little Big Man* with Dustin Hoffman in downtown Nairobi. There were so many subtitles in five languages we could barely see the movie. The theater was nearly empty and we sat in the back row drinking red wine. Heavy kisses, my hand up her shirt and her hand down my pants, just as I had always imagined it when I was fifteen. She had no coherent explanation for why she was in Kenya but she seemed to know Nairobi well. We walked across a large park toward the University dorm where she was staying, sat under a tree in the dark, no one was around, and ended up making love. It was sweet.

After that she came to my hotel every day, an airy room with a balcony and a view of the city. I told her about Deirdre, Phaedra, Arroyo Hondo, etc etc and she told me about growing up in Tampa and the love of her life who is in prison. She trimmed my beard and helped me apply lotions for the bugs that I had acquired in Ghana; it was as if we were married. There was something bovine about her, her broad face which I had seen as happy now seemed blurred and unhappy to me.

Marilyn packed up her things, stuck out her thumb and took off for Walsenburg. Alone! Now I know what alone really means. It frightens me. I've always sought out what frightens me the most, flung open the doors of my mind one by one. Stared into that darkness. Going slowly is the answer. Not pushing it.

Death hovers over me and Alexander on black wings. This baby is so close. He could go back so easily. His hold here is transparent as the veins beneath his skull. His soft spot, the open place between his skull bones, the vulnerable brain underneath.

If he died, I don't think I could be philosophical about it. I'd scream and cry and claw the earth.

I said to Harvey, "you have a morbid attitude towards death." He said, "Well, I'm afraid to look. Because if there really isn't any afterlife, I'll just die."

Dear Roget,
I've lost weight and my beard is getting long. I have fleas, lice and crabs, and I went to an Indian druggist – it seems that most of the stores here in Mombasa are run by Indians. I had to show him where each creature abides and then he pulled the appropriate powder or lotion from the shelf. I apply them studiously and they are helping.

The dance halls are filled with black and chocolate and

coffee-colored and rose-colored prostitutes some young and pretty, some old and wretched. After malaria, I have no fire, no thoughts, am just glad to be alive. But the women are sinuous, some of them.

Dear Jim,
Another successful raid on town. And back to my hideout in the valley with my goodies. Sure is fun spending money when you have it, although the welfare is only eighty-seven dollars a month and doesn't go that far.

You think Africans have a funny idea of sleep. Babies have no respect at all. I've resigned myself. But I'm only functioning with half my head, like a painless drunk. I left Alex sleeping in his cradleboard in the car and I was standing in the basement of El Mercado pricing a sleeping bag from an old man when suddenly I felt my milk coming. A geyser of milk shot out right through my dress in a white fountain and all over the floor. I was so surprised! As the man stared, aghast, all I could do was exclaim: "My baby!" Clutching my package to my breast and hurrying out, I didn't dare look back. What a shock to have your body expose you in public like that when you are trying to be modest and respectable. It made me snicker.

I've had it with Dr. Spock. The kid crying under one arm while with the other hand I'm scrambling through the book. I've decided to write my own:
Ms. Experience Says:
1. Don't take your kid to bed with you. He'll puke and pee and you'll wake up feeling all sticky.
2. Don't pick him up every time he cries. Your dinner might burn.

3. *Be inconsistent so he can adjust to real life.*

I'm oddly touched by his puny pathetic self-determination, the vitality and will that activates his tiny body, demanding, helpless, earnest. Maybe I won't sail him down the river in a little boat. I'll keep him another day and see how it works out.

Dear Harvey,
I'm trying to put the malaria in perspective. It was serious but somehow I knew I wasn't going to die. Yet *something* died: my sense of invulnerability. I realized I was going to die of something, someday, a simplistic thought but not real until you see it up close.

What a long dream life is, Kodjo's life shot through with illusions, my life, with even more. In Dixcove I was dreaming a limestone fort and a wide moonlit sea. Here in Kenya, on the island of Lamu, I am dreaming a shabby hotel and a small, sleepy village.

I will go to Ethiopia and Israel as planned, then on to my sister Bunny's in Montainville, may spend some time in England. I was supposed to meet my mother in London but our dates don't work out.

Dear Jim
Got your letter from Ghana. Thank heaven you survived malaria. It sounds horrible. I laughed at the part about your clothes lying in the courtyard.

You say when you had malaria that it felt as if someone had pulled the plug out of you. It happened to me in the outhouse about ten days after Alex was born. I was straining to *poop when there was a sudden gush of blood. It didn't stop. Death in five minutes. I panicked. Not NOW! I've got this baby. Everything is so good. A good day to die? I ran shrieking down the hill, calling Alicia at the top of my lungs. I ran into their house without knocking. Alicia and Harvey had me lie down on the rug. That's about all I remember. Bleeding on their expensive rug. And H. saying in an ironic tone, "Women and their plumbing!" I guess it just stopped. We didn't rush to the ER. And I didn't die. Alex would have missed me. I can't remember ever being so scared.*

Dear Phaedra,
Lamu is a small Swahili town, with mixed Bantu-Arab people. The island has no cars or trucks; people get around on donkeys and go to other islands in dhows, stout little boats with sails. As always, a rural setting calms me.

At night I go to a chai house and have shishkabab – a few pieces of fatty meat for a few cents – or a meal of curry, rice, coffee and cake, for thirty-five cents. Men are playing chess and shouting, and I grow dizzy from the Indian sitar music coming from speakers. One of the men gestures to me; do I want to play chess? I shake my head. I have become shy. And I cannot imagine playing chess, all that thinking and plotting.

A wedding ceremony tramps by singing and I thought of you and wondered for the thousandth time how you and the baby are doing.

Yesterday I walked out of town on the ocean side, past the village of Shella and up the beach. There was no one and nothing except ocean on one side, high sand dunes on the other. I went further and further, as if I haven't already gone far enough, trying to escape from my escape. I climbed the highest dune and could see a dhow sailing towards Somalia. I went down into the hollow formed by two high dunes and took off my clothes. The world was reduced to walls of sand and, overhead, sky. Me in the center, naked, hard to say what I was feeling, a kind of blankness that felt like a conclusion, a solution.

I masturbated in the sight of the sky, into the sand.

Then I returned to the shore and went swimming. The Indian Ocean is warm, with little waves lapping on the beach. I stayed close in and paddled around in the shallow water. Apparently I have finally come to the end of swimming far out.

Dear Jim,
By the time you get this it will be at least three weeks later. No, I'm not unrecognizably changed. The only difference is that the bulge inside me is now outside. Thank goodness. I waltzed to the Romance of Motherhood (I'm not denying the miracle) for two weeks before I crashed.

Ken was here yesterday. He brought Alex a little "jumpsuit." Things were very relaxed between us. I liked the way he handled Alex, quiet and gentle. He said when he saw "those crooked toes," he knew Alex was his. His toes are the same way. Crooked.

"And he's bald," Ken said. "That runs in my family."

I laughed. "In my family too."

Yes, I am changing, not because of the baby, but through the experience of giving birth. Letting go. Nothing to lose. I hardly care what people say about me anymore. I like people. If they don't like me, what the heck! I guess I can take it any way it comes.

It will soon be the day of your birth. All I can give you is my best wishes for a happy day. Or a sad one. But a full deep one. You will be thirty-one. And what will I give you for your birthday? My love? You already have that. Something practical? No. Something magic. That's practical. I love you! Goodnight.

Dear Roget,
Harar, Ethiopia. It took me two days to get here, a train to Dire Dawa and a van to Harar. Things haven't changed much since Rimbaud's time. The town is still surrounded by green, but the walls are gone. My first sight, a block off the main square, was a man lying on the sidewalk covered by a dark cloth. As I looked closer, it was crawling: a covering of flies.

I've hired a teenage boy to come with me. He speaks rudimentary English and helps me order meals. He says (I think) that Amharic has no word for yes, which explains one of the reasons I am having so much trouble. He is slim, sharp, but very shy.

I've met a Norwegian man who has lived in Ethiopia off and on, a short man with a long face who looks like Max von Sydow. He's one of those foreigners who have become appalled by and fascinated with the barbarities of the country. Marriage, he says, is a calamity, for there is no contract and the man can walk away. There is one doctor for every 70,000 people. Hangings are public; the last one was of a man in a dungeon for twelve years. They asked him what he wanted and he said a banana; then they hung him.

The Norwegian goes on and on, relishing the darkness. Certain people are excluded from contact, witches and men with the evil eye. Babies are buried on platters. All the teeth were pulled out of a girl's mouth because of "the worm in the gums." Castration for the bride.

My Nordic friend is enthusiastic about the women. "You can have any of the waitresses in the cafés," he said, "They all do it for extra money."

"I don't believe that," I said, thinking of the handsome women in the café where I usually eat.

"Yeah, yeah. It's true. The women in the alleys: forty cents. Forty cents. But I wouldn't touch them. Disease."

I went to look at the women in the alley. They were dirty and furtive. I too would not consider touching one of them. But forty cents: the amount aroused me.

Dear Jim
He is sailing along, enjoying his "vacation" in Africa, being alone, exploring his soul, getting a grasp on his own identity, when WHAM! BAM! The U.S. Mail yanks him back to the unresolved relationships at home, the sticky ones he had freed himself from to get an objective view. Now the time is nearing when he must return and work out these relationships: best friend, ex-wife, two stepchildren, ex-mistress, lover and lover's child. He finds himself anxious, even afraid.
    What next? South America!

Dear Harvey,
In sweltering heat, I walked out of Harar and sat under a tree to write in my journal. Two men in the field below me were talking to a third man. They appeared to be two army officers, and the third man a recruit. Then the third man ran up the hill, got to the top, turned and ran down. The two men stood on their sticks, talked to him again, and he ran up the hill, ran down the hill. My first thought was this was some sort of initiation. But as it continued, in the intense heat, I realized that it was punishment. I watched the man run up the hill, run down, there was no more talking. There was no drinking water. His instructions were clear. And finally it dawned on me, this was not punishment. It was torture, an efficient torture using the available hill and the available heat.

I stood up, making my presence obvious, but that had no effect. The officers saw me but the man continued to run up and down the hill. I glared at them. I stomped around. He ran up the hill and down the hill. The two men sat under a tree. They were settling in for the long haul. When I left they were still at it. Perhaps it was meant to end in death.

Dear Jim,
First, do we agree on the life principle that we should all try to love, understand, accept, tolerate each other and try to live together in northern New Mexico? Ye gods! Well, nobody here seems to want to leave town.

The stars are still shining bright, the river runneth cold with melting snow. All that continues. And inside the house a fly on the window crawling across my grand view of the mountain. Should I say it's wrong? It shouldn't be there? But it is there.

I'm glad you're my friend. I'm glad I'm yours. I'm happy to be frank with you and confident in your openness, honesty and understanding. Interested in what you are feeling. Glad to share your moods, your views, your discoveries, your questioning.

Dear Harvey,
After Ethiopia I went to Israel for ten days, then caught a ferry to Marseilles and a train to Paris. Now I am staying with my sister Bunny, her husband Jacques and son Marc. They live in a modern house outside the village of Montainville. Marc is nearly three, is speaking French as much as English, and speaking two languages has perhaps confused him. Jacques is frustrated; he had declared when they first met that he would be CEO of a company by the time he was thirty-five. He is thirty-four, the marketing director of Lawry's Foods International, and is obviously not going to make it in time. It is causing some strain in the marriage.

I told Bunny that I was not going back to Deirdre and the kids, and that I had something going with a woman named Phaedra.

"A woman named Phaedra," she said, trying not to scoff. "You only go with women with exotic names?"

I laughed, for it was true.

"I couldn't do it," she said.

I wasn't sure what she meant, and I wondered what

she would make of it all if I mentioned that Phaedra was pregnant with another man's child. No, not pregnant: she has had the baby by now.

Dear Jim,
I headed down to the hot springs with Alexander on my back.. We picked our way down the steep, rugged trail to the springs. In the pool, three women, two men and two blonde, blue-eyed laughing babies, including the family that lives down the road from me, Gary and Cheryl Walker with their baby Lichen. The air was cold, for the sun had dropped behind the cliffs, but I couldn't resist going in with Alexander. What a privilege, introducing him to the world. At first he clutched me, afraid of falling. The babies were splashing and laughing. I took him gently aside. When we all fell quiet Alex lay on his back in the warm murky water. While I supported him with one hand under the back of his skull, he stretched his arms over his head and stared at the blue sky for almost half an hour. Satori.

I'd like to give you a child of your own. I'm indiscreet to say that. It's fair to at least replace yourself in spite of Harvey's horror of the population explosion. I'd like to give you a girl. Let you watch her grow through these months, be part of that miracle.

But what I would like to do even more than create a child with you is to collaborate on a book. After all, we're all writing the same one. I almost regret having burned your early letters from Spain and Morocco. But I know there's plenty more where they came from, and I have your recent ones.

fly on the window crawling across my grand view of the mountain. Should I say it's wrong? It shouldn't be there? But it is there.

I'm glad you're my friend. I'm glad I'm yours. I'm happy to be frank with you and confident in your openness, honesty and understanding. Interested in what you are feeling. Glad to share your moods, your views, your discoveries, your questioning.

Dear Harvey,
After Ethiopia I went to Israel for ten days, then caught a ferry to Marseilles and a train to Paris. Now I am staying with my sister Bunny, her husband Jacques and son Marc. They live in a modern house outside the village of Montainville. Marc is nearly three, is speaking French as much as English, and speaking two languages has perhaps confused him. Jacques is frustrated; he had declared when they first met that he would be CEO of a company by the time he was thirty-five. He is thirty-four, the marketing director of Lawry's Foods International, and is obviously not going to make it in time. It is causing some strain in the marriage.

I told Bunny that I was not going back to Deirdre and the kids, and that I had something going with a woman named Phaedra.

"A woman named Phaedra," she said, trying not to scoff. "You only go with women with exotic names?"

I laughed, for it was true.

"I couldn't do it," she said.

I wasn't sure what she meant, and I wondered what

she would make of it all if I mentioned that Phaedra was pregnant with another man's child. No, not pregnant: she has had the baby by now.

Dear Jim,
I headed down to the hot springs with Alexander on my back.. We picked our way down the steep, rugged trail to the springs. In the pool, three women, two men and two blonde, blue-eyed laughing babies, including the family that lives down the road from me, Gary and Cheryl Walker with their baby Lichen. The air was cold, for the sun had dropped behind the cliffs, but I couldn't resist going in with Alexander. What a privilege, introducing him to the world. At first he clutched me, afraid of falling. The babies were splashing and laughing. I took him gently aside. When we all fell quiet Alex lay on his back in the warm murky water. While I supported him with one hand under the back of his skull, he stretched his arms over his head and stared at the blue sky for almost half an hour. Satori.

I'd like to give you a child of your own. I'm indiscreet to say that. It's fair to at least replace yourself in spite of Harvey's horror of the population explosion. I'd like to give you a girl. Let you watch her grow through these months, be part of that miracle.

But what I would like to do even more than create a child with you is to collaborate on a book. After all, we're all writing the same one. I almost regret having burned your early letters from Spain and Morocco. But I know there's plenty more where they came from, and I have your recent ones.

Dear Phaedra,

Bunny gave me, proudly, as if she herself had written them, a stack of letters tied together with an elastic cord. I fanned them and saw a mass of colored stamps. They had been forwarded from Africa. She insisted that I unpack so she could give my clothes to the *au-pair* to put through the washer and dryer. We spent the afternoon talking about family and reminiscing about our childhood. The letters sat on my lap, pressing on my penis through my thick corduroy pants. I was dying to read them right away but I thought it would be rude. Or perhaps I dreaded what I would find. Had Deirdre collapsed? Had Alexander's birth been difficult? And where was Harvey, and with whom?

Around dusk, Bunny announced she had to go to the village to shop for dinner. I wanted to read the letters but instead I played with Marc, a grinning boy who was delighted with this new toy – an uncle – which is a bit large and rough at times, and a bit dark and hairy, and whose eyes glitter like Rimbaud's with reflections of rivers and jungles, or so I like to think.

Finally I went to the back bedroom, put the letters on the bureau, took another long hot shower, and drying off, looked at myself in the full-length mirror. I hadn't realized how scruffy I looked. I had shed the last of my narcissism in Harar. As always, I didn't consider the man in the mirror to be me, who was in my mind a finer and more thoughtful human being.

There were more than a dozen letters, some of them dated back to June. They had been sent to Rabat, Rabat sent them to Accra, Accra to Nairobi, Nairobi to

Montainville. One from Harvey, full of wry passion for Glenda's goldenness and another woman's intelligence – she has even read Racine. Two from Roget describing the comings and goings of the cast of Taos characters. Two from my mother. There was one letter from Deirdre. A tape from Evelyn, thirty minutes of a thirteen-year old's rambling about her watch and what she had for dinner. A letter from Alicia and a tender letter from Paul, the guy I met in New Orleans. A half-page note from Bob from Nairobi, sounding lucidly stoned, and also one from Lucille in Nairobi, the woman I wrote you about, hesitant and affectionate. Four profound letters from a new mother in Arroyo Hondo which wakened my love. One of them included photos of her and the baby, another of her alone, one of Deirdre with her lop-sided grin, one of Harvey in a tweed jacket smoking a pipe.

I laughed when I learned that Roget was clearly in love with Glenda who was in love with Harvey but Roget was marrying Elaine; Deirdre was down, almost hysterical. Harvey rushed back to Alicia when she threatened to return to Mexico. Deirdre had found a house and was content again. And Glenda . . . and Roget . . . and Harvey . . . and Phaedra . . . and now another one, Alexander, just a baby.

Alexander! You write, "No one told me about the pain and work and worry." I think the ladies tried to tell you. As for my role in his life, be assured. I feel a lot of tenderness towards children and like being with them. I don't think I will ever again go through a love-hate relationship like I had with Ewar.

I try to look ahead and wonder. I will tell you the depth of my silliness. I already think of myself as Alexander's father.

I've thought about what you wrote, about having my child. We'll see.

I miss you Phaedra. Your laugh and your arms and your eyes. And other parts too. I gaze into a corner of the room as if you were there, and sometimes as I fall asleep, I talk to you. I am not ashamed. We are all such children.

As for walking on water – when we were at the ponds at Ojitos, you never saw me walk on water. That's not because I can't. I just don't want to. I wonder why Jesus was so wary of getting wet.

Love,
Jim

It's coming to the surface, how I really feel about Ken and why. I'm not proud of it. I recognize the flailing of my wounded ego. It's weird because last week we were on the friendliest terms. I felt very loving and forgiving. But this last meeting with him really set me off. As his facade drops away, I see the real man beneath. His callousness. His falseness. His condescending attitude towards me. Why should I care if a man I don't respect doesn't respect me? I don't. But our mutual pretense at spirituality? Bullshit! He pretends to care and I pretend not to. Harvey said, "Have you ever told him?"

"No," I mumble. "What good would it do to express my feelings of resentment?" But I'm really fed up with his ego game. Bored. Also, I think I am outgrowing my idea of how things should be and beginning to accept them as they really

are. That's important. Today I found myself running through the snow, tossing snowballs for Zoe the dog to chase. Laughing. She was all happy and alive. It felt so good. But swooping down from behind the curtain was that black wave of disapproval: my parents and Ken. Keeping me from being totally present. The past is such a clouded depth. The future so nebulous. I'd rather not know.

Alex is doing better, his digestive system settling down. Ken looks at him, "Well, he's becoming a little person."

"No. He's already a person. He was a person the minute he was born, his personality already formed. It's just a matter of getting to know him."

For the first time Alexander didn't wake me for his dawn feeding. I was counting on him. I was late for the dentist. And now he only poops about once a day instead of every time I change his diaper, so I only have to do laundry every three days. I'm hauling all my water from Harvey's.

Dear Roget,
I realize that I have made a mistake. I wrote Deirdre that I still loved her, and I do still love her, but not *that* way. I didn't mean to say we could be together again. I thought that I had made that clear but obviously I hadn't. I thought I was being gentle but I confused her. A new beginning. We used the phrase several times, me meaning a new beginning living our lives apart, she meaning a new beginning together. How can the same words mean such different things? I should have said, "I don't love you anymore. Goodbye."

Me – I've learned to eat, write, read, cook and answer the door with this little bundle on my arm. He has transformed from a quiet solemn thing into a real baby, screaming and demanding his right to survive. I was riding high the first few weeks. Then he got colicky and I sank into postpartum depression. My milk nearly dried up. Wind rain, cold, mountains of laundry and night after night without sleeping till I was so exhausted my face turned black, the floor kept shifting under me like a ship. I grew incoherent; my sentences came out backwards.

Then a miracle. I tried him on solid food for the first time. If he could just keep something down I could stop worrying. And yes, he absorbed the Pablum. Even slept for a few hours. I had no idea his digestive system could handle real food so early. No, I'm not complaining. I'm confessing. In spite of it all, he's gained three pounds this month. The bigger he gets, the better I feel. He's still too close to life/death for me to feel comfortable. There!

Then Alexander blessed me with one of his fleeting smiles. That makes it all worth it! He likes me to sing to him and tell him stories. His eyes aren't quite focused yet, hardly open much. And where is his consciousness? Recording it all, picking up every wave and vibration. It's like watching a flower unfold petal by petal. In spite of everything, I am enthralled.

Dear Phaedra,
You are right, wise girl: I am afraid of all of you. I wish you lived in Japan, Deirdre in Peru, Kelly in Alaska, and I could drift from one to another at leisure. As it stands, I feel like a carcass being shipped in to be the main course. I

know, I am not so important to any of you, except as that steer whose throat you would like to slit.

You ask me about Deirdre. Last I heard, from a letter I got in Nairobi, Evelyn will continue to live with her father and Ewar is leaning towards living with me. Deirdre also said that she has renounced all rights to me, as if I were a movie script, and then in the next paragraph asking if we will sleep together when I get back. You would never ask me not to, for that would be against your rules, those rules you deny having, but I am telling you now, I will not sleep with her. I want to stay clear of her in that way. I want to do what is best for her and me, which isn't sex. We have to find another way to love each other.

Dear Jim,
A few days ago Deirdre came close to accusing me of breaking up your marriage. I had to remind her that you two split up months before I came into the picture, that it was Kelly you had an affair with, not me. "Oh yes," she wailed, "but you're the one he wants." She asked how I would feel about the three of us living together. Plus Alexander and Edward, the five of us? This is too creepy. I am not sure I want anything to do with any of you. I spent as much time as I could in bed dreaming and all conscious hours walking in Deirdre's shoes, imagining what she's going through, taking on her suffering. Shriveling with guilt. Wondering if I had done the wrong thing, feeling all over again the loneliness and horror of loneliness that I experienced when my third husband left me.

Speaking of Phaedra, I say to Bunny:
"From what she's told me, her childhood was hard. She never had a real home. She's been married three times and each was more or less a disaster."
"She sounds nuts."
"She's a little nuts, but she is also the sanest person I know."
"I could never do what she is doing, having a baby in a mud house."
"You keep saying that, that you could never do this, never do that. You can do as you please."
"That's just it. I don't please anyone."
"A pun. A pun!"
"I don't get it.. Oh, yeah. Ha-ha."

I took Alex to a pediatrician, Dr. Anderson, who comes from Los Alamos once in a while. He said not to worry, "he's gained eleven pounds, five ounces."
"Tremendous!"
A VW van pulled up in the driveway and out spilled three women, all clutching babies about the same age as Alexander. My sisters from the Hog Farm. We had all given birth about the same time. That made me feel almost normal. The only two I remembered with certainty were Moe and Sesame. For two or three days we sat in the living room in a circle and talked, nursed our babies and changed diapers. We fixed meals and ate together. We compared birth stories and babies and all agreed that none of us would trade our babes for anyone else's. We all thought ours was the best. (Of course mine was the best. Definitely.) By the time they left I felt calm again.

Dear Jim,
So now you have a beard? I'd really like to see how you look with a beard. I made a mustache for myself out of the ends of my hair. Thought I had "mustache envy" for a while. No. It feels too funny.

First of all I want you to appreciate the fact that I've given up buying Pall Malls so I'll have the postage for this – my Earth Shattering Revelations!

Having just read your letter, I feel strangely elated. Secretly happy. I don't know why. Funny that you think I'm ready to gobble you up while I'm wondering how I can squeeze you into my tight schedule. It's so placid and uncomplicated living alone. You get to have it all your own spoiled way.

Deirdre said last night that she's nervous about seeing you again because though she is prepared to see a different man, "not the same one that left," she's hoping/fearing, "Will he see that I've changed, too?"

You both feel very wary. I believe that in her heart, what she really wants is to get clear. Not to have to go back again. That's what she says, that she just wants to get through it this time.

Dear Jim,
This desire to merge seems to be a longing to merge with something higher and finer than ourselves. Talking to D., I was trying to express that I couldn't take you away from her. I didn't have you. Neither can I share you, because you are not mine. Neither is Alexander mine. I'm not even mine. I'm God's creation. As for writing for Alexander, no, I'm writing for me. Always, for me. It's my story. He just happens to be the catalyst. It starts out, "One day this little person shows up at

my door. Ah, he says, you may not remember me, but I'm an old friend of yours from way-back and I've come to live with you for the next fifteen or twenty years."
  "Say what?"
  "Fifteen or twenty years. Seeing as we're such old friends."
  "Well, what can you do?"
  "I can fart and burp and cry and poop and throw up."
  "Okay, you can stay. Since we're such old friends."
  If I don't write this story I end up telling everyone and boring them to death.

Dear Jim,
No, Deirdre and I each keep our letters to ourselves. (Except for that one of mine she opened and read. She apologized). Then the other day I started reading one of your recent letters while riding in back of the VW van with Deirdre and Joan, driving to town. The first line of your letter said, "You want to live alone, but on the other hand, you don't. You want to live with someone – maybe me, but on the other hand, not me, but someone like me."
  I burst out laughing. I couldn't help it. "What is it?" Deirdre asked. I looked up quickly. "I can't tell you." I felt like a callous fool. She said it caused her "a little pain," but it passed.

Dear Phaedra,
What a drama it will be, to enter again the Arroyo Hondo arena, lions, gladiators, blood-thirsty spectators, hotdog vendors, saints, millionaires, racists, dope fiends, dope friends, pig rustlers, paper rustlers – the whole wacky gang

in a valley called Deep Ditch.

Let's spend the night together.

I love it – you got an offer to receive Time for fifteen cents a week, and you explained that we get Eternity and it's only ten cents.

How much does Life cost nowadays?

Dear Jim,
I got up in the night to re-read your letter. The first time I laughed till I cried. Now I'm just smiling and snorting. The first time I read it I was down at Harvey's doing the laundry. Glenda dove for it before I had opened it. "I'm addicted to these!" Big grin.

"NO!" I said. "I've got to censor it first."

Your sister Mary and William were drifting through the room. Glenda said, "I think it should be open." But dammit, it wasn't written for the masses. I really did feel a need to censor it before they read it. I did read nine tenths of it aloud and we laughed. Cries of "Far out!" and "Right on!"

Your letters are being handed around at quite a rate. You'd laugh – everybody wants to get into the act. We're all starting to write to each other – the lost art – and it's really fun. Some clear and beautiful thoughts are coming out of it. True deep communication and understanding. I'm for it!

I saw D. today, briefly. She doesn't seem either shattered or furious. She seems more real to me all the time. I believe her heart is pure. (Mine isn't!) We didn't talk about you. I didn't want to. She just mentioned a line out of your letter to her that said, "While you are still suffering and in labor, you haven't given birth." She was deeply moved by it and asked if

those were my words.
"No."
She waved her finger in the air. "I'm gonna do it!" I believe her. I'm sure glad it's none of my business.
You realize it will cost me a fortune to mail this. I kind of enjoy scrounging. I'm a natural. Sometimes it's more interesting than buying things.
I love you, too.

Dear Harvey,
I wrote to Deirdre: "We're free, we're clear, we are no longer man and wife." And she wrote back "Yes, we're free, we're clear, and we are no longer man and wife, AND I AM SO GLAD. How glorious! I don't NEED you anymore. I don't NEED anyone. You've experienced this but I never have. It's so beautiful. Thank you. THANK YOU."

She says she sees through my serenity. That makes two of us. It is her goal, to be serene, not mine. I want to live. She used to want to live too but now she is afraid. She is the first to say so. Being "clear," being serene, has become for her a refuge from the turbulence of life, of love.

My father believes that I am giving in to my most selfish tendencies. He doesn't say so but I can imagine it showing on his pained face. He would be pleased if I returned to Deirdre and got a job; he'd be pleased if I divorced Deirdre, married Phaedra and got a job. Anything but this wandering around. His country is Normalcy, and new lands make him afraid. The adventurer is, for him, by definition, selfish.

I'm laughing on the outside, but I'm laughing on the

inside. I said that.

I am (laughing on the inside). There is something comical about all of us running around in circles: Roget says it's a melodrama and I agree. I want no part of it. Bunny and Jacques, Roget and Elaine, Kelly and Robert, Harvey and Alicia, poor dears, not to speak of . . .

[Not finished or sent]

Dear Phaedra,
Go to one of those sex-crazed Taos physicians and get an IUD or a loop or diaphragm or a plug or a flamethrower and do it today because Bunny said she is leaving Jacques and wants to leave the 19th and then she said no, she wants to leave the 28th and my blood was up for the 19th and it won't go down. Now she says she is definitely leaving but she can't say absolutely for sure if it will be the 28th or perhaps in a year.

And he spake and sayeth well then I'm going hometh because this waiting aroundeth is killing me. And he went and he tooketh himself up to Paris and did booketh a flight to New York for the 20th. And he willeth catcheth a bus to Denver and travel and go and be in the land of the Deep Ditch in November.

Well as far as I am concerned the dress rehearsal is over. Take off your dress. Try Dr. Shorter and if he says he is booked up tell him the situation. Sob if you have to. He knows me – I taught his daughter at Da Nahazli School – I taught her everything she knows! Did you know that Dr. Shorter carries a gun in his belt? Some wacked-out hippies threatened him. Don't tell him I told you. It's a secret between him and me and the rest of the town.

Dear Jim,
I'm full of myself tonight. Dead tired, but resolved. I've washed both sides of the windows. Now I can see out as well as in. Isn't life an exciting experiment? I see it as a chess game. The moves may be planned somewhere else, but it is here that they must be played out.

Dear Phaedra,
I got your letter in answer to my letter about your letter today.
    She: (blithely) How long ya gonna be away? (This was back in May. Do you remember?)
    He: (tragically) A year. Two years. Maybe forever.
    She: I bet you're back by November.
    Do you remember, predicting that I would be back in November? And I've been thinking, I'll show her; I'll wait till December. But I can't.

Dear Jim,
I think, if I did nothing else, I'd like to write you letters the rest of my life. It feels so good. I love you so much. Don't be afraid of closeness. I won't eat your heart. I'm too busy bleeding, and enjoying it.

Postcard to Harvey
Bunny's dog Tambour came in and started to eat the hair clippings on the sheet. I had never seen a dog do that. And why is he called Tambour, which means drum in French?

I am leaving Montainville. I gave myself to my sister for ten days and I was tired of it. I want my own life back, my new one.

It's very quiet this cold November evening. I am lying in bed reading. I hear a knock on the door. I slip out of bed barefoot and go to see who it is. Because, after all, what lands on my doorstep is mine.

Home Sweet Home

I knocked. No response.
I knocked again.

It was November 22, 1971, a cold night with snow on the ground and beginning to fall again.

We had never bothered with locks and keys. I pushed the door open. This was, at least nominally, my house. Then I was standing in the dark of the kitchen.

A woman appeared and put her arms around me. I held her tightly for a moment but she broke it off.

When I started to say something, she shushed me, whispering:

"Do you want to see Alexander?"

She led me down the hall and into the tiny bedroom. I saw by the light of a nightlight a cradle hanging from the ceiling, about waist high.

I knew from Phaedra's letter, the one that had been forwarded from Addis Ababa to my sister's house in France, that her son had been born on September first.

"He's ten weeks old," I said.

"Eleven, and he's quite a handful."

He had wisps of blond, almost white hair on his head. His face was calm in sleep, and his frame, tiny within his jammies, was delicate.

I felt something for him, a shared courage, to be in the world.

Looking back, it seems improbable, something that might be invented years later to explain subsequent events, but it really happened. It occurred right then, in those first moments together. Without any trepidation, I became Alexander's father.

I am lying in bed reading Dune. *Knock on the door. I go into the kitchen. A tall dark stranger takes me in his arms and embraces me.*

"No," he says, "I'm not that one; I'm the other one."

I am thoroughly confused but I am hugging him back, responding to his vibrations in spite of myself, to his warmth. I draw him into the light of the bedroom.

"Jim!" With a beard. I hadn't tried to imagine him with a beard.

I just hug him and weep.

"Who'd you think it was? You thought it was Harvey didn't you?"

"Don't be silly."

We go into Alexander's room and over Jim's objections, I wake him. Jim gazes at him, a strange expression on his face.

I started to say something and Phaedra shushed me again. We went into her bedroom and looked at each other as if for the first time. I saw a twenty-nine-year-old woman who had recently had a baby. Her face, beautiful as ever, was also thin and anxious. She saw a tall man, thirty-one years old, with a beard and thick glasses.

"Did you get my telegram?" I asked.

"I haven't been to the post office in two weeks."

I had telegrammed Phaedra from Paris. In a spirit of bravado, I had written, "Me: there in ten days. You: foam, diagram, IUD, whatever it takes."

Now, in her presence, that telegram seemed crude.

Her lukewarm greeting in the kitchen, not going to the post office in two weeks: it crossed my mind that she had lost interest in me or had a lover. Then I remembered, she was raising a baby and must be exhausted.

There were twin beds and we felt so new to each other. we agreed we would sleep apart.

In the morning, there we were, either reunited lovers or an old married couple, me with my unplucked eyebrows and milk-stained nightgown and he in some sort of dirty sweat pants and top. We did a really weird thing; we showed each other our imperfections.

"Look," I said, showing him my "skin disease," the rash that was spreading on my neck.

"Yes, well, here's me," he said, and pointed at his toenails, which were crusty and dark with fungus.

As if we were afraid of idealizing each other and wanted to get the worst out of the way.

He emptied the contents of his duffle bag onto the bed, sorted through old clothes and books and notebooks, and put aside some items: seashells, a necklace, a headband, and a dress.

"Are you really giving all this to me?"

"No, I'm just pretending to give them to you. Tomorrow I'm going to take them all back and give them to Deirdre."

We listened to the rush of the waves in the seashells.

When I fed Alexander, Jim knelt beside me and stroked my arm and the baby, as if he had read the parenting book that suggested he do that.

I sat in the living room and the two dogs, Apollo and Zoe, came to me, sniffed me and, a bit puzzled, recognized me. I caught a glimpse of the two cats, which had belonged to Deirdre and me and now seemed to belong to no one.

I looked around the room where Deirdre, Evelyn, Edward and I had lived for two years. It was still small, dark and dusty, but it was also elegant in the way old adobes are. Harvey's Navajo rugs lay on the floor, black Indian pots on the mantle, and a kachina in a niche in the wall.

"The VW in the driveway," I asked. "Who does that belong to?"

"Me. Deirdre gave me three hundred dollars towards buying it, after the baby was born. But it isn't running."

"You and Deirdre get along then?"

"She's been great. She took me to the hospital when I went into labor and stayed with me the whole time."

I watched as she arranged her dress, gathered Alexander to her, and pulled him under her breast. To me, they seemed archetypal figures, Mother and Child, elemental and eternal. I knelt beside them and hoped I wasn't intruding.

Our first day together and we weren't. Jim took off to see his sister and Deirdre, Evelyn and Edward. I scrambled to put my life in order. I got a guy to tow the VW to town to be repaired, asked Roget to take me shopping and bring me home. Tired, I nursed Alexander and went to bed early. I hoped Jim would return but had a feeling he wouldn't. He was with Deirdre and his two stepchildren, and she was, after all, his wife. Wasn't that the way it was supposed to be?

Before going to see my younger sister Mary and Deirdre, I went to Harvey's house to shower, and found Glenda repotting house plants.

"My god!" she said.

"No, it's only me."

Glenda came from a wealthy family but her lifestyle was simple and rustic. She was keeping goats in the backyard and milking them for cheese.

She blurted out that she and Harvey were having an affair.

"You and Harvey," I said, trying not to sound skeptical.

"Yes. Very. Me and Harvey," she gushed. She had golden hair, a golden body, and she quivered with amazement to be involved with Harvey. I wondered if she understood that it would not be for long.

I walked several miles to the valley of Valdez. Below me, strung out along both sides of the Rio Hondo, low houses and trailers sat among fields and orchards. Following Phaedra's directions, I found my sister's house. As I trudged across a snowy field, I saw her in the distance hanging laundry.

When I waved, she waved back.

"Howdy," she shouted.

Mary looked like a Plains Indian, with nearly black

hair in a braid down her back, her face dark and angular. In fact she sometimes claimed to be part Cherokee or, forgetting, Cree.

"Howdy," I replied as I approached, enjoying the moment. "You don't recognize me, do you."

"Oh my god. Jimmy. I didn't . . . a beard!"

We hugged deeply. Then, in a rush, she said that she was three months pregnant and that she and William were going to move into a stone house in El Salto, up higher in the mountains.

We went into her house. Low and dark, it smelled of incense and patchouli. Her husband William, a thin, scruffy young man with a beard longer than mine, greeted me nonchalantly. Although he claimed to be psychic, it was clear that he didn't recognize me. As my sister and I talked, he lay back in a pile of cushions off in his own world, which consisted of certain mysterious homeopathic remedies and "light readings" which revealed to him a person's inner being.

"How did you get here?" she asked.

"Well let's see, I flew from Paris to New York, took a bus to Denver where I ran out of money so I hitchhiked. Snow started to fall outside Colorado Springs and I got a ride to Pueblo, another over La Veta pass to Fort Garland and a final one with a couple in an old Chevy who drove me to Arroyo Hondo."

"Oh shit," William said quietly. He had just realized who I was. After some banter, he and I went outside to split firewood for their woodstove. I picked up a log to put on the chopping block and without thinking, raised it above my head as if to brain him with it. He laughed and raised the axe above his head. Mary snapped a photo of us.

I went to the tiny post office in lower Hondo and there they were, two letters Jim had written from France and the telegram from Paris saying he was on his way. The letters were beautiful, full of descriptions of the French countryside and how much he loved me.

This was better, but then he wrote that although he is attracted to the idea of family, he must be alone and he knows that I too must be alone. I had to laugh at this; did he forget I had a baby or did he just not realize what that means? I was unable to match the three of them: lover from last May, the letter writer in France and the man with the beard who was in the twin bed this morning. It would be easier without the beard. I wondered what the beard was hiding?

I went down a dirt road, around a bend, and across a plank over an acequia to Deirdre's house. No one was home and I let myself in. This house was even more cramped and dim than our Hondo house. Although there were clothes on hangers and books and toys on shelves, it didn't feel like a home, although Deirdre had clearly made an effort to make it comfortable and pretty.

I raided the refrigerator. There wasn't much: milk, left-over soup in a plastic container, lettuce, tomatoes, half a loaf of bread with mold on a corner.

A car pulled up, and soon Deirdre, Evelyn and Edward (or Ewar, as he was known by practically everyone) were in the room. Deirdre was not surprised to see me. I had told my mother I was returning and she had told Deirdre. She held me briefly, as if warmly, but it was detached. Perhaps she wanted to show how independent she was. Or maybe she just hated me.

Evelyn, my stepdaughter, was thirteen.

"Hello," she said, and startled me by sticking out her hand.

"Hello," I replied, and shook her hand.

She had grown taller but was still more a chubby girl than a young woman.

"Hello," Ewar said (age ten), imitating his sister, but he couldn't pull it off. He rushed into me and we held each other tightly for a long time.

I handed out presents: two African comic books for Ewar, a bracelet for Evelyn, slippers for Deirdre. Although for me they carried a whiff of tumultuous, open-air markets under hot African skies, they seemed now, in this shabby room, cheap third-world merchandise.

Deirdre and I sat at the kitchen table and talked about her parents and sisters and brother and Harvey and Alicia and Glenda, both of us avoiding the subject of what I was planning to do. She kept looking at me oddly, because of the beard. And I kept looking at her. On one hand, she was Deirdreen, the woman I had loved for eight years, delighted and cheerful, words that were attached to her like Homeric epitaphs, but as always there was an undercurrent of something else, something remote, sad, even false, and now beneath that, a third layer, of genuine dismay and suffering. I had always thought of her face as round – a round merry Irish face – but now it appeared to be square and pinched.

"How are you for money?" I asked.

"I'm fine. I'm teaching at Da Nahazli and David sends money for the kids every month. What about you?"

"I'm okay too. I left five hundred dollars in an account here and I'll use that, but obviously I'll need to find work."

She said that she and the kids were expected back at Da Nahazli, the hippie school where she taught and the kids attended. Before going, she brought out two journals, laid them on the table, and said that I could read them if I wanted.

I was devouring the first journal before they were out the driveway. Her handwriting was large and chunky, with bursts of emotions. "There's no going back!" and "How I suffer!" To emphasize statements she used exclamation points or underlined them two or three times. When she got to Marin County and entered into Janov's Primal Scream therapy, she became more reflective. Prompted by one of the therapists, she wrote about her hatred of me, of her first husband, of her parents, of me again even worse, in fact, of me most of all. She wished me dead. Then she had a good long scream.

When the therapist tried to seduce her, she went to an ashram called Ananda in northern California, where she lived in purity with Hindi devotees. In another ashram, things were not so pure. She had several sexual encounters, and these were topped by the day, when she was walking in the fields near the ashram and met a newcomer, a young blond man who was wading through the wheat. Without a word they undressed and had sex. It was the best sex of her life. The next morning, at breakfast, best of all, they did not say a word to each other.

Her writing was bare and uncomplicated, statements of acts and feelings, a sort of shorthand that felt as if it were painful to write. It was painful to read.

The next day, Deirdre and I were cautious with each other. She appeared haggard, but she acted cheerful and upbeat. She looked earnestly into my eyes and asked if I would sleep with her.

I said no, I couldn't handle it. She had earlier told me about a young man named Jim Fellows and when I met him, I knew he was interested in her. He was ten years younger than her, an earnest young man with a narrow face and long hair. I suggested that she go to him. Her face lit up. It was as if that had not occurred to her. I stayed with the kids and she took off. I read *Huck Finn* to them and we told stories and played our games as in the old days.

Deirdre returned the next morning, radiant. She said they had had great sex, and this time, I could tell, it was true.

We fell into a pattern of walking and talking every few weeks. We were still close, still loving each other. We talked about life, love, time – all the big themes that we had always talked about. We agreed that our relationship didn't have to be defined. She said that she wanted to be back with me, and if that couldn't happen, she could even consider returning to David, her first husband.

"I want to be settled," she said. "But I know there is no going back. There is only going forward."

"Strictly speaking, there is no going forward. We can only be here, now," I said, joking about Ram Dass' book *Be Here Now*.

Years later, after she became a Buddhist nun, she said in an interview, "My marriage ended . . . and everything fell apart. I couldn't feel any ground under my feet . . . the groundlessness I felt had a fearsome and panicky quality to it. It was devastating. . . I went into a major depression. The pain was intense, and there was nothing I could do to get out of it."

In the same interview, she said "There were a lot of communes around, and I explored them all. One week there'd be a Hindu swami in the neighborhood, the next a Zen roshi, the next a Native American teacher, and the next a Sufi master. I really didn't distinguish between them."

Stranger and stranger. I was down at Harvey's doing laundry and taking a shower. Drying off, I saw Deirdre's VW van pull up. I went to rush out to see if it was Jim or Deirdre or both, but I restrained myself, finished dressing, my fingers trembling.

I headed downstairs, brushing my wet hair, and there were Evelyn and Glenda. Evelyn greeted me warmly and patted Alexander on the head.

"Hi Phaedra. Your baby is bald!"

And then Deirdre, and behind her, Jim came whirling into the room. He moved to embrace me but I jumped back.

"It's alright," he said, but was it?

Jim phoned Harvey in Santa Fe and arranged to stay in "the round house," a one room studio Harvey built in the piñon trees up the hill. By then Deirdre was upstairs showering. Jim thought she might be crying but when he went to the foot of the stairs to listen, she was singing.

That night, Phaedra and I had the house to ourselves. After she nursed Alexander and put him into his cradle, we ate a big meal and smoked a joint. As I had done hundreds of times before, I laid paper, kindling and logs in the fireplace and started a fire. She put on music, lit sparklers and danced for me. She was dressed in the white and brown striped dress from Mombasa and wore the Ethiopian headband with its tin ornaments hanging over her forehead. I thought she might start taking off her clothes but the dance was demure and somehow artistic, like a turn-of-the-century interpretation of Air or Water.

Jim built a fire and we smoked some grass and I decided to give him a belated birthday present. I put on Nights In White Satin, lit two sparklers from the stove and danced barefoot in the living room. My legs were weak as water, my body wobbling. The sparklers burned out. I threw myself down on the cushions in front of the fire.

I smoked more than usual and suddenly I was exhausted. I wondered if I was making the same mistake again, centering myself in a woman, losing the sense of myself that I had regained in Africa. Then paranoia kicked in. I realized that I was being punished for my transgressions. Everyone was just stringing me along and couldn't wait for me to leave again so they could resume their lives. I doubted their sincerity, which was bad enough, but what was worse, I doubted my own. Wasn't I just playing with Phaedra and Alexander for a while, enjoying the drama of having a new family, before I did something impulsive again? She would then see me as I really was, a coarse sensualist, a cynical womanizer who abandons women and children as soon as they come to love me.

"I don't feel clean enough to even touch you," I mumbled, and I went out, walked down the driveway to try to clear my mind. When I came back, I kissed her and went to bed in one of the twin beds.

Jim started talking about schizophrenia and how he feared he might be prone to it. The dope was kicking in and making him paranoid but I didn't know how to explain that to him. He left to clear his head, came back in and kissed me and went to bed. I got out my guitar and sat by the fire and played "Gentle on my Mind" and "The House Song." I fell asleep in front of the dying fire.

The next day, I decided to walk to Valdez again to see Evelyn before she returned to San Francisco. Phaedra offered to come part way and I hoisted Alexander in his carrier onto her back. Struggling through the snow that lay deep in the shadow of the canyon, she looked like a squaw leading the expedition.

We propped Alexander in his carrier against a log and sat by the little Rio Hondo, which was beginning to ice over from the freezing nights. We didn't speak but we stole glances at each other.

Part of me felt that we three belonged together and that it would happen that way, but I was not about to say that to her. The events of the last four years had taught me that I was often mistaken about the future, that I wasn't in control of it, and I wasn't in control of myself. As for her, she was not the kind of person for plans or promises.

I put the baby onto her back and we continued deeper into the canyon. It was as if we were moving deeper into each other. All of a sudden, my doubts left me. I knew that this was what I wanted, this woman, this baby, not just for now but for the future.

Jim was going to hike to Valdez through the canyon to spend the day with Evelyn and he invited me along part way. Shaking all over as I got dressed and got it together – my Indian dress and Alexander in his snuggly. And we were off.

My image of myself kept changing as we walked. I'm an Indian. I'm Phaedra. I'm the fool on the hill. I'm Alexander's mother. I'm Jim's lover. I'm his friend. I'm silent. I listen to myself talk. It's all unreal. Who am I in relation to this man? I wonder if he's decided he doesn't want me anymore. I am afraid of saying the wrong thing. It is all shifting so fast I can't get a fix on it and somewhere, I am inwardly detached from it all. And wondering that I feel so detached. And not understanding this man's silence or what he is feeling.

We continued up the river and stopped at an S bending through the clear banks of snow and he spoke my exact thoughts so calmly: "Do you realize how lucky we are to be here? To live here? This is our backyard."

"Yes!"

The snow, the cliffs, they were so beautiful they made me gasp.

"What a friend you are," he said. "I love you so much, it frightens me."

We kissed and Alex fussed and we went on. Past an island into the heart of the canyon.

"Let's sit down over here," he said.

I didn't understand; I thought he was in a hurry to get to Valdez.

"Till what happens?" I asked.

"Till nothing happens," he said, and I laughed.

Evelyn and Ewar were at a friend's when I got to their house. Deirdre and I had a conversation about where things stood. She had prepared her statement, but before she made it, she asked if I had read her journals.

"Yes I did, and I have to say, you are incredibly brave."

"It wasn't all true. I didn't have sex with all those men. I made that up to make you jealous."

"The guru's handsome heir-apparent, on the cushions?"

She shook her head.

"The young man in the wheat field, who never said a word?"

She smiled her crooked smile and shook her head again.

"I thought that part was beautiful," I said.

"I guess that's how I want it to be."

And suddenly we were our old selves, laughing and

ironic.

Later, she said that she knew I loved Phaedra, and that she loved Phaedra too. And Alexander was a dear thing too. But Ewar missed me terribly and for him, I was his real father, and he needed me, needed me to be his father. So she felt that we could make it work, the three of us, her and Phaedra and me. The house was a little small but if the boys shared the small room we could make it work. What did I think?

I was caught off-guard. Deirdre had always worried about being too conventional, too much a coward, and consequently she had pushed herself to do things that she was afraid to do. But living as a three-some? This was taking it to a new level.

I said that I didn't think it would work. I laid it on myself, that I had enough trouble staying with one woman, forget about two. Which was true, but not all the truth. I didn't say that I felt no desire for her. And I didn't say that I wanted to be, and intended to be, faithful to Phaedra. The hypocrisy of that was just too great, even for me.

Midmorning, I heard the tramp of boots; Jim's bright face was grinning in the door. He told me about his day and night at Deirdre's, how they had talked honestly about the situation and when Evelyn and Ewar came home, they had played board games and he had even read to them the way he did when they were little. He was very happy, telling me about the conversation with Deirdre and things he did with the kids, how natural it all felt. Although he was stroking me, I was holding my breath, afraid that he would become her husband again, for the sake of the children.

He went on, couldn't seem to stop, said that when my name came up, everyone was open. Evelyn had been informed and Ewar was allowed to catch on gradually. When he did, he said to Jim: "Well you'll still be my father."

"Of course I will."

This took the pressure off my heart. Ewar needed a father and Jim was a good one. Nevertheless, I felt confused about him, wary, just as I was almost afraid to open his letters. Part of me determined to stay on my guard with what I said, lest my words betray my inner turmoil. Although often and often words spring to mind, I will say nothing.

He went out to split logs into firewood and I saw the whole picture of them as a family again in contrast to me. I wanted to be his family, but at the same time, I wanted to retreat into my stubborn independence, to my determination to go it alone, now and always, just me, and now me and Alexander. Without the risks. Without the heartbreaks. Without the partings. I felt myself withdrawing to a distance, hurt because I would never be part of what they had, sitting at a table playing board games, sitting on the couch reading to each other. I wondered if he had told them silly stories as he used to do, and for that matter, where had he and Deirdre slept?

I felt so cold, so isolated. One part of me was saying That's good; that's really good, that they can be open and natural and happy together, and what does it really matter where the man sleeps? The more love the better. Look how happy he is. Be happy for him, not sad for yourself, not sorry for yourself. It's ridiculous.

Then he burst back into the house with an armload of firewood, proud of himself.

"Splitting logs," he announced. *"It's like riding a bicycle. I love it."* And after he dumped the wood in the wood box, came over and kissed me, as if he had the right.

The Hondo House

Phaedra and I were still shy with each other, still not sure what the other was feeling or thinking. I took a flashlight and retreated to the studio in the piñon trees. In the morning, I lit a fire in the woodstove and surveyed my new domain, a round room without electricity or plumbing. There was a woodstove for heat and cooking, and a kerosene lamp for light. The floor was flagstone. Windows faced west, with a glimpse through the trees of high desert and way beyond it, a string of small extinct volcanos.

The next night I lay brooding in the studio and wrote Phaedra a long letter, saying how I was not going back to Deirdre and how committed I was to her (Phaedra) and Alexander. I walked down through the piñon trees with a flashlight and gave it to her. I lit a fire in the living room and we lay down on cushions and, finally, made love.

Deirdre and Phaedra were running out of firewood and I put together a wood run. I borrowed a big old flatbed truck from Harvey's construction company, cleaned and sharpened the company's McCulloch chainsaw, assembled cans of gas and bottles of oil and mixed them together. Phaedra declared she was coming with me and off we went in the dawn, but not before I knocked her new thermos off the back of the truck and broke it. We went to Garrapata Ridge and cut wood there for an hour with a Hispanic man. The saw kept stalling and he helped me clean the filters. After he left, I really went at it and cut a lot of wood. Phaedra propped Alexander in his cradleboard up against a tree and cleared branches as I cut them off. Around noon the three of us sat with our backs against a fir tree and ate lunch. The plain stretched westward, covered in snow that was streaked with ravines, broken by the gash of the Rio Grande gorge, more like an abstract painting than a real landscape.

Jim and Alexander and I went on a wood run. While Jim loaded up the equipment, I took a tab of acid that that I had been saving for a day I could spend outside, preferably up in the mountains, to clear the cobwebs out of my brain.

Should I tell Jim? Not right away – let's see how it goes. Don't want him to be worrying about me when he's busy doing what he has to do today. My tripping might be a distraction to him. Besides I'd like to quietly and secretly enjoy it by myself.

Jim has the truck ready in the driveway. I'm bringing the baby in his cradleboard, coming on to the acid. My legs wobble a little. I see the frost on the trees, a breath of crystal whiteness. I take a deep breath and inside me exalts.

Jim joins me by the truck, leaping up in back in a flurry

to get going – tossing a piece of rope off the back and crash! our first calamity of the day. The new coffee thermos I'd left sitting on the back of the truck falls to the ground and breaks. Jim is disgusted with himself.

"Nothing lasts," I say.

There is a pattern of frost petals on the window. The little bell on Alexander's hat is jingling brightly as we bounce down the road. I love the old red flatbed truck, the rhythm of the engine, the jouncing and bouncing, the springs in the seat. But the road is tricky – frozen ruts of mud leading through stumps and fallen branches. It doesn't seem possible we can actually drive over all this and not get stuck. Jim spots a pickup ahead of us and, alongside the road, neat stacks of logs. "Umm –" he says, eyeing the logs, "I wonder if he cut all those already this morning. He certainly is efficient." So Jim admires efficiency.

Just like that, my take on Jim changes. The beard, the glasses, the brown corduroy pants, his quiet unassuming manner, are all a mask. In his red and black checked jacket, he is a flare. He is intense, and he wants firewood.

Jim comes back to the truck. "He says the wood up on the ridge is probably better than here."

Alexander is quiet now and I prop him up against a tree in his cradleboard about fifty yards away. I've been anxious to help Jim and now prepare to do so, but I've only gone on one wood run before, with two hippies from the Hog Farm. They strolled into the woods, smoked a joint, then one cut a limb off and rested while the other one lopped off the branches with an axe. I follow Jim into the brush and immediately I see that he and the Hog Farmers don't work the same way. He throws himself into the tree with his whole body, the saw becoming an extension of his arm, his will. A cloud of blue smoke rises from the log, a flurry of woodchips fly through the air, the saw is all the way through the log and triumph! He falls back, a gleam in his eye. For with Jim, on his high energy level, even cutting wood is a challenge. It is a sensual, sexual experience. He excites me, biting through that log with his buzzing monstrous yellow chainsaw (that doesn't cut right). I move in to lop off branches with an axe but I get in his way as he dives for the next log.

"Let's not work too close together," he says, which sets off a whole chain of acid images crystallizing in some lines from The Prophet – *for the trees cannot grow in each other's shadows* – and – *let the pillars of the temple stand together and yet apart.* Yes he's right, I think, and draw back.

"I didn't really expect you to work," he says. "I thought you just came along for the ride."

"I thought you just came along for the ride," I say, meaning the acid trip, meaning life itself.

He doesn't understand, and says, "You mean you thought you and Alexander were going to do this by yourselves?"

"Well, I did come to help you if I can," I explain. "Certainly not to be in your way."

"I think you should take care of Alexander," he says, and I am glad to do that. I run back, get my baby and take a little walk up the evergreen path through the dazzle of fresh snow.

By noon he is exhausted from struggling with the wood and the saw which does not perform up to his expectations. We sit with our backs against a Douglas fir and eat tuna fish sandwiches and blueberry cheese cake. Jim holds Alexander on his lap and absently plays with his fingers. The vast purple snow-streaked plain lies below us like the surface of another planet. I make a mark on the tree so we can find it again.

When we got home, I split some wood into kindling and then left for the studio. Just as I was leaving, Phaedra told me that she had taken LSD that morning. I was amazed, upset, angry. I felt it was too great a risk. Working with the saw, axes, wedges – I knew how out of it I was on acid, how I went off into space and time not of this earth. Anything could have happened. I remembered her coming too close to me when I had the saw running and my asking her to move away.

When I expressed my discomfort and anger, she laughed nervously, was surprised at my reaction.

She said, "At Woodstock when I worked with the Please Force, we were able to stay focused on helping the crowd because most of the acid we dropped was mixed with a hit of speed. If we had dropped pure Owsley's Orange Sunshine, we would have come unglued and left the planet."

"That's all fine, but we were out cutting logs in the woods, not tripping at some music festival."

She asked me if I had realized she was stoned and I admitted that I had not. She laughed again, this time knowingly, and I felt foolish, because everything had gone smoothly. Except for breaking the thermos, which had been my fault.

Jim splits some of the wood and brings in armload after armload, stacks it by the fireplace. "I love splitting firewood; it requires both delicacy and strength." Then he collapses on the couch with Alexander. I fix him a cup of coffee and he tries to play with Alexander but Alexander just spits up and cries and

Jim's eyes turn inward instead of outward to the joy of life – and they're both so tired it's no fun anymore.

I try to put Alexander to bed but after the loud cold bewildering day he refuses, fights sleep, just cries and cries, and Jim flees the house to go to the studio. Maybe he feels a little guilty about that, and wonders about Phaedra, stuck with the squalling brat? Maybe he thinks "Well, it's her brat, not mine, thank God."

And Phaedra? Well she too is glad that Jim has a place to flee to, that he can go relax and write and think, because that makes him happy, because she loves him and wants him to be happy. Feels happy herself when he's happy.

Once he is gone, she gives her undivided attention to her son, sings to him, reassures him with her singing, watches the stars beam out of his eyes, smiling when he smiles, laughing, getting warm. Soon he's drowsy and ready to sleep.

For some reason he didn't explain, Harvey invited us all to dinner: Deirdre; Jim's sister Mary; Roget and Elaine; George and Joyce Robinson; Jim; and me. It was a nutty affair for no one wanted to talk about the various elephants in the room, Harvey's affair with Glenda, Deirdre and Jim's breakup and his living with me; Mary being pregnant and her husband William's absence; George's becoming a Christian and working for the unchristian Harvey. Gentleman that he is, Harvey seated Jim and me opposite each other in the middle of the table, Deirdre at one end ("like a deposed queen," he said later) and himself at the other end. There was much chatter about The Fountain of Light. Everyone poked at the thawed veggies that Harvey and Jim had grown two years ago and frozen in an immense freezer in the basement. Deirdre re-

counted some sanitized versions of her adventures in communes and ashrams and I spouted about how glorious giving birth to Alexander had been. In other words, it was social and false and yet despite everything, there was not a single snide remark and we had a good time, except perhaps for Jim who sat closed off and saying little.

Afterward Jim said, "The house was too warm and I ate too much."

"A desperate evening," Harvey said with a chuckle.

After dinner, Harvey said he had some important things he wanted to talk to me about. We went out onto the front porch and sat on a two-seater swing in the freezing air.

"What are your plans?" he asked.

I wasn't sure what he was asking. My plans for what? Money? True, I was drawing down my savings. Sticking around? Fleeing?

"Who are you sleeping with?" he asked.

"Well, let's see: Glenda of course. Kelly. Deirdre. Phaedra. My sister Mary. Apollo the dog. I would have slept with Mariposa the pig but we sold her to a farmer for their Christmas dinner."

"Will you be serious for once in your life?"

"Just Phaedra. We're going to make a go of it. I love her and I adore Alexander."

"Good," he said. "That's what I thought, but I wasn't sure. I have a proposition for you."

It turned out he had three propositions for me. One, he was buying a Porsche and I could have his old BMW so I wouldn't have to keep hitchhiking.

Two, Phaedra could continue living in the house rent free.

Three, what was I going to do for work?

"I have no idea. Maybe some landscaping in the spring. Construction. I don't know. I can try teaching but I only have a California certificate so I don't know if I can teach in New Mexico."

"What will you do if those don't work out?"

"Will you get to the point for once in your life," I said, imitating his irritable tone.

The third proposition turned out to be an offer of employment. Harvey had bought the Taos Plaza Theater and was renovating the interior, which had been gutted by fire in 1969. He had hired an architect and he needed someone to oversee the work.

"You want me to be the owner's rep?" I said.

"Is that what it's called? Yes, I want you to represent me on site, keep me informed and help me make good decisions."

I took a deep breath. After years of delinquency, I was being asked to buckle down and do a real job. What about my poetry? My daydreaming?

I turned and looked at him.

"You have saved me, again."

A week later, Harvey became more specific about my new responsibilities. As the representative of the owner, I was to bring a movie lover's perspective to the project, and he hoped I would manage the theater after it opened.

Right off he said we had to go to New York so I could

book some movies.

In New York, the first thing Harvey did was to declare that my clothes were too rough. I had thought I was looking good in clean khakis, white shirt and one of his jackets, which, it was true, was too tight and too long. He took me into a shop and bought me a sports jacket, slacks and a tie. I went into the corporate offices of Warner Brothers expecting to book movies for a 202 seat, one-screen theater in Taos, New Mexico that had burned down and was currently under reconstruction. I waited a long time in the lobby, not realizing that they didn't know what to do with me. Finally an executive came down and took pity on me, explaining that movies are booked in regional offices and the regional office for Taos was in Denver, not New York. I should, he added helpfully, plan on booking movies about a month before the theater was to open.

I realized that I had to start thinking things through for myself rather than relying on Harvey.

Harvey had booked two rooms in an unassuming but elegant hotel. Although I enjoyed having him to myself for the first time in years, we went our separate ways much of the time. When we were together, we went to restaurants of his choosing and prowled used book stores. One afternoon we went to see *Dirty Harry* with Clint Eastwood, a violent cop who breaks all the rules to trap and kill a psychopath. We came out of the theater into the sharp winter light of Manhattan too stunned to say anything. After a block, we both started to talk at once.

"That was the most . . ." I began.

"I think that was . . ."

". . . fascist movie ever made."

". . . a brilliant example of movie-making."

We didn't laugh, dismayed and almost angry at each other. He couldn't understand how I could ignore the craft, no, *the aesthetics* of the director; I couldn't understand how he could stomach the glorification of torture and murder. Twenty years later, not so idealistic, I saw the movie again and enjoyed it immensely, as a psychological thriller.

On the last night, I got a phone call from a woman staying at the hotel.

"Do you remember me? We met at lunch yesterday; your friend talked about New Mexico and El Greco and some other stuff and you hardly said a word."

"Yes, hello, of course I remember you. You're in town to see your stepson, who is a stock broker or something."

She offered to come to my room. I was polite but remote, explaining that I was already in bed and was leaving the next morning.

Went to the good ol' P.O. on my way to town and behold! A letter from the wandering Jew. I was in such a hurry to open it I ripped the end right off. He'll be back from New York on Sunday. Says he misses Alexander, but not me. "Ha!" he writes. "Ha!" to you, too, Mr. Levy. I miss you. Didn't for a week, but now I do.

I don't know if he got my two letters. He's not enjoying New York or being "a hick businessman." But he's honestly trying to do the job.

I re-read my two worst journals last night, trying to decide if I dared let Jim read them. They were the two after Alex was born, the postnatal blues ones. In reading them again I realized that it's not so much a change in hormones, but a feeling of death hovering over me. Birth - death, that thin line. I excuse myself on the grounds that Alex was sick with colic and jaundice, and I was exhausted and drained, more than I had ever been in my life. The first baby is always a trauma. You have to readjust your whole life. And there's no way of preparing for it. You just have to do it.

Jim asks if it would have been easier if he had been here. Maybe, but I think it would have been hard on him and he wouldn't have enjoyed it. I think it's best that I did it without him. The only part that makes me sad is that I lost faith, not only in him, in everything.

So, I was wrong about Jim. He has been super good to me, has helped me so much, I'm ashamed of ever having doubted him. I might have been reacting based on my negative experiences of other men. Okay, we don't want to be hung up in the past, do we? NO! But I realize that being with a man who truly loves me and responds to my needs is a new experience.

I was writing in my journal when I heard a car, jumped up. A knock on the door, the sound of boots in the hall. With a click and a shock and a high wave of exuberance, he's here!

I run into the kitchen, leap at him, arms and legs wrapped around him, laughing. We can't talk, just hug each other. Just look into each other's faces. We have a little party, some wine, listen to music and sit and talk like two adults. As he calms down, he becomes a little subdued, handsome in his city clothes, more mature, quieter, and very tired.

    I was aware of feeling whole within myself, that the mystery of me should not be in hiding, but in being honest, having confidence. I'm growing. I'm aware that things I theorize today I may throw out tomorrow if they no longer ring true.

    In silent, mutual consent, we went to bed. The goodness of loving, the purity of our bodies taking delight in each other, giving ourselves to each other. Black wings swoop down closing us in a cocoon of satiated exhaustion. Knowing that there will be more: writing, the sky, music, talking, so much richness to share. We laughed and talked and hugged each other. Letting go, not trying to control things. This was a true reunion. I have committed myself to a mystery I may never solve.

    Some nights we got stoned. "It's amazing to me," I said, "how you can quote from poems and songs. I can't even remember my own poetry. I am so stoned. What time is it? I know what you're saying and I feel the same but . . . is it too early to say?"

    "Yes. I can't say what I can say," she said, and snorted. "Sorry, I'm really blotto."

    "I was thinking that we are meant for each other. This is really happening. I can at least say that. I can say more, but I won't. We've created certain rules, haven't we?"

    "Unspoken rules," she said.

    "And it's too early to start breaking them."

    On another night we wandered through the snow looking up from this planet encircled by stars. We shared these moments: stars, sunrises, the moon covering the snow with a cool bluish dust, and we held each other, not for comfort but because we felt connected to the cosmos.

Jim popped in and out, discussing comic sketches we should film. The dogs barked. I peeked out the window. Deirdre's car was pulling into the driveway, her face strained with her sweetest smile. She and Jim talked briefly, then Jim came back in to report the conversation. She had written him a letter about how sexually passionate she is. He thought that perhaps in the ten days he had been away in New York she would have had a chance to gather strength. "But she's still holding on," he said, his face sad and concerned.

I gave Jim the two "depressed" journals. It was a big step for me, letting anyone read those things. He went out to the casita where he was going to work on his Ghana story, but couldn't resist the journals. He came in later to say in a cool tone that he had sensed that I was feeling alienated and it was a very moving story.

After I put Alexander down for the night, Jim and I sat on the couch, me crocheting.

"I was hurt," he said about the journals, "to read how little faith you had in me." But then he thanked me for letting him read them. He said, "You're really beginning to believe I love you. You seem amazed. But you don't feel worthy, do you?"

I said, "Like everyone else, I sometimes doubt myself."

He said he can't imagine me being irritable. And there's a part of him I haven't seen yet. "Moody," he said, "and cynical. I lay for hours on the bed in the hotel room in New York, doubting myself."

We experience each other as "known" but also as

strangers. Jim says, "Sometimes it appalls me that I've let a stranger get so close to me. How did this happen?"

We plunged into a long discussion about writing. Who were we writing for? Why and how? He said, "I want to be free to take up horseshoeing if I feel like it. It would be awful to feel I had to write to prove my worth." I talked about the original purpose of my journals, to balance my writing, to understand human nature by understanding my own. The self-analysis, introspection I find necessary.

The job at the theater was part-time: I went in on Mondays, Wednesdays and Fridays, leaving Tuesdays and Thursdays for writing and weekends for helping Phaedra with Alexander and doing chores. The architect and contractor said they needed to be able to reach me so the phone company ran a line from Harvey's barn and gave us a "temporary" phone number which still exists.

With a steady income, I asked Phaedra to drop welfare and food stamps. Between her check, which was $87 a month, and my pay, $3.75 an hour, we were living on $370 a month, which more than covered our expenses. She wouldn't consider it; she wanted to be as independent as possible.

We had a few good friends, Harvey and Alicia, and Gary and Cheryl Walker who lived in a tumble-down adobe next door, which they were fixing up. They had a blonde toddler, Lichen. And classy Glenda with the cheekbones, crystal blue eyes and long blonde hair. She was Phaedra's first friend in Taos who tried to fix her up with various men and arranged for her to be the night watchman at the Taos airport.

Our closest friend was Roget Thomas, from our *Fountain of Light* days. He had an elfish air, a broad forehead, penetrating brown eyes and a goatee. His accent was distinct, but he had a perfect grasp of English. He was surprisingly articulate but often obscure when he waxed philosophical. He would carry on in abstractions for five minutes, then rubbing his goatee he would say, "That's the question, isn't it?"

Elaine looked like a school teacher, with her cat glasses and long hair ratted up on top. When they came for dinner we served steak and potatoes and Phaedra's blueberry cheesecake. Afterward, we danced or Roget and I wrestled. Sometimes we played a game called spoons, a variation on musical chairs, which consisted of sitting on the floor in a circle with spoons in the middle, short by one.

The four of us played intense games of poker, hearts and canasta. I gave some thought to the theory of these games and started winning a lot. Elaine was a serious card player too and liked to win. She and I argued about the proper strategy and not surprisingly, Phaedra and Roget got annoyed by our competitive spirits and didn't want to play anymore.

I arranged with Deirdre to meet her for drinks at the Sunshine Bar. It was one of Harvey's businesses and he had asked me to check it out and give him a report. That evening it was half full of Taoseños, mostly Anglos, a few Hispanics, and two Indians. The jukebox played continuously.

I jotted down some observations about the operation to give to Harvey. Deirdre and I had our drinks and looked at each other wondering what we were doing there.

"Come on," I said, "I'll take you home."

It was good, how comfortable we felt on the drive to her house. We reminisced about our days in Berkeley and Sonoma, careful not to talk about our year in Mexico, and I felt that we were old souls who had survived the worst and could now relate on a new footing.

I went down to the big house to take a shower and give Alicia one of my stories to read. While there I felt a sudden urgency to see Jim. I decided to go to town. I called a local teen who agreed to baby sit. But I didn't have the key to my car: Jim had it. So I asked Alicia if she wanted to go dancing. We drove into town in her new BMW, like a ship floating through the night.

The Sunshine Bar was crowded and noisy and we couldn't get seated for a while. I stood by the jukebox peering around trying to spot Jim and Deirdre without them seeing me. I wanted to spy on him. I was all excited. Alicia caught me peeking and laughed and shook her finger. She said, "Jim's not here."

The jukebox was blaring ". . . alive, alive/ wanta get up and jive/ Wanta wreck my stockings in some jukebox dive." A few couples were dancing on the small dance floor.

I looked around for a dance partner, studied their faces, but couldn't find one as handsome, alive or interesting as the man who was out somewhere with his ex.

When I got home, Jim was lying on the bed with Alex.

He laughed, said it was so perfect that I wasn't here when he got home. "It just served me right."

He asked me if there wasn't an element of anger in my going out. I said no, I was all dressed up and wanted to go, so I went.

"Okay," he said.

He slept on the couch and I retired to my room. On my desk I found a note that made my heart soar, a confirmation of his feelings. "I love you and I love your journals too."

I gradually get to know Phaedra's ways, how she tap-taps the top of a soda can so it won't squirt up when she opens it; the exhilaration she exhibits when she takes Alexander in his carrier and rides Harvey's horse around the field, the wind blowing her bangs back. She cuts vegetables on the counter, not using a cutting board, the same way I do. I discover something that I hadn't realized before: the curl on her forehead is similar, almost a mirror image, to the way her upper mouth curls up.

She is gifted, eager, temperamental. Underlying these is her goodness and honesty, and it is the goodness and honesty that I love, not the temperamental side.

Zander – that is what Ewar calls Alexander – is a delight. He peers goggle-eyed over the rim of the back carrier, or gnaws it. He is resolute like his mother, and yet there is a fragile being in there who looks at the world with wonder and doubt. He grabs my finger and won't let go. On the days I have him, he is content for hours, while we dance together or sit on the couch and "talk." After a while he misses his Mom and begins to fuss and then we both long for her.

The day after I shaved off my beard, he didn't recognize me until I picked him up and whispered in his little ear, "It's me, silly."

That did it; he wrapped his arms around my neck.

Phaedra looked at me funny too. "So it's really you," she said.

When someone stole some of the firewood from Harvey's house, he and I agreed it was probably hippies from the commune Reality Construction Company, for no Hispanic would steal someone else's firewood. The commune was gone but a pile of battered vehicles still lingered on and a small group of desperadoes – the ones with guns – who jacked deer out of the hills. They were urban radicals who justified stealing by saying that private property is the tool of capitalism. They were really just thieves, too lazy to cut wood themselves, whereas the hippies at New Buffalo were too idealistic to steal. At least in the beginning, when the founders were mostly middle class couples with children. As for the ones at Morningstar, they were too stoned.

I wasn't sorry to see the communes dwindle. A guy named Bob Armitage died of tuberculosis and county health agencies banded together to screen all the residents of the three Hondo communes. At Morningstar, a girl delivered a still born baby, and at New Buffalo, a child walked across a sky light, fell through and died.

The long windows in the living room sagged on their hinges with big gaps at the top where the cold air blew in. We didn't even have curtains. In the deep cold of the New Mexican winter we woke to the windows frosted with lacy patterns while we huddled in front of the kitchen stove or the heater in the hall. Jim placed coals from the fire on a cookie sheet and slid it under the car so it would start in the mornings.

In summer the house had running water in the kitchen sink, supplied by a gravity feed that brought it from the irrigation ditch. But in winter, we both trudged down the steep front hill with two buckets, a white enamel one with a red rim and a vintage bucket that must have come from an antique store. I often found myself down on my knees beside the Rio Hondo scrubbing poopy diapers and rinsing them in a pail before taking them to the laundromat for the final wash.

We had skunks that lived in the crawl space under the house. If we left the front door open they would sometimes wander into the kitchen and eat kibble out of the dog food bowls. They would also eat duck eggs if they had a chance. We put up with them until a couple moved in together. Their domestic bliss was short-lived. They quarreled and sprayed each other. Of course the smell permeated the whole house. Eviction time. But how? They only came out after dark. When they emerged we planned to run around to the back of the house and block the crawl space with a rock

One night when we were both in bed, a skunk emerged. I'm not sure how we knew. Maybe the dog barked or it sprayed. Jim grabbed his handgun and I grabbed the .22. We ran around the house in opposite directions. It's a wonder we didn't shoot each other. I smacked into the skunk first, took a shot and it fell over. Without the stink. We filled in the hole in the crawl space and that was the end of that.

For the record, that's not how I remember it. Yes, I grabbed my .38 and she the .22, and like morons we raced around the house in opposite directions, but it was me, holding a flashlight on top of the revolver, who shot the skunk dead.

It was time for my sister, Mary, to have her baby. She was examined by a hippie doctor in Mora but would have the baby at home attended by a midwife. Mary, William and I read obstetric books and prepared everything in advance. The house was a primitive, stone structure without electricity on the slopes of the Sangre de Cristo mountains.

I was very nervous, but Mary, William and Deirdre, who would also be present, were committed to new-age ways and believed that a homebirth was more natural and healthier.

I drove to Peñasco, about eighty miles away, and picked up Rose Medina, the midwife. I was surprised to discover that she spoke very little English. We got to the house around nine in the evening and found that Ewar was there, which bothered me. I also wondered about Deirdre's presence, first at Alexander's birth and now Mary's baby. She hadn't wanted children with me, and I had not pushed her on it.

Mary was comfortable and we were all cracking jokes. Deirdre sat with the mother-to-be and talked to her. William baked newspapers in the woodstove to sterilize them and I spread plastic sheets around. Rose started giving Mary instructions in Spanish and I stepped in and translated as best I could. When she examined Mary and rubbed her with oil, Mary didn't like it, waved her off, and kept moving from place to place like an animal searching for the right spot.

Ewar fell asleep in the loft, came down and fell asleep again in the corner. While we were standing outside for a breath of air, Deirdre took the opportunity to tell me she was having an affair with a younger man who considered her his guide.

Mary pushed and grunted for an hour. William supported her back and Deirdre her knees. I held a kerosene lamp and a mirror so Mary could see the birth. We all shifted around, anxious and unsure but Mary was calm and in charge. She waved us off as she had done Rose; she didn't want to be touched. Then things got hectic: she groaned, panted, moved to a new place. By now I became genuinely frightened. I thought of ordering her into the car and rushing her to Holy Cross hospital in Taos. We might make it.

First the black hairs plastered on the head, which came out a way and then receded. Then came out further. Receded. And with another contraction, the baby was born.

"Is it alive?" Mary asked.

I looked, heard a gurgle, and said yes.

I burst into tears, and then Deirdre was crying.

"A boy or a girl?" my sister asked.

"A girl," Deirdre said, through her tears.

I had never seen Mary so radiant.

Rose Medina, cool as a grape, stepped in and took over. The cord was around the baby's neck and she swiftly removed it, tied it and cut it. She washed the baby's eyes.

The afterbirth plopped into a pan and Mary and William examined it with great interest. Thinking about our Morningstar neighbor who said he liked afterbirth soup because it had so many vitamins and minerals, I later buried it.

Mary had her little girl on Sunday, May 21, 1972 at 1:35 a.m. Rose produced a little scale and weighed the baby. She weighed six pounds, eight ounces.

I was putting in much longer hours renovating the theater. It had burned down on Thanksgiving night, November 27, 1969 around two in the morning. Later that same morning, the Taos Community Auditorium burned too. Everyone remarked on what a coincidence it was and everyone suspected that it was not a coincidence, that an arsonist had lit the fires, perhaps a puritan who blamed the Plaza Theater for showing racy movies and the Community Auditorium for staging indecent plays. Another theory was they were torched by teenage boys with a grudge and a taste for fire.

I tried to cooperate with the architect on the renovation, Bill Mingenbach, but he had never designed a movie theater and didn't seem to care about movies, and I, although a movie junkie, knew nothing about architecture and even less about construction. Harvey hired the two of us because that was how things were done in Taos – it was better to hire the known ignorance than a qualified outsider.

The fire had gutted the interior so Mingenbach had a free rein; unfortunately he was a man who had little control over his own cleverness. Because the theater was in the basement with limited space, the distance from the projector lens to the screen was only twenty-two feet. He said that we could increase the distance by a few feet if we tilted the projectors straight down and bounced the movies off a large mirror suspended from the ceiling. I thought this a horrible idea and nixed it – the one certifiable contribution I made to the project. Later, after I became a projectionist, I realized that if we had tilted the projectors ninety degrees down, the oil would have leaked out of them.

Harvey drifted in and out of town with a variety of ideas, some brilliant, some impractical if not outright dopey. He seemed determined to make money and lose it in equal amounts. He was lobbying against a new coal plant in northwestern New Mexico and was getting death threats from developers and their Mafia backers. *The New Mexican* carried an article about his possible run for the New Mexico Senate. He started two companies in Taos, Pelican and Ponderosa, which were to renovate and run the theater, build low-income housing, and initiate several other community enterprises. He asked me to be president of Pelican, which I declined but, out of guilt, I agreed to be vice-president.

What I really was, was consiglieri, a fixer. My first act, with Harvey's permission, was to fire the less than competent Taos attorney and hire a big firm in Santa Fe. We also hired a new business manager, who served Harvey well for years, and we recruited Sally Howell, a local and savvy business woman, to sit on the Boards of both companies, a position from which she lectured us on how inexperienced and foolish we were. She and I and George Robinson, who was her lieutenant, became allies and tried, not very successfully, to make the companies profitable. The pattern was, Harvey developed grandiose ideas, we began to implement them, then, recognizing their impracticality, scaled them back. At the end, staring a fiasco in the face, Harvey ended with a generous gesture, either selling the remains to a friend or to the Town of Taos at a ridiculously cheap price or just giving them away. Thus the people of Taos had surreal opinions of him, as either an egomaniacal developer or the most generous of gentlemen.

A girl from New Buffalo came over to visit. We got stoned, exchanged gossip. I had propped Alexander up in an armchair because he looked so cute. I was a few feet away as he rolled forward and fell on his forehead. I caught him on the rebound, poor kid. He cried lustily. I smeared his head with ice cubes but couldn't tell where he hit. I think he was more scared than anything. Me, I was shaking all over.

I got a letter from my mother, saying she had cataracts in both eyes and had to have two operations costing about $3,000 after Medicare payments. I offered to find the money although I wasn't sure how I would do that. Worse case, I would swallow my pride and ask Harvey for it, and he would give it. Even worse case, I would ask my father for it but he wouldn't. I felt helpless and regretted that I didn't have a high-paying career bringing in $12,000 a year.

We celebrated the Fourth of July. That day there was a tre-

mendous storm: Two bulbs in the house blew out. Heavy rain and then hail covered the ground like fish eyes. The ditch overflowed and ran down the road to the river. I took Alexander out into the lightning and thunder. He looked nervous but didn't cry.

We were going to go to Taos Junction to see the fireworks but Roget, Elaine and Elaine's daughter Renee arrived with armloads of them. We collaged for hours and then went outside and set off fireworks. At midnight Jim fired his .38 into the sky along with the rifle shots from the village.

Our idea of a good time: Put Zander in the back seat, drive to Questa, have hot pie a la mode and coffee, and play pool. Phaedra had never played pool. On the first try, she beat me.

On my off days, I wrote stories and essays: *Deirdre*, about our breakup; *Elements of Nighttime*, concerning more of my dubious adventures; *Glass*, a story set in New Orleans; *200 Tons of Sunlight*, a lyrical prose poem; *Os Sertões*, an essay about Brazil's national epic; and *Fort Metal Cross* about having malaria in Ghana. Phaedra helped me revise *Blas Blenio*, a story about an Indian in northern Mexico who hunts wild boar. I wrote poetry about the acequias and cemeteries of northern New Mexico, the eerie light of San Francisco, and the sunlit streets of Haifa, where I had wandered for days looking at movie posters and at men playing pool in green light.

Despite all of this activity, I felt that I was not a real writer. I didn't send these pieces to magazines and I had no interest in publishing. I felt that the writing was third-rate, some of it overwrought, some of it amateurish. About six years later, in a period of depression, I threw them all away. Only a few poems survived.

Dear Jim,
As for selling your writing, I thoroughly understand how you feel. I'm not shattered by rejections anymore, but it's hardly worth the postage. The stories I write are for myself and my friends. I don't need to be paid and published to validate my worth as a writer; it's worth it to me a thousand times over. That's why I persist. Edgar Cayce was a psychic healer but he didn't earn his living by that. He never accepted a cent. Instead he built himself a small trade as a photographer. I have faith that there will always be some way to pay the bills without sacrificing our souls.

I was reading Chinese poetry, mainly Tu Fu and Li Po, from a book that gave three versions of each poem: the original Chinese, a word-by-word literal translation, and an English poem version. From these, I was able to guess at what the poem meant and I translated a dozen poems.

> You came into my dream
> so you know my longing for you.
> Are you dead in my dream or alive?
>
> I can almost see your face.
> Where are you
> the waters are deep
> the waters are insane

This was about Harvey. At that time, he was living in Santa Fe, Washington D.C. and Mexico City. He dashed into town, gave me a short story or a poem to read, and was off to Mexico, then to England. Our sporadic friendship drove me crazy. He showed up, we smoked weed, drank wine and danced with Phaedra and whichever girl he happened to be seeing. On some nights we stayed up until three or four talking about literature and life. The night after he ended an affair, we went to La Cocina and drank Wild Turkey and Ezra Brooks to compare them, then Chivas Regal and The Glenlivet to compare *them*, then broke into El Cine café (which he owned) and stole bread, turkey and mayo for sandwiches. The next day he was off again, for months.

Dear Phaedra,
I am feeling perfect about you, knowing and trusting your strength and honesty, knowing and trusting my love for you and feeling perfect too about Alexander. It is a cold dreary day, the sun sounds like the distant bark of a dog, and you are the flame I go to. You're so large and warm, immense in your solitude, a mountain with many paths.

Alexander adds a sense of innocence to our lives and a purpose; and I no doubt add something, dirty footprints on the kitchen floor and the illusion of strength, but it is you who impart to the walls that essence that makes a house a home. Things gleam after you've touched them. The glass in the window tries to be as transparent as it can be and the table to hold things up even better than before. When I open the icebox in the middle of the night, there is a tuna fish sandwich looking brave, ready to do its duty. Books open more easily after you've read them, but that's because you put them open face down, straining their spines. I hear your footstep sharp and sure as the moon stepping out from behind a cloud. Alexander and I look up but no, it is a furtive something; the moon slides again behind the cloud and the earth darkens. We return to the diversions that men amuse themselves with while waiting for blackbirds to return; we sniff the air for signs of rain and keep one eye on the road.

Dear Jim,
I love you so! And I appreciate your help with Alexander, not just changing his pants or taking him off my hands, but really being a father to him. Loving him, playing with him, teaching him things. You're a good man, Mr. Levy. I'm glad I accepted this job. I'd like to stay on for a while even though you do make the most outrageous passes at me!

Thank you for your nice letter and all the kind things you said about me making the house glow. I suppose the only real magic there is or ever will be is in the loving care. I'm a simple person. It gives me a great deal of satisfaction to care for our little home, to see the plants green and blooming, the dogs' coats shining and tails wagging, the ducks cuddling down in fresh yellow straw. The beds neatly made, rugs shaken, windows clear, the clothes neatly ironed and mended and hung in their proper places.

This, of course, isn't how it is, and like a sunny day, appreciated after a cloudy one, I enjoy it most when the energy I put into it doesn't leave me exhausted.

Whatever is beyond this life, I strongly suspect it is so similar that we'll hardly notice the difference once we get used to it. Like Dorothy in Oz.
Yours,
Miss Dreamwood

Soon our lives changed. Deirdre and her friend Jim Fellows set out for a Sufi camp in the French Alps to study with Lama Chime Rinpoche. There she met Chögyam Trungpa and began her road to becoming a Buddhist nun. Her days as a mother more or less came to an end. Evelyn, age fourteen, was living with her father in San Francisco and Ewar came to live with us. Deirdre left Calle the dog and Karma the cat with us also, and they joined the other animals, the ducks and chickens and Zoe the German Shepherd, Apollo the mutt, and Leif and Eric the cats.

Ewar was eleven, skinny, usually jovial but sometimes sulky. I was incredibly glad to have him with us. I enrolled him in Da Nahazli school for the fall. David offered to pay but I was having none of that.

Glenda came over and we three got stoned. We dressed in costumes, in long dresses and head dresses, Jim in overalls and a straw hat.

"I'm having a vision," he whispered to me, "of you as an incarnation of Summer. I've never seen her so lovely."

We walked in the moonlight carrying a tall pole tied with a scarf at the top, danced in the driveway and held hands in a circle, inventing patterns.

Worn out, we sank down on the couch.

> "This is the best movie ever," announced Glenda.
> We thought about that.
> "How long are we going to wait here?" she asked.
> "Until nothing happens," Jim said, repeating our old joke.
> We burst out laughing.
> "Only idiots laugh at nothing," Jim said in a dry manner.

One Saturday I spent all day in Harvey's workshop making a table out of discarded pine planks and a cabinet out of old apple crates. I drew rough designs and built from them; the power tools made it easy to cut joints. At the end of the day, Phaedra and I sat at the new table in the late sun and drank a bottle of Boone's Apple Wine and had soup and sandwiches, apples and cheese. I fed Zander Gerber's green beans. Phaedra was in a white and red Mexican blouse, the red sharp against her dark hair. She flashed her eyes this way and that, she laughed, she mocked herself, and we went to bed. We were in bed fourteen hours, loving, reading, talking, listening to Prokofiev's *Alexander Nevski*, Shostakovich's First symphony and his cello concerto. In the morning, Zander joined us, kicking and laughing.

I had started keeping a journal from Alexander's point of view. I called it My Side of the Story.

> *Whew! It sure is hard to get hold of a pen or pencil around here. Mom keeps taking them away from me because she thinks I'm going to fall and stab myself or get lead poison-*

ing or something. She doesn't know what I really want it for.

Mom keeps a diary and so does Dad. Why shouldn't I? It will make it easier to remember all this stuff later on when I have to tell my analyst.

My name is Alexander and I'm two years old, the age of reason. I have blond hair and my eyes are turning brown. I have cut two teeth on the bottom so far and am working on the top ones. I'm learning to stand up by myself now, use my spoon, hold my glass and talk a little.

I live in a little adobe house with blue window frames. The house sits on top of a hill overlooking a field. Below is a creek lined with tall cottonwoods and out the bedroom window I can see the mountains. It's nice here and most of the time I'm pretty happy. Mom and Dad take me for walks and visiting people and other places. I love to ride in the car. I used to fall asleep all the time, but now I like to look out the window.

I know what it is to look out my bedroom windows at blue and white mountains shining against a crystal sky. At a cold clear river bubbling its way to the sea. The hawk soaring. The placid sunlight. I love it all: the wind at my window at night on dark wings, howling wild tales of the mountains. My good and beautiful son. These ridiculous loving animals. Even the goldfish with their bright scales flashing, swimming gracefully among the shells of the Indian Ocean. And Jim is so warm and generous and fine and capable. Not that he doesn't have his weaknesses too. His troubled relationship with his father. The breakup of his marriage. When he is down, he comes and casts himself weary on my bed. Out of him flashes from time to *time a good-natured boy.*

Yes, there are times he's down, doubtful, afraid, paranoid, or just high and coming in too fast for a landing with that surge of energy. There is no bitterness in him, no resentment, no sense of being wronged by life. He's not self-destructive. I can see him as an old man, grey-haired, but his eyes full of life, his face lined with his journeys. I'd like to go on with him till the end.

Yet, we were sitting on the couch one night talking, as we so often did, when Jim popped this question, close to my face, his big hands lifting my hair. "How long do you think this love will last?"

"So you want it to last, but you don't really think it will?"

He became lost in thought. I felt confused. What was it exactly he was saying to me? It will last if it works. If it doesn't, it doesn't.

He mentioned the welfare and food stamps again today, wanting me to drop them, offering to pay me those amounts.

"Why not take money from someone who loves you?"

"But then you'll be stuck at the theater."

"I'm stuck there anyway, for at least another year."

I should find out what inspired this new offer, because I feel disinclined to take him up on it. Why change the status quo? It's working fine right now. The only thing that would, of necessity, change, is if I had his baby.

Yes, I was thinking about "marriage." Another child with my maiden name on the birth certificate? But what's in a name? Scratches of ink on a piece of paper? The word "marriage" is veiled, but seems to intrude on both his consciousness and mine.

The Plaza Theater re-opened on September 3, 1972 with *Sitting Target*, a British thug-flick so forgettable that even *VideoHound's Golden Movie Retriever* does not list it. Only a handful of people showed up and I imagined nights, weeks and years of a dozen patrons and bankruptcy and disgrace. We flooded the county with 7,000 calendars that announced the movies for September, putting them in grocery stores, gas stations, on telephone poles and in windows. The movies came and went, more and more people came, and much to my surprise, we had a real business going.

Tuesday and Wednesday nights were film club nights. Figuring that Taoseños were hungry for great art, Harvey insisted that we show the finest movies in the world; he felt that if he was going to be a business man, at least he would be a classy one. We formed a film club that people could subscribe to and we showed older movies like Fellini's *8 ½* and De Sica's *Bicycle Thieves*, as well as current art movies: *Walkabout*, *Sunday Bloody Sunday* and *Garden of the Finzi-Continis*. *Death in Venice* drew seventy patrons and we thought the club had taken off, but after that few people came and fewer subscribed. It hit rock bottom with *Discrete Charm of the Bourgeoisie*, the Buñuel film eviscerating the middle class that we showed to two people. *Dirty Harry* and *Fritz the Cat*, on the other hand, sold out.

While managing the theater at night, I continued to oversee the renovation of the rest of the building during the day. I had never worked so hard in my life. Harvey moved the Plaza Theater Bar to the second floor and offered me the job of running that too, but I felt it would be too much. As it was, I hired and supervised staff, ordered movies, purchased supplies, and sold tickets. When I counted the receipts, I soon realized what every theater owner knows, that profits come, not from the sale of tickets, but from candy, drinks and above all, from popcorn.

After the customers and staff left I put music on the stereo and turned up the volume. I walked around the theater to Cat Stevens and to Santana's "Black Magic Woman" and "Oye Como Va" while inspecting the carpet and chairs for tears, sweeping up popcorn with the magic carpet sweeper, and looking for passed-out drunks between the rows of seats. I was gratified to have had a hand in rebuilding the theater and I felt a keen happiness to be supporting Phaedra, Alexander and Ewar. I swelled with pride as I moved through the theater doing the most mundane work. I can still taste the sweet love I felt for my new family. In Phaedra, I had found my "hardheaded woman" who was loyal and independent, mild and fierce; in Alexander a loving and loved son; and in Ewar, someone I could love and, in doing so, relieve some of the guilt I felt about trashing my first family.

In the middle of September when Alexander was a year old, he and I flew out to San Francisco to visit my parents. They were waiting for us at the airport. Dad had gained more pudge around his waistline. In his orange shirt he looked like a pumpkin. Mother was graceful in a striped shirtwaist dress that buttoned down the front. Her short curly hair had turned white. (From living with Dad?) She was weeping.

"She always does this," Dad teased. "Both ways. Coming

and going."

Mother smeared her cheeks with a tissue and forced a smile. *"It's not true."*

But it was. They hadn't seen Alexander since he was eighteen days old. Dad enjoyed having Mother all to himself and pushed his three grown children away, picking fights, writing nasty letters, first to one, then another. Of course he wouldn't let Mother come to visit us alone. She never did anything alone except go to work or sneak off to the mailbox while he was napping.

But now, to my surprise, he welcomed me with a big smile and an honest hug. It was a short drive home. He and Mother were living in a small three-room trailer in a nondescript trailer court a block from the post office where Mother sorted mail. The week of our visit they gave up their bedroom for us and slept on the couch. For the first two nights Alexander and I found it hard to sleep with the jets roaring over night and day and the traffic humming on the freeway. But we soon got used to it.

Dad had a full itinerary planned for the week and chauffeured us around. The first day he drove us to Golden Gate Bridge where we sat in the soft grass in the warmth of the setting sun and watched the ships go by. On another day we climbed into Dad's big yellow car to visit Muir Woods. The forest floor was quiet and cool and the air smelled fresh. A narrow stream sparkled through banks lime green with ferns, backlit in morning sunlight. We crossed back and forth on little wooden bridges. Dad kept snapping pictures. Mother brought up the rear, tucking in Alexander's blanket, peering into his eyes. *"You look so cute, Alexander, with that little turned-up nose and that wisp of hair on top. Are you cold?"* I don't think Alexander really saw the trees, but he was quiet. I picked a red and yellow leaf and gave it to Alexander to chew on. Mother took it out of his mouth. "I don't think that's a good idea. It might be poison oak."

The next day I had a red rash all over my face. But Alexander was fine.

We followed the path back and forth, down and down, until we came out of the forest onto the paved road.

From Alexander's journal (by Phaedra)

Finally we came out of the those big red trees onto the paved road. Below us was something alive, twinkling and blue heaving in the sunlight. "Alexander, look!" Mom said. "The ocean." There seems to be lots of oceans around. Mom and Granddad and Grandma were too tired to climb back up the hill. Granddad said this is where we should stick out our thumbs. He took me in my carrier up on his back. "Who wouldn't stop for an old man with a baby on his back?" He laughed and stuck out his thumb.

Mom stuck out her thumb, too. Grandma said, "You all look so silly."

The shiny cars spun by. People stuck their noses in the air or looked at us funny. Mom said, "I think the rest of you should hide in the bushes."

Granddad snorted. "Oh, you want me to hide in the bushes? I wouldn't even fit in the bushes." (He is pretty round.) "Why should I hide in the bushes?" Then he answered himself. "Because I'm short and squat and evil looking."

Mom laughed. "I didn't mean that."

Finally a van pulled over and the driver said get in. We drove up a curvy road to the parking lot where Granddad left the car, and off we went to have dinner.

I was hungry, so Mom gave me some cheese and grapes and bread in the car. That was her mistake. By the time we got to the eating place, I wasn't hungry anymore. It was there that I had my moments of glory. I got to sit in a high chair at the head of the table. I had an audience of seven people at the next table who were trying to have a peaceful dinner. I started off with a slow rasping scream and held the note as long as I could. All seven people turned and stared at me. "Shhh!" Mom said, and stuck an ice cube in my mouth. The little girl smiled, but her mother sniffed and said, "Permissive."

Then a woman in an apron came and brought me three cookies on a plate. I took a couple of bites, but I didn't like them so I tossed them on the floor. Mom picked them up and set them back on my plate. Does she really expect me to eat stuff that's been on the floor?

Granddad ordered a rum and Coke. I turned my plate upside down on the tray, banged on it and screamed. Everyone was looking at me and I felt pleased. Mom took the plate away and stuck another ice cube in my mouth. Granddad was smiling, his eyes wide. He said, "This couldn't be the same child that usually eats with us so quietly. He's a little dynamo of destruction."

Grandma said, "He's acting like a spoiled brat."

Granddad ordered another rum and Coke. Then the food came. Mom tied a bib on me and gave me a piece of lettuce. Flooey! I spit it out. The same with the French fry. Grandma's eyes were darting around. Mom kept say-

ing in a low voice, "Stop it! You're terrible!"

But Granddad was chuckling. Mom offered me some of her milk. I took a mouthful, held it for a minute, then opened my mouth and let it dribble all over her lap.

I tipped Mom's glass backwards, spilled a nice puddle on the tray and splashed with both hands. The milk shot up in the air and splattered Mom and Granddad. He was laughing. "I never saw anyone take a bath in his milk before," he said. "And it all started when I took that first drink."

Back in the car, as we were driving home, Grandma said, "Never again!" But everyone was laughing, so I think I was a hit.

Another day Dad took us to the beach. We hadn't planned to swim, so I wore cut-offs and a T-shirt. Mother bought Alexander a little shovel and a pail and he sat in his blue corduroy jumpsuit and dug holes in the sand. About fifty yards from shore a craggy shaft of bare stone rose from the ocean. Dad said in an offhand way, "Why don't you go climb that?"

Still competing with my little brother to impress my father with my fearlessness, I trotted out into the waves and swam to the rock. Barefoot, it was no big deal to climb to the top. But it was taller than it looked from shore. By the time I reached the top I was tired and out of breath, dismayed to find there was no place to sit and rest. I peered over the top – a sharp drop down the other side. Holy kaboley! I looked back to the beach where my parents sat in the sun beside little boy blue. I wasn't even sure that they could see me. Did they even watch where I went?

In the rush and ebb of the waves below, a stranger swam

back and forth, shouting, "Come down! You're going to fall."

The thought had not occurred to me until that moment. I glanced down fifty feet of jagged rock to wave-torn teeth waiting to savage me. The wind roughed me around. A shrill of fear rang through me and set my body quaking. I clung like an insect to my bare perch. My legs wobbled. Damn! How could I? How could I have climbed up a dangerous crag and left my baby on the beach? With my parents. If I fell and died in the rocks below, they would probably raise him for me. The thought galvanized me. I took a couple of deep breaths and tried to steady my hands.

"I won't fall! I won't!" I whispered. "I can't. Please, God!"

I had no idea exactly how I got up there. Face to the rock, I reached down blind with my bare toes to find a hold. What if I got trapped? But each time I searched for a niche, my toes found one. Slowly, I clambered down. Weak with strain and adrenaline, I lowered my scratched limbs into the forgiving waves. With a shaky sigh, I paddled for shore. I wasn't a little girl anymore, ready to risk her life to impress her father. I was a mother. And I'd better start acting like one.

On our last evening Dad drove us out to Point Reyes. It was windy, but we enjoyed the bracing walk along a grassy path to the edge of the cliff. The ocean surged dark below and the city lights across the bay twinkled in the blue evening haze. Part of me would always love the ocean, but I was irrevocably married to New Mexico. Not to mention in love with a certain man. I had played that down as much as possible.

In the morning Dad drove us to the airport. He was right. Mother was crying again. The day before she had cautiously suggested that I might do better if I moved to Felton.

"California is nice. You could have your own circle of friends."

Inwardly, I scoffed at the idea, imagining how Dad would alienate any friends I made. Chase off any potential mates. And chase me off too. Now I understand how lonely Mother was, what she would have given to have us close, to be part of Alexander's growing up. Maybe she sensed that she wouldn't see us again until Alexander was twelve. But I had a life on hold, a lover, waiting. I gave Mother and Dad a hug. Told them I loved them. With a sigh of relief and a smack of guilt, I climbed on the plane.

The winter was a hard one. Most nights were below zero and the windows, which had no curtains, frosted up with ice each morning. Gary and Cheryl Walker talked about moving to Mexico. Mary, William and their baby, whom they had named Ona, moved to California, to waves and oranges. The harsh winter united us with our neighbors. We borrowed sugar and flour from each other to save trips to town. We pulled each other's cars and trucks out of the frozen ruts.

Neither of us minded the outhouse, which we used around noon in the winter when it was warmer and in the morning in the summer, when it was cooler. We dipped lime from a bucket in the corner and dumped it down the holes. To amuse ourselves, we collaged pictures from magazines on the walls, of Nixon and flowers and cougars. It was fun in a grim sort of way, but we agreed that on the list of improvements for the house, indoor plumbing was a high priority.

In the summer, we showered under a canvas camp bucket

behind the house. Just filled it with warm water, hoisted it up over your head with a rope, turned on the spigot and voila! Shining drops in sunlight and teasing gusts of wind on your goosebumps. But in the winter, we tried various ways to bathe inside. One winter we hauled a huge green bucket of water from the river up the hill and heated it on the stove. I had great hopes for this method, especially when I first stepped in. It was great to have warm water up to my knees. Too bad there wasn't enough room to sit down.

Next, we bought a kiddie wading pool, rigged up a ring of PVC pipe, hung it from the ceiling with a shower curtain around it. Then the canvas bucket. Brrrrr! Being enclosed in a shower curtain did nothing for the chill on my wet skin in the frigid living room. We reverted to sponge baths in the kitchen.

An assortment of people came to the movies. Christians came to see *The Bible*; cowboys to *Pat Garrett and Billy the Kid*; cops to *Magnum Force*. Some movies, such as *Jeremiah Johnson* and *Jaws*, attracted what felt like the entire county. Matinees, which played at 1:30 on Saturdays and cost fifty cents for everyone, drew families and young teens and a young Pueblo widow with three children.

Some patrons came every week regardless of what movie was playing. Henry, who was mentally challenged, watched comedies and thrillers and kids' movies with the same exalted expression on his face. Chuck, from New Buffalo, whom everyone called "a beautiful sweet guy" while shaking their heads, drank Scotch from under his coat and fell asleep. Dennis Hopper and his posse swept through, packing and loaded, too wired to watch an entire film. He was a hairy and incoherent bandito deeply committed to drugs and alcohol.

The plaza was at that time still the heart of Taos. It had a barber shop, hardware store, insurance company, small bookstore, five and dime, army surplus store, drug store, a hotel, restaurants and bars. In fact, there were an improbable number of bars and liquor stores, and starting around nine in the morning, motley Taoseños of all stripes – artists, ski bums, pilots, bartenders – started drinking in Tano's bar or La Cocina or another of the bars. There were drunks on the street too, who would shake your hand for thirty minutes if you didn't know how to extract yourself.

After dark there was often trouble. Nelson from the pueblo and his drunken wife were arguing in the lobby and she bit him on the cheek. Blood flowed down his face and I made a note to get the carpet cleaned. A big Anglo redneck started a fight with a Hispanic and when I broke it up, wanted to fight me. I tried to calm him down while Loretta from concessions called the cops. William from Lama Foundation, which was the enlightened commune, tried to seduce every woman he came across by using the direct approach. He said to Robin Appleby, "Why don't you come home with me?" She spit on his shoes.

During the day the plaza was for the most part a peaceful place, but come nightfall, it was a different story. Drunks were either very happy or very belligerent, and young men and women were bored and restless. While Phaedra was with me, a group of drunk teenagers were taunting people coming out of the theater. When I asked them to leave, one of them picked up a cinder block and threw it at a glass poster case. Someone must have called the police because chief Fernando Rivera showed up, all five feet, seven inches of him, and grabbed two of the teens and flung them to the ground. A third one approached him, thinking to help his buddies, and Fernando said, "Leave now or I'll arrest you too." The kid hesitated and Fernando stood up, grabbed his hair and pulled him down in one swift motion, then handcuffed all three. Phaedra handed me the cinderblock, which had somehow bounced off the glass case.

In the winter I was often the last person to leave town. On bad nights, even the bars closed early. I drove home across a flat snowy plain guessing where the road was. My banged-up BMW, which Harvey had discarded, was not the most reliable of cars, mainly because I used it to play tag with other cars across the mesa and to herd cows and horses out of our fields. It didn't occur to me to carry a flashlight, blanket, matches or water.

One night the dirt road leading to our house was blocked by a horse lying on the ground. I got out and tried to get it on its feet but it was so weak from starvation, it wouldn't get up. I was pretty sure it was a horse abandoned by one of the communes. I walked home, got my .38 and a rope, walked back, and shot it in the head.

Morningstar had an old white mare. Sort of. It just grazed around the mesa and nobody paid much attention to it. Maybe gave it an apple once in a while. By the end of November, there was nothing left to nibble on but dried yellow grasses. In the late afternoon the mare wandered downhill into the orchard. When I went down with an apple, she bolted across the stream, then stumbled and collapsed.

Apparently someone from Morning Star or Reality found her. They brought a bale of hay, stuck a flake under the mare's nose. But it was too late.

On his way home from the theater, Jim found her lying in the road. He got out of his car, stroked her neck, tried to roll her onto her back, twisted her tail. Nada. He came home and got his gun, shot her, tied her front legs to the fender and hauled her body into the field.

"This is awful," he said. "When was I appointed to be the horse killer around here?"

In the morning when we drove by, all that was left of the horse were the sawed-off legs and the head propped up in the snow. Later we heard that at Morningstar they ate that skinny mare for Christmas dinner.

By February 1973 I had had it with the theater, bored with the routine and stressed by the responsibility. The weight of the theater had been on my back for over "a whole year." It was nothing compared to what most people do, but for me, devoted to daydreaming and writing, it had become too much. When Harvey proposed leasing the theater to an entrepreneur named Bill Whaley, I jumped at the opportunity to be unemployed.

Whaley was half business man, half impresario, with one of his selves usually getting in the way of the other. He wore a sports jacket and a fedora like a costume and hid behind the brim of the hat and an ambiguous smile.

The last movie I showed was *Burn*, a movie by Gillo Pontecorvo starring Marlon Brando as a mercenary. After the second showing, I counted the tickets, changed the marquee, and locked the front door. It was February 28, Harvey's birthday. I joined him at Antonio's bar in the La Fonda hotel. It had always been one of my favorite moments in life, walking away from a job. I thought I was finished with the Plaza Theater once and for all. We sat and reminisced about our prep school days and the year we spent in Europe. Eli Walcott joined us, an old timer who used to be an artist and was now drinking himself impeccably to death. When Harvey went to the men's room, Eli said "The trouble is, Jim, now I have no one."

I had three beers, Harvey had four tequilas. We went back to the Hondo house where Phaedra joined us in drinking a bottle of Ohio Sauterne. We smoked dope and roared with laughter until three in the morning. I don't remember what we laughed so hard about, something about the way his mother opened the front door to guests. He gave a hilarious demonstration. And we laughed about not being able to remember what we were laughing about.

Dear Jim

I really enjoyed Harvey's visit the other night – the terrible punning, the bad jokes and the "literary talk."

You're a nice big warm thing and I like cuddling up to you at night. I'm glad you're finding solace again at the studio. I love Alexander and Ewar and even those silly dogs and troublesome cats. I love you and me. I peek through a crack in the door and see you down on your knees in blue overalls painting the bookshelf white. Alexander hovers around you like a large bee. I love even the vicious ducks. That duck chases me through the mud all the way to the outhouse and I run because it really bites. I know I'm bigger but it doesn't know that. I'm afraid of what it thinks it's going to do to me.

Bluesox

Jim offered to buy me a vacuum cleaner but I said I didn't mind sweeping. We did buy an old wringer-washer and plunked it in back of the casita. I liked hanging the wash on the line to blow in the wind, under the blue sky. I enjoyed gathering in the fresh-smelling clothes to sort and fold on the bed. When I remarked to Elaine that I liked doing laundry, she crooked an elbow at me and took a drag on her cigarette: "I like getting it done."

I also enjoyed washing and shining the kitchen floor, running my hands over the patterns in the oak, giving it a little loving. In summer I waxed it to a shine that lasted until the first set of footprints. Then I switched to oiling it. Dusting, I enjoyed not so much. Several inches of dirt in the ceiling above the boards, used for insulation in the old days, was constantly drifting down on us. I felt oppressed by the weight and darkness of the old adobe; it gave me pleasure to buy a white vase with Chinese flower patterns and set it on the kitchen windowsill. The whole room seemed to lighten. But overall, I had so much more than I had ever dared to dream of. Our adobe home with the blue window frames was "my blue heaven."

From Jim's journal

    Sunday afternoon in Arroyo Hondo and nothing to do. The blue sky travels overhead like newssheet. Marcos Ortiz is fixing the hydraulic lift on his tractor. The dope dealer comes by in his VW. Mrs. Chacon opens the grocery store. Matthew is splitting cedar for his cook-stove. Cave Dave is sitting on a rock in the canyon. Two hawks float over the cottonwoods. Dennis Long's band is starting a new piece in the shed behind his house. The peyote feast is beginning at New Buffalo commune. Ida Martinez has her Self-Help women over to sew. Three cars of Chicanos block a pickup full of hippies and beat them with two by fours. Village boys shut off the acequia Atalaya and are snatching fish up from the mud. Ruth is kissing Fast Ed in a teepee. Father Prieto is going over parish accounts with Clodoveo Chacon. Morningstar is playing basketball against a Raza team from Arroyo Seco. Tony Garcia has eluded his wife and is headed for Celso's bar. Three hippie kids sneak into Mrs. Chacon's store to steal candy. Finley is beating his horse. Tahiti is blow-torching bronze discs together. The bleeding hippies are at Dan's and Peggy's getting bandaged. Albert Christianson is illegally irrigating his carrots and peas. Justin is repairing his old Mercedes. The Rio Hondo is traveling towards the Rio Grande. Nick's dog Spark is sniffing Sandra's dog Windsock. Toby is pulling tufts of hair out of his own face. The dope dealer has arrived at Reality. Nonnie, Carlos and Ramon are teasing an enraged cock behind the church. Jackson is laying a Mercy trap for the skunk that has been eating his chicks. Mrs. Ortiz is pulling in white sheets off the line. The winos are returning to Morningstar in triumph – they scored some bourbon! Matthew has gone back to splitting wood in the bright Sunday sun.

We were walking along the river and on the way home, we saw a red VW Bug backing out of Harvey's driveway. It spun its wheels and zoomed up the hill. A bunch of hippies hung out of the windows, shouting and laughing. We started towards the house. A man was standing astride on the roof of Harvey's house, looking around, as if he had just landed. Jim handed Zander to me. "Take him back to the house. I'll go check it out."

I went into the house and through the living room, but seeing nothing amiss, I went upstairs into Harvey's bedroom. I could barely see in the dark, but I could hear someone breathing. I reached down beside the bed and dragged up a young man who was crouched between the bed and the wall. He had dirty blond hair and a large bowie knife strapped to his side but he was about a head shorter than me and seemed harmless. He lost his balance and staggered against me.

"Are you drunk or stoned?" I said, not really wanting to know.

He mumbled something. I herded him downstairs, where he slouched down in a chair at the head of the long table. When I asked him who he was he said, "Jason. I'm really sorry, man."

He added that he was from the Hog Farm, and that his pals were friends of Phaedra's.

"Look," I said. "No harm done. Just leave and we'll

forget about it."

"Hey man, I'm totally wasted. Do you have anything to eat?"

I heated up a can of beans, which he wolfed down.

"Okay, Look. Time to leave, or I'll have to call the sheriff."

He mumbled some more. So I called the sheriff's office and explained the situation. They said they would send a deputy.

I turned back to my guest. "A deputy is on the way. Go right now and you'll be fine."

But he was so tired, he said. He sat down in the living room. A deputy arrived, listened to my account, then ordered the young man to stand up. He frisked him. Much to my embarrassment, he found an Indian necklace under Jason's shirt and more jewelry in his pockets.

When I looked around and saw drawers hanging open, I realized that Navajo rugs and Hopi kachinas were missing. I also realized that the red VW Bug we saw screeching out of there was involved. I called Harvey in Santa Fe, and he called the New Mexico State Police.

The next day Harvey and a State policeman named Ben Salazar went to the Hog Farm, where the young men and women denied any knowledge of a robbery. On the way back to Santa Fe, Harvey and Salazar passed a red VW Bug and pulled it over. The driver wouldn't allow them to look in the trunk so the trooper held the car and called in for a warrant. Before it arrived, the driver struck a deal: he'd open the trunk if no charges were brought. Harvey said he wouldn't press charges if all the artifacts were returned. In the trunk Harvey found one of his black and red Navajo rugs. Back at the Hog Farm, Harvey laid the rug on the ground. The hippies brought out the rest of the rugs, Kachinas, pots and jewelry and lay them on the blanket. Harvey checked off each item, loaded everything into the deputy's car, and it was over.

Harvey got back his collection of artifacts and never blamed me for the bad behavior of my so-called brothers who had ripped him off. I didn't mention that when I was housesitting for him the year before, those same "brothers" came to take showers and then, while I was in the kitchen cooking, almost drove his tractor off a bridge.

A week or two after the robbery, a busload of ragged Hog Farmers showed up at our house, mostly men, gray-faced and sullen. Blond Steve and the rest who had left Jason behind. Now Jason was in jail. And it was our fault! Capitalistic pigs! Since Harvey had gotten everything back, they demanded that we drop the charges.

Jim explained in patient tones that we had not brought any charges. The deputy had caught him and taken him in. It turned out that Jason had violated his probation.

I sat at the table clutching my baby, eyeing them thinking, Some robbery, you idiots. Leaving this guy behind. Not to mention taking advantage of my trust. Never again. You are not my brothers.

Dear Mom,
I think of you and your battles with the avocados. Maybe you were not meant to be an avocado tycoon. But last year

was so good. I can almost smell the orchard, the dust, the trees. I love to walk in the trees and look out between them at the shining ocean.

The theater has been leased and I'm looking for a job. I could stay on at Harvey's company since we've decided to go on renovating the other parts of the building, but that's work I'm not qualified for, supervising construction and costs. I've had an offer of work as a carpenter working two days a week or three. I'd make about $200 a month, which is enough, with Phaedra's welfare and food stamps. I keep asking her to give them up and she won't. It's the one thing we disagree about. I think she feels it leaves her independent. As you know, I can live on practically nothing. Phaedra told me that when I was in Africa, Harvey said: "Jim thinks he's rich."

Deirdre announces that she is going to London to continue to study Buddhism with Lama Chime Rinpoche. "Never to return," she says, laughing nervously, as if it is only a joke. I am relieved that she is staying away, for I am tired of her mood swings. Ewar will stay here with us. But if she settles down, perhaps she'll send for him.

He and I have been running a mile circuit together, to the Hondo church and around past Harvey's house. He has better wind than me. I taught him how to drive the tractor. We've also been landscaping Harvey's house for three dollars an hour. One night we went to a movie and stopped at a bar on the way home but the bouncer wouldn't let him in. I said he was my son but the guy just shook his head. Ewar has matured a lot. Phaedra cut his hair and he looks like a man. He does his chores without grumbling. As for school, Da Nahazli doesn't give him homework, and he resists my efforts to teach him.

Zander is my delight. We play continuously. He throws a ball, wrestles, sings, runs in circles around the chair, hides and seeks, and of course has little cars and trucks. He is stout, brave and rather delicate in his feelings, pouts when hurt but rarely cries. He is no longer a baby but a boy, busy, curious, babbles all day, "mommy, daddy, cuck, shoe, hot, baba."

Jim lifts Zander

One day I kept Ewar out of school and he, his friend Hoski, Alexander and I went up the canyon between Hondo and Valdez and spent the day there. The grass coming in green, the sky blue, the river swift. The boys climbed a rock slide and raced boats in the acequia. Alexander slept in the shade under the trees. I mused all day, on the edge of boredom, delighted to do nothing.

Dear Jim,
Let's see. Date the letter, he says. Orient yourself in time and space. Right. Saturday March 10, 1973. Out in the casita. The sun is bright and the wind whistling around the stovepipe. Flies buzzing on the window sill. If March can come in like a lion, spring can roar!
 So now you're a bum, Jim. Be true to yourself, that's what I always say. It's usually good for a laugh. It's nice to get letters from you again.
 I take a walk back up the canyon and run smack into a killer from Reality. I see him through the trees, coming heavily down the side of the hill. I duck out of sight hoping he doesn't see me, but the next turn in the path brings us face-to-face. It is a tense moment. I see he has something large and heavy and brown around his shoulders, a headless deer, already gutted out. The feet are tied together in a professional way.
 He has a green silk handkerchief tied around his head and when he smiles at me I notice a wide space between his front teeth. It makes him look good-natured and dumb.
 "I see you have yourself a deer!"
 He grins and nods and offers me the liver. I say, "No thanks, I'm not making that kind of a run today. Where are

you coming from?"

"Up in the mountains."

"Where are you going?"

He looks startled. "Where are you from?"

"Down the road apiece." I jerk my thumb, wondering if Jim is waiting to collar this guy when he comes out of the canyon.

A second one comes down the hill, a short guy with a Confederate cap and bushy beard. He's carrying an old army rifle. He smiles.

I ask, "Are you guys from Reality?"

They look at each other.

"Yes."

"I hear you don't have much to eat up there."

"Right."

"Well, goodbye," I say and start off.

"Hey, what's your name?" shouts the one with the deer on his back.

"Phaedra."

"Oh, I thought you were someone else."

Harvey put his house up for sale, and when it didn't sell he rented it to Bonnie and Michael Kaufman. Bonnie was a slight, wiry woman with freckles, short hair and a lively character. Mike, fresh out of med school, was tall, thin and elusive. Their daughter Jemery, with reddish blonde hair, was the same age as Alexander. There were also five dogs, most of them rescue mutts. Bonnie said she planned to raise Arabian horses. We were pleased that we would have a family across the river, that our son would have a playmate.

Phaedra finally dropped her welfare and food stamps. We were doing fine. We were poor but had little sense of it. Harvey continued to give us the little adobe rent free and I made some money doing landscaping and carpentry, although I was terrible at both. We grew some vegetables, not very successfully. With an old Kenmore sewing machine, Phaedra made nightshirts and pants and shirts for us, as well as pillow cases, curtains and quilts. I wore work shoes until the nails came up through the bottoms, then hammered the nails back down and stuffed the insides with newspapers.

For a year I was busy finalizing my divorce from Deirdre, writing immortal stories and poems, and mostly enjoying myself. I wrote a great deal, stories called A Death, Mrs. Ababa, Dunes, Weir Speaking, My Father, which was a story from Alexander's point of view about my going to Ethiopia and never returning. It was unclear if I died of misadventure, suicide, or just wandered off. I thought it romantic. Phaedra helped me a lot, especially with structure. She was busy writing a novel that she called "a political romance," bringing up Zander and also mostly enjoying herself.

Even as I wrote, I believed that the pieces were third-rate, that all of the characters were simply me thinly disguised. These stories went into the dump years later.

We occasionally hired a babysitter, smoked a joint, ate too much pizza at the House of Taos, then went to a movie. At first, the evening was spoiled by my checking the focus and noticing the bulb burned out in the red exit sign, but I gradually forgot about them and returned to losing myself in the movie.

I saw a snake in the orchard and looked hard at it. It coiled and rattled its tail in the grass and struck at a stick, so I called Phaedra to bring a shovel. It didn't have a flat head or fangs so I knew it wasn't a rattler; it was probably a bull snake imitating a rattler. Still, to be sure, I was going to kill it. Phaedra brought the shovel, but with her help, the snake escaped into the thicket by the apple tree.

A lizard in the house. Skunk down by the river. Deer in the evenings. Two bears in the plum hedges. Karma the cat brought in a mole. Neighbors saw a mountain lion. We are keeping a neighbor's little mare for the summer with Glenda's paint. Phaedra likes to ride the paint bareback up and down the driveway.

Harvey hired us to clean his cabins at Los Ojitos and after we did, we went swimming in the ponds. Los Ojitos, the Little Eyes. We had the place to ourselves. Phaedra put down a blanket under a fir tree where Alexander could sleep. Then she and I rowed into the middle of the pond where there was a float with a nest sitting on it, and a single duck egg. Iridescent blue dragonflies flew around us, red-winged blackbirds swooped into the willows, hovering and screeching above their nests. A dead rotten bird floated in the water. No matter; we dove in and swam among the water lilies and floated on our backs looking at the trees and the mountains and the clouds.

When Alexander woke up, Phaedra placed him on my chest and I slid into the water. At first he was nervous, clutching me with his tiny talons, an alarmed look on his face, but he soon relaxed, and we splashed and laughed. Naked Phaedra, naked Alexander, naked me, the three of us on the float in the middle of the pond, sharing it with the duck egg.

We didn't pay much attention to the daily news until the scandal of Watergate. We were not aware that President Nixon and his aides had formed a secret group called the White House plumbers to perform break-ins, but in April of 1973, the news was everywhere. In July, the country learned that Nixon had taped conversations in the Oval Office. We had a small radio that sat at the back of the kitchen counter and we were glued to it day after day listening to the five o'clock news.

In August Taos made the headlines with the Eddie Gaudet story. Gaudet was a Creole who was living at Morningstar commune, a short, bearded man with a big mouth and a predilection for firearms. He had once been a cop in Louisiana. The FBI showed up and started asking his whereabouts. Rumor had it that he had been drinking in a bar in New Orleans and had threatened to shoot President Nixon on his upcoming trip to the city.

First came the police helicopters thud-thud-thudding overhead, followed by press helicopters. Then State police and the secret service staked out a camp on the other side of the river. Every day parties went out hunting for Gaudet. They came to our house twice, asked permission to look in the outhouse and the chicken coop. We peered out the windows as they held their rifles ready, kicked open the doors of the sheds.

"It's just like a movie," Phaedra said.

Most people in Taos sided with Gaudet and enjoyed the spectacle. Gossip trickled in: an FBI agent spotted him in the hills and there was an exchange of gunfire. The outlaw's old lady sneaked off into the hills every night with food and wine. Alternately, they said Gaudet used secret tunnels leading into Morningstar and visited his woman every night.

After nearly a week, the cops escorted Gaudet's old lady and cousin into the hills and negotiated a surrender. Within days they discovered that Gaudet hadn't been in New Orleans when the threat was made; the charges were dropped. But he was immediately hit with a new charge: assault on a federal officer for the one shot he had fired.

In court Gaudet admitted that he had fired one warning shot in the air. It all came to nothing. He was released. Most of the country believed that it had been Nixon's people trying to divert attention from Watergate.

My mother and I went to Paris in September to visit my sister Bunny and her husband Jacques and son Marc. We stayed in their apartment in Saint Cloud for nearly three weeks. On the way home, we stopped in England briefly and I met Deirdre on the Oxford-London train. She was still studying with Chime Rinpoche and had decided to become a novice nun. She was herself, outwardly cheerful, inwardly sad and dour. She gave me volume two of Painter's biography of Proust for my birthday, and wrote, "Jimmy I love you," in the book, and signed it Dierdreen.

She used her old nickname, but reversed the e and i and misspelled her own name. I wondered if it wasn't a sign of how much she wanted to be someone else.

During our visit, the Arab-Israeli war of 1973 broke out and inexplicably, I decided to go to Israel and join the Israeli army.

Dear Mom,
I came into Taos on the bus on Saturday at noon, a crystal clear fall day, snow on the mountains, Phaedra, Ewar, Alexander waiting on the sidewalk. Phaedra told Alexander I was coming but he didn't recognize me. When I held him, he was looking over my shoulder looking for me. I put on my glasses. Then he recognized me, and he said, in a matter of fact way: "Daddy."

Phaedra had a miscarriage while I was in Paris. She seems nonchalant about it but I think she is more upset than she lets on. We had our doubts last year but now we know we want to have a child. Well, patience, right? We shall see.

I am still determined to go fight in Israel. Phaedra has applied for an emergency passport. I know you don't understand and I hardly understand myself, but I feel that I must go.

I had more than one disaster while Jim was in Paris. I knew he was going to see Deirdre and I was still worried that he might get back with her, but I said nothing. Had I asked him, he would have reassured me. It was only a train ride. Nothing more.

As it was, I felt like Cinderella, left at home to take care of Ewar and Zander and the animals. I had never been to Paris. In fact, I had no longing to go to Paris, but I felt left out. A weakness in my character, no doubt. At some point his mother had remarked to me, "You'll get your chance." I wondered if that was true.

It was late September and, as usual, I planned to drive out to Taos Pueblo for San Geronimo Day and the climbing of the pole. But I messed up by smoking a joint before I left the house. On the way to the Pueblo, I was gazing off at the mountain. I came around a blind curve and saw a car was stopped dead in the road. Someone was asking directions out the window. First I pulled out to pass, but a car was coming, so I pulled back in. Zander was in the front seat, not even belted in. I took off my glasses, reached an arm across him to keep him from falling and, bam, we smashed into the back of the car.

Neither Zander nor I were hurt, but he cried. I only dented the fender of the other car, but took out the radiator of our old car. There we sat, engine steaming. The day spoiled. Someone called it in. A tow truck came. Somehow we got home. The other driver was found responsible, but that didn't make me feel much better.

Ewar and I were not getting along. He disappeared for whole days at a time. I had no idea where he was. He sneaked out at night. When I caught him and scolded him, he said, "You treat me like I'm a criminal."

Meanwhile, Bonnie remarked to me one day when I was down there visiting, "I think I'm pregnant."

I smiled. "I think I am, too."

I had noticed that my breasts were sore. I thought of that afternoon with Jim under the cottonwood trees beside the river. What a great moment to conceive a child, the one we had been waiting for. I was beginning to wonder if I could get pregnant again. A year ago I had stopped using birth control. We had decided to try for another baby.

I was feeling overwhelmed when Manuel Ortiz, from down the road, let his cows out. Maybe he even herded them across the river and towards our orchard, which had once been ejido, or common land, used for grazing and picking herbs. I trotted down to the orchard where the new trees had just taken hold and begun to grow. They were not fenced and I thought the cows might destroy them. I chased the cows out and came back to the house, breathless. Half an hour later, I had major cramps and then a miscarriage. I locked myself in the bathroom and wept. I felt totally crushed and defeated, an irresponsible mother and caretaker of the land. I dreaded having to tell Jim when he came home.

Dear Bunny,
Mom and I got back safely and have resumed our lives. Thank you again for putting up with us for almost a month. You and Jacques were great, very patient of our ways. And yes, I agree, you were right to stop her smoking in the apartment.

Phaedra had a tough time while I was gone. She had a miscarriage, and although she didn't seem too upset, I think she was. She also had an accident with our car, and she and Ewar got into it over his behavior; he kept going out without telling her where. She tells me all this with a lighthearted humor, because she is an amazingly resilient woman.

We are not going to Israel to fight. She had her passport photos taken and she applied, but it hasn't come through yet. I called the Jewish Agency and they said they are taking only single men eighteen to twenty-four years old. I wanted to say, Ha, I'm not married, because Phaedra and I are not, but then remembered that Deirdre and I still are. I don't know what silly dream it was, to go fight for "my people." Please don't laugh – it was a powerful feeling. I suppose it was some literary fantasy, like going to fight in the Spanish Civil War. I feel a little stupid. I wonder if I was seeking some cheap identity?

Within a month of Jim's coming home, I felt my breasts swell. I was pregnant again. When I told Jim, he was astonished. "Are you sure?"

I patted my stomach. "Yes."

"Just like that?"

"Just like that."

Dear Bunny,
Mom phoned twice in thirty minutes, again last night, frightened but stoic about the upcoming eye operations. She goes into the hospital Tuesday and has the operation the next day. I feel that I should go out but I have no money, have several job applications in and want to be here in case I am called for an interview. Mary is going and I am very grateful for that. She will watch the dogs and be there when Mom gets home.

The big news here is that Phaedra is pregnant! We are

excited, to say the least. Last year she said she wasn't ready but this summer we both said let's go for it and now it has happened. I already wonder how Alexander will take it. He touches my heart, the way he saunters around the yard in his brightly-colored yarn cap and fringed buckskin jacket. (I refer to them as "fringe benefits" and think I'm funny). He comes from the sandbox and takes my finger to drag me over. I won't go and he looks so sulky. Then he wanders off and sits in the sandbox "reading" the Jesus cartoons that George gave us.

I really must find work. Most men, in the middle of their careers, have fleeting moments of contemplation, but I have fleeting careers in the midst of one long contemplation. I'm thirty-three, old enough for the senate but three years short of the presidency.

Dec. 31
Dear Phaedra,
I haven't written you in so long, I mean a letter from me here to you here, an interoffice memo as it were. I feel shy. I guess there are little crevices of my mind still hidden from you, little cubicles that contain brightly-colored wrapped little boxes in which are brightly painted little boxes which contain still more little . . . and then a tiny note that says look under L in the dictionary. In short, I love you more than ever. I love your swelling body. It's almost as if there are two of you. Your face is more beautiful now – did you know? It's the baby. Should I feel jealous? I can't make you beautiful like that. Oh well – I'm not jealous. I'm glad. It's like watching a flower opening in slow motion. Someday

in summer there's going to be our healthy funny baby.

Listen mother, I'm so glad it's you. You're so good. You know how you weren't sure you could trust me to take care of Alexander and then you found out you could, so I realize that I trust you completely with *it*, whoever *it* is, and I wonder if other men feel the gratitude towards their women for going through all this. I look at you and shake my head in amazement – I see you withdraw, the two of you – to some secret meadow of sweet contemplation and I see that for you it has already begun; for you it's already real and you'll remember now as the beginning of his or her life, while I don't feel that but must wait, watch you, smile, be ironical in the face of your preoccupation. Sometimes I want to help you and other times I want to distract you towards me, wanting you to wait on me, and sometimes I am content to cheer quizzically from the sidelines. Well I love you, I love your sweet shape, I love your misty eyes and your sleepiness and your "I feel so big." I love less your maniacal drive that gets the couch reupholstered in one night but enjoy it when it's done. I love your courage that tells me not to worry. Knowing that you are not afraid makes me not afraid (and when you are afraid of the cold face at the window, I feel positively heroic, ready to fight off demons).

It's the last day of the year and I'll make no resolutions except to give up control. Like Muslims I'll end every statement with "god willing." You taught me carefully; I'm the product of the Greenwood school of Que Sera Sera, the Let It Be institute of higher learning. As for us in our nest, we may be washed away by the next full moon, and if we are I'll be comforted by your cackling voice from the stars saying "Why not? It was a good idea at the time." (Fade cackle as she is borne away). But what better day to write you a letter without a resolution or vow – *no vows* – and yet to whisper into your silken ear how you matter to me and are spirit to me and how much I love and respect you.

The three of us, plus one more

Journal
David phoned, saying Ewar wants to stay in California. They have already visited the public junior high near his house and Ewar is due to start. It hits me hard. I feel a sense of great loss. We are given only so many opportunities, and I have definitely blown this one. I destroyed the marriage and now this. I had hoped to salvage something.

A week later, I still feel a sense of being left, left behind, which is ironic and pathetic because I was the one who left them, several times and then for good. I am bewildered, and I know that I am not seeing into the heart of things.

Harvey,
You casually mentioned that you might have to take our house and property bac, to sell. You see into my dark; consequently you miss my light. I love this house and property and I feel desperate when I think of losing it. This is my home. I finally have the passion for my own place, a passion which you thought I lacked and with good reason, given my rhetoric about not owing anything.

I feel I have within my grasp the chance to live a sane life, me, who was in all honesty a little insane. My fear is that I'll let it slip away through some stupid act.

Don't tell Phaedra and me that due to this and that, the land is lost. I ask you, please do not play with our future. This is by far the largest thing I have ever asked of you. If you want it for yourself, that is different. It's *yours*. But for it to go to a realtor and then to some anonymous homebuyer: I feel horror. It would be like selling a child to a stranger.

Dear Bunny,
Alexander is in a contrary phase. If I say "Let's go" he says "No go." If I respond, "No go" he says "I am going."

We have decided on names. If it's a girl, Sara Caroline; if a boy, Benjamin.

I have sent Deirdre the divorce papers to sign.

Dad sent a photo of himself and the interview that was published in a magazine – did he send them to you too? I put the photo above the stove, to come to terms with him. He is exhibiting his wedding ring and he looks very handsome and satisfied with himself.

I continue to write a novel, now called *The Mnemonist*, about a man whose wife was murdered. The cops are worthless so he chases down two suspects, a hippie and a Christian.

Journal
We had a party; Jim was the cello and I the violin. We ate ice cream, danced, smoked dope and drank and had a fist fight in slow motion (I won). We pored over Bruegel's paintings for a while and Jim says "Look at that dog, at those eyes. Down through the centuries right out of the page. Look, he's staring at your grilled cheese sandwich!"

He tried to convince me he was psychic by guessing the name of the record I was going to put on. I kept telling him I believed in him but he got all excited. The party was fun but when it was all over we both felt sick from too much food and drink.

Journal
Two guys from Reality Construction commune showed up on foot in a lather: one short guy and one tall. They said a friend had blown his fingers off while trying to unjam a 12 gauge shotgun with a comb. We drove up to Reality and I met Steve, who had wrapped his hand in a cloth. We looked for the two missing fingers and couldn't find them. Then I drove the three of them to Holy Cross hospital where a doctor stitched up Steve's hand and gave him a

bottle of pain pills. Steve was "good in there" as Hemingway would say, in pain but stoic.

Back at Reality, we sat in a circle drinking bad wine. The short guy was friendly and a bit dumb, and the tall one, a tooth missing, had an edge. They cooked deer meat from an animal they had shot five days ago and hung on the north side of the house. As we ate our meat, they passed around Steve's pain pills.

"I think Steve's going to need those," I said, but no one cared, not even Steve. They laughed when they recalled how we had looked for the missing fingers, our heads bent down to the ground. They forgot the story about trying to unjam the gun with a comb and said they had been having fast draw contests with their guns and the shotgun had gone off.

When I left they gave me a large piece of venison for my trouble.

"Is this a buck or a doe?" I asked.

"I don't know what you mean." Grin. "A doe."

When I showed Phaedra the leg of venison, she said taking it made me a party to the crime. I said let's make the crime a party.

Dear Mom,
Well at least I have employment again. Roget, the Frenchman, I think you met him on your visit, is moving to Zuni to run a grocery store, and I am taking over his job at the theater as head projectionist. Pays $4.50 an hour and at a little over half time, it will come to about $450 a month. I hired him last year and now he is hiring me. I will work for

Bill Whaley, who leases the theater from Harvey.

I started last week, showed *Fiddler on the Roof* four times. Afterwards went to Antonio's bar and had a rum and coke and felt quite satisfied with myself. Next morning I was divorced by Judge Wright, with George Robinson as a witness. I felt close to George; I had served as his witness at his divorce the previous year. The Final Degree says that the grounds are "inconpatibility" – which is misspelled, so typical of Taos.

The snow continues to melt; the roads are full of mud and water. Gary Walker and I pulled George's truck out yesterday and the three of us stood yakking and throwing stones into the ruts. Some are filled with water so you don't know how deep they are until it's too late. I drove into one that was three feet deep and had to attach a handiman jack to a tree, run a chain from it to the car, and jack the car backward onto "dry" ground. And so on, day after day.

Journal
A spring thaw, the roads an incredible mess. It's no longer a question of how bad but how deep is the mud! Jim pulled a guy from Arkansas out; his long Olds was half under water and had a flat. Glenda and Jim both got the BMW stuck (twice in one day, up by the fence) and a neighbor had to jack the car out. Glenda got her truck stuck too so we're all parking out by the Hondo church.

Harvey was selling off most of his land in Taos County. If we wanted to stay in our house, we knew we had better buy it. I had vowed during my college days never to own property or have a mortgage, but that was when I thought the universe gave us truths to abide by rather than beings to love. I asked Harvey if he would consider selling us the house. I explained that we couldn't afford to pay very much at first, but that we would make steady payments for as long as it took.

"You don't have to buy it," he said. "I'll give it to you."

I couldn't believe it. Just like that, I owned a house.

But it took me only a few moments to realize that I didn't want him to give it to me. I wanted to buy it, to make it real. I explained that if he gave it to me it would just be a game.

He understood that, so he said, how about $10,000? I knew that was dirt cheap, but it seemed a lot to me, almost overwhelming.

I said yes.

"But it's for you," he said. "I don't want it ending up in the hands of one of your women."

One of my women? Like my mother, who had called me "a bolter," Harvey still saw me as a womanizer. Given my record, I could hardly blame him, but what a grotesque misunderstanding. I loved Phaedra and Alexander with all my heart, and they were the commitment of my life.

Three weeks later, his attorney in Santa Fe sent me papers to sign. The sale was for the house and 105 acres, from the center of the Rio Hondo all the way north to the Carson Forest. The title would be in my name only. Cost: $6,800 at 4% interest over twenty years, bringing the total to $10,007. That came to $41.22 a month, to be sent to Harvey's accountant on the first of each month.

$41.22 a month for twenty years – I took a huge breath. Then, betraying all of my anarchist principles, I signed the paper.

Buying the property gave me a whole new perspective. We decided to add two rooms to the house and a bathroom, although we still didn't have indoor plumbing. Alexander would move into one of them, and the baby into the little room. Writing now was put on the back burner. It was a choice I made consciously, grimly, to give Phaedra and the children a stable place to live, that they could count on.

We didn't have a blueprint for the new rooms, just a rough design. One of the rooms would have a skylight. I bought adobe bricks but mixed the adobe mortar myself. Straw, mud, water, thrown into a wooden boat – then heavy hoeing for twenty minutes. Brick by brick, the outer walls went up, leaving spaces for a door and windows. The floors and interior walls were made out of the cheapest pine I could buy. Phaedra helped me when she could but she was very large.

I didn't know how to build a house. When I got stuck, I walked down to Gary Walker's and asked him what to do next. He drew something on a scrap of paper, how to join two planks or how to frame a window, and I went back and did it. Two hours later, I returned. He drew something else and I did that.

Journal
Bonnie's baby and mine were born within two weeks of each other. Some things were meant to be.

The second baby is usually easier than the first, and this one was so much easier, I managed just fine. It's very different having a baby with the big, enthusiastic father standing beside you holding your hand.

But in this respect, I had both babies the same way. I went down to the Rio Grande, swam across and back. Once. When I got home, my "leaky membranes" let out a splash on the bedroom floor. Then the labor pains began. I lay on the couch and practiced Lamaze breathing for several hours. When I thought the baby was so close it might be born in back of the car, I said to Jim, "Let's go."

When we got to Holy Cross, they set me in a wheelchair. It was cold in there. I shivered in spasms and ground my teeth during the contractions. They turned off the air conditioning and prepped me for the birth.

They wheeled me into the delivery room four hours later and Jim came with me. He stood beside me the whole time and held my hand. The baby was so large they had to do an episiotomy but I barely felt it – the contractions were so intense. At last I pushed her out into the world, heard her first cry, held her on my stomach until the placenta emerged with one last painful push. I pushed so hard that I broke a blood vessel in my eye. But the ordeal was over. Sara's life just beginning.

When I had her to myself, I removed the blanket and counted her toes the way most mothers do. She had a splattering of red birthmarks on her face, but I knew those would fade. Her hair was reddish and her forehead fuzzy, but I knew *the fuzzy would disappear too. Her bone structure is good and she will be beautiful.*

Back home, huge sunflowers were blooming at the west side of the house. I held her up in front of them, my own blossom. The sunflower faces were bigger than hers. I felt joyous.

Dear Mom,
Okay, here it is, blow by blow. Phaedra, Alexander and I spent the afternoon swimming in the Rio Grande. Phaedra sat in the water like a hippo and got bright red. We came home around 4:30 and she discovered she had "leaky membranes." I think that is what she said. Then cramps, then labor. We dropped Alexander off at Gary and Cheryl's and arrived at Holy Cross at 9:30. The ward was empty and cold, until an orderly turned on the lights and turned off the air conditioning. The pains were coming every two and a half minutes. Dr. Knudson arrived at 10:30. He and I dressed in the doctor's room: white gowns, baggy pants, caps, masks, and odd slippers with long laces. No gloves for me however.

Phaedra was made ready in the delivery room. She worked hard and her face was distorted. She pushed so hard against the bed that it started to move across the room. She popped a vessel in her eye and it scared me, to see her eye turn so red.

Sara was born at 11:15 in the evening.

I left Phaedra at 1:30 and went to the Plaza Theater bar and had a sandwich and a drink. I announced Sara's arrival but felt foolish, for the bar was nearly empty. I was inordinately proud that she was so big and sturdy. I had another drink.

When I was driving home, a semi crept up on me until it was right behind me. Coming down the hill and around the curve into Hondo, I had a flat in the rear right tire. The semi was lumbering down on me and I was afraid to pull over. I rode on the flat for several hundred yards. All I could think of was how sad it was that Sara would never know her father. When I finally pulled over, the semi roared past. It took me an hour to change the tire because it was dark and I was on a slope and somewhat drunk. I got home around four.

Two days later. Sorry, I didn't mail this. It's been crazy. I took five nights off from work to help Phaedra. Sara doesn't cry; she squeaks. We have started calling her "squeaky door." So she is with us. She looks shrewd. She looks up at me when I am holding her as if to say, Just who *are* you? I like it when she snuggles against my neck.

I look at her birth certificate with wonder. "Sara Kay Levy born to Phaedra Greenwood and James Levy at 11:15 p.m. on Friday, July 5, 1974. On the back, "8 pounds, 12 ½ ounces, length: 23 inches." Even more wondrous are the ink prints, baby's footprints and mom's thumbprints.

Journal
President Nixon resigned August 9. We whooped it up.

Jim's mother Kay came to visit us and stayed in a motel in town. We went by to visit. Zander seemed dismayed at not being the center of attention. I hung out with him a little on the swings, but my breasts were so swollen I was in pain.

Kay invited me to go with her to Picuris Pueblo to see an Indian dance. She stood back from the circle, looking on as if from a great distance. She startled me when she said, "I can't imagine ever growing really old."

We also took Kay down to the Rio Grande, to our favorite sandbar. It was a rough walk on the path along the bank on the east side. Jim asked me to catch up to her and take her arm, which I did. But she pulled away, annoyed, not wanting to think of herself as an old lady who needed help. She seemed to enjoy watching Zander play in the water, and Sara, all of thirty-two days old, laughing. She also seemed to enjoy the picnic we brought in an old-fashioned basket.

Journal
I call her Sweet and Sour Sara. The first three months she was like someone's dour aunt. She looked at us as if to say "Humph!" But after a while she smiled a little smile and then a bigger smile that lit up her eyes and her whole face.

She laughs aloud with a little squeal at the end. I play silly games with her like "Lean to the left, lean to the right; stand up, sit down, fight fight fight!" She always smiles at that one.

Nothing is so sweet as Sara in the morning, all rosy and warm with sleep, her hands walking up and down my breast like delicate spiders. Nursing her is bliss. I feel like a space station with the baby spaceship trying to dock and hook up to refuel. Or I feel like a tree, with branches and roots, as she sucks with strong rhythmic gulps at the milk ducts in my breasts. Now she is teething and occasionally gives me a hard bite with her gums.

She's very sturdy and doesn't complain of much, loves having her pants changed and gets fussy in wet diapers. She likes to watch me dance and listens to me sing. She'll sit patiently in her rocking chair for an hour and watch me wash dishes while I rock her with my foot.

She's alert and interested in everything, especially her big brother and the animals. She tries to pat Leif the cat and tonight Zoe the dog lay her head down beside the rocking chair and Sara stroked her ears. She likes to sit before the fire all wrapped up in her colored afghan like an old woman with her dreams and memories.

Phaedra cut my hair. I sat in the middle of the living room with a sheet over my shoulders and she clipped the wildest of my locks. A clump fell on the sheet and I was alarmed to see that it was white. I held it up to my eyes and it turned out to be light shining on it. She was quite good; she did Alexander's and Ewar's too and we looked spiffy for a week. It was in fact Phaedra whose hair was turning. She now had long silver hairs on her head. She watched them appear and I was unsettled, not by the silver hairs but by her watching them so intently. One night I noticed two lines down from her nostrils to her mouth. This led to an earnest discussion about the meaning of life.

To supplement my wages as a projectionist, I worked as a bouncer at the bar next to the theater. It brought me into contact with a lot of people I wouldn't have met otherwise: an ex-whore about forty with tangled hair and ravaged face; Billy Eddison, on crutches who said he was dying of a liver ailment, so we refused to serve him. Jimmy Santistevan, the manager of Old Martinez Hall, well-dressed, very drunk, demonstrated for me how to throw people out. He offered to take over the bar and clean it up. He wanted to fight – the drunks, me, anyone. And there was the alcoholic with a long sorrowful face who always wore the same jacket and hat. He came in every day and spent six or seven hours drinking. One time his daughters and sons-in-law joined him and they all got loud and combative and I had to remove them all.

Alfred Johnson sat for hours alone. He was an art framer married to a younger woman. He said they take turns babysitting while the other one drinks. Before he left, he gave me money to buy her drinks if she came in.

Chuck and William from New Buffalo danced with the recently divorced Challis Taylor, who danced hugely with anyone who asked her. Her ex came in on another night and said to me, "I never enjoyed sex with that woman in all that time."

"Oh come Walter," I said. "Seventeen years with a woman and you didn't enjoy sex with her? You're either a fool or you're lying to yourself."

I had my own method of getting rid of drunks. I sat down with them and started talking. I asked if they had always been a heavy drinker. When did they first start? Were their parents alcoholics too? I was friendly and concerned. After a while they got up and left.

Journal
I am more relaxed with Sara than I was with Zander and am enjoying her as an infant more, reminding myself in the colicky times that they grow out of babyhood so quickly. I squeeze

her fat little legs and kiss her stomach and tickle her and kiss her neck and make her laugh.

When she cries she cries in rhythmic hiccups that build up and up till she bursts into a loud wail that shakes the glass in the windows. (Someone said she sounds like his chainsaw). This is when she is hungry or wants to be held. She is highstrung and robust but seems good natured. She can't stand being in a room full of people talking. When I take her to a meeting I end up walking her in the hall. She smiles at herself in the mirror. Her first toy is a Raggedy Ann doll given to her by Julie and the kids. I propped it up in the corner of her cradle. When I looked again she had grabbed it by the leg and dragged in under the covers.

Building the roof of the new rooms was the hardest part. I did it in the fall but it was still hot. I bought vigas and trimmed them with an adz. Five or six friends came over to help. We lifted them up to the height of the roof with a back hoe, then rolled them across the walls and into place. Then Phaedra served everyone pizza and beer.

I wired the rooms for electricity but I didn't install the furnace or the heating ducts because I was afraid I would do it badly and blow us up. I hired a local plumber and to pay him, I went to First State Bank for a loan. They turned me down; I had never borrowed money before or financed anything and didn't even have a credit card. They said if Harvey co-signed they would lend me the money. So he co-signed and they lent me $500. I paid it off early. The next time I went in, I asked to borrow $1,000. Perhaps this was to install bathroom fixtures. They said no, I had never had a loan on my own, but if Harvey co-signed, then I could have the loan. I threw a fit. They backed down, loaned me the money. Adult joys.

I got into a frenzy trying to finish the rooms before we left for California at Christmas. I dismantled the cabinets in the hall where the door would go, dug a hole in the adobe wall with a pick axe. I was possessed, could not stop, until I broke through at eleven at night, ecstatic and exhausted. I was surprised but delighted to find that the level of the old floor and new one matched perfectly, not needing a step.

On our trip to California, as we were driving through the Mojave desert, a hundred miles out from the City of the Angels, we noticed a brown smudge on the horizon. "Oh my god! What's that?" I said. Jim gave me a look. "It's smog." "And we're driving right into it." A pause. "We are." "How can people live in that?" Jim blew out a breath. "I don't know. But they do. Millions of them. We're only staying there for five days." He grinned at me, "Once we're inside it, we won't even notice."

Which turned out to be true. But then, Norman and Jeanne's house was perched on a hillside above the Stone Canyon Reservoir, looking down on the smog. As we sat in the shade of the palm trees on the patio by the pool, enjoying an evening glass of wine, I felt compelled to say, "The smog has really gotten bad." Norman took a sip of his wine and gave me a complacent smile. "It's not smog, it's fog." He turned and looked down, "Of course, there is a little smog mixed in it."

Home Sweet Home

In Los Angeles we spent two days at my father's house, a ranch style house overlooking a reservoir and smoggy west Los Angeles. His wife Jeanne went to visit a daughter while we were there. The pool was heated to eighty-eight degrees and I swam at seven in the morning and again at eleven at night. Sitting on the patio, Dad spoke of people in his profession unable to have close relationships, preferring the one-way relationship of psychoanalyst-patient. He worried about the kids messing up the furniture. He couldn't remember Sara's name and called her Sara Lee. Couldn't remember that we had named her for Kay. That's when we started calling her "the Cake." I called her upside-down cake, angel food cake, short cake. Towards the end of the two days, he was anxious to have us gone and did not conceal it.

At Mom's we got caught up on family: Mary and William breaking up, Mary blissed out over Movement of Spiritual Inner Awareness, or MSIA, a cult in L.A. where she was living. Deirdre had adopted a new name, Pema Chödrön, and had shaved her head and was wearing the robes of a Buddhist nun. Mom joked that I drove her to it. "After marriage to you, what else could she do except become a nun."

Mom was entrenched in her habits. She drew a bath of scalding hot water, then let it cool down before getting in. She looked old, lumpish, and tired, and her thick lenses gave her an owlish look. She had a drink, said goodnight and slammed the door to her bedroom.

Zander went into the back room at my mother's house and discovered little bottles of liquor. He spread them out in a neat row and began to sample them. We didn't realize it until we went to a restaurant for dinner. Going to the restroom, he staggered. We realized he was drunk. Twenty-five years later, he said that being in the room, seeing a slur of lights, was his first memory. He was three years, three months old.

We drove home through snow all the last day, got home at five o'clock. The house clean, the animals fine. Phaedra and I were delirious to be home, puttered around the house. Zander and I put together his big Christmas wagon. Phaedra quickly moved Zander's posters and rugs into the new skylight room and he went to sleep there. Sara was installed in the little room next to ours.

The new rooms were handsome, and it was a new sensation, wandering through the house looking for Phaedra. Two phonographs going, one in the living room, the other in the back room, so it was like passing from one world into another.

We settled in, snow outside and the light of the fire on the walls. We were warm and saturated with love. Four fat hearts – it seemed unlikely that we were together, but inevitable.

Early January was very cold, always below zero at night, and dropping to thirty below a few times. The coyotes came down closer behind the house. Even at below zero, there were tiny insects in the snow. Then in the third week of January, a thaw, and the fourth week, almost spring like, a thunderstorm, lightning and rain. Buds sprang out on the cottonwoods. I spent one warm afternoon napping on top of a sleeping bag in the yard.

Jim and I talked half the night about the ferries we had been on over the years. We got excited and decided to write about them, in alternating stories.

We wrote longhand and I typed it up on my old typewriter, using a red ribbon for my part and a black one for his. The manuscript still exists, in two colors.

One night we stayed up till 4 a.m. rearranging the living room. I admired the muted sparkle of mica on the walls of our neighbor's house. Polly Schaafsma said they plastered their walls with a slip coat of clay called tierra blanca that came from a special pit in the hills south of town. Jim and I thought tierra blanca might look elegant on our living room walls, so we drove out there with buckets and helped ourselves, like everyone did. We plastered one wall in the living room but were not happy with the results. It had looked good at the Schaafsma's, but on our walls it turned gray as cement. We decided to paint the living room off-white instead.

Then we painted the concrete floor red, and also the floor of the casita. Jim took Alexander in Harvey's pickup to Pilar Hill and shoveled from a steep sandy bank a load of fine sand for the sand box. Zander often played in his sandbox by himself with a pail, a shovel and a dump truck. He didn't mind being alone.

One freezing night we walked in the moonlight and found three horses in the winter wheat. The next morning there were five. We drove up to the two communes to see if they belonged there. Reality was deserted, with derelict cars outside and furniture, clothes and shoes strewn around inside.

We went to Morningstar where we found about twenty people and had a cup of coffee. A bearded Che Guevara type in fatigues, a tall girl, a burned-out young man, several kids and dogs. They said the horses were from Reality. When we said no one was there, they said there were still a few men living there, probably hiding from us. The Morningstar house was clean and neat. When we got home, we thought our house looked a lot messier.

Stepping Up

Phaedra and I took Alexander to school at Los Niños preschool, which was held in a room at the back of the Presbyterian Church. Jackie, the teacher, was very creative, and Alexander enjoyed art projects and playing with the other children. Phaedra was the aide.

I left them at the school to run some errands, then picked them up, went to the dentist with Phaedra, walked in the park with Alexander and Sara Kay while we waited for her. Got home at 3:45. At four, Mom's friend Frances Holman called. She said that Mom had had a stroke. This was on March 10, 1975.

I called St Francis hospital in Santa Barbara. The nurse said she was in a coma, that there was only a slim chance of her regaining consciousness. I staggered against the wall, and sat down on the floor.

I called George; not there. I called Sally Howell and asked to borrow money. Threw clothes in a bag. George called. Before I said a word, he said, "When do you want to go?" By 4:45 he was here. We left, picked up a check for $75 from Sally and cashed it at La Cocina restaurant. He dropped me off at the Albuquerque airport.

I tried to rent a car for when I would arrive in L.A. but they said no, because I didn't have a credit card. I got angry, explained the situation, and they relented. Landed in L.A. at 11:45 p.m.. Harvey met me at the gate, had already rented a car. Phaedra had phoned him in San Francisco and he had flown down.

We drove to Santa Barbara. I strode through the lobby of the hospital, third floor, down the hall, rang the bell at intensive care unit, walked into her room alone. Screens were monitoring her heart and other things, and there was an oxygen tube down her throat. Grayish color, bruised arms hand and chest from the fall. Hands and feet very cold although her temperature was 103. Heart steady. Pressure high. Eyes open, locked to the left.

I went to tell Harvey. Cried in his arms. He drove to Mom's house to use the phone and try to locate Bunny and Mary.

It was now two in the morning. I sat with her, cried again, held her hand, kissed her and stroked her face and hair. I talked to her, told her how much I loved her, assured her that everything would be all right.

In the morning, called Phaedra. Phaedra tracked down Mary in Berkeley. Mary would catch the next plane down. I called Bunny in Lille, France. She said she would wait twenty-four hours to see how Mom was doing. She didn't trust my sense that Mom was dying so she called Dr. Klosasser.

At nine Dr. Klosasser and Dr. Rack examined her, then told me there was no hope. They asked me what measures I wanted to take or not take. I said to continue the intravenous but not anything else. I felt no doubt; I knew that my mother would not want to exist in a coma.

I waited with Mom. The nurses were very considerate,

brought me breakfast which I didn't eat and offered me coffee and juice, then helped Mom as much as possible. Harvey came at ten, stayed awhile, left again. Came back with Mary at four that afternoon. She took one look at Mom and said, "She's not there," and citing urgent business in L.A. left. Harvey returned to New Mexico. I went to Mom's house but couldn't eat. I showered and shaved and got dressed up, returned to the hospital around 8 p.m. I hadn't slept in thirty-eight hours and had eaten practically nothing. Around midnight I returned to Mom's house and slept in a chair in her room.

Wednesday. I went to the hospital early and stayed until four. Although she was still in a deep coma, her foot moved. One eye flickered occasionally. She arched her back and strained. But I knew that she didn't know I was there. Nevertheless I talked to her, explained how I felt, that there was nothing left unsaid or undone between us. We had not always been there for each other in the physical sense but we had never doubted the love. Kissing her face and hand, I told her that I loved her and always had.

She was sixty-six years old. I was thirty-four.

I wanted for her what she wanted for herself. I wanted her to die. In a larger sense, she had been ready to die for some years. Things had not worked out for her. Her marriage had become stale, possibly as early as the mid-1930s, certainly by the war. Moving to L.A. in 1945 and the long years there had been treading water for the sake of the children. It was a sobering thought, one that only now really came to consciousness in me, that Bunny and I and then Mary had lived in a loveless house all our young lives. That is not accurate: not loveless. Our mother loved us. The lack of love was between our parents.

I looked out the window at the world. It had rained and a puddle of water had formed on the roof below. The wind ruffled the water and the sunlight sparkled on the surface. I felt a moment of peace, of acceptance, which turned into something resembling joy.

Mom's cousin Ruth came at eleven in the morning, stayed till four. She and I went back to Mom's house and she left for L.A. I returned to the hospital around eight at night, sat and watched. I tried to read and fell asleep. A nurse came in around eleven and found me asleep half on the bed.

She touched me on the shoulder.

"She's gone," she said quietly.

I started up, ashamed that I had fallen asleep.

Doctors came and verified it.

I stayed with her, held her hand, talked to her.

Bunny and her husband Jacques arrived from France about fifteen minutes later. They had been driven by our father from the L.A. airport, but he had chosen to stay in the car.

I walked down the hall to meet Bunny, averting my eyes. She cried and went to the waiting room. Cried more. Nurse brought water.

We went in to Mom. "Poor Mom," Bunny said. She was straightened out now, under clean sheets.

We went outside into the night. Dad was in the car with Marc, Bunny's young son. He started the engine, I don't know why. Bunny hammered on the window,

"Open the door, damn it."
"Symbolic isn't it," I said.
Bunny laughed.

The night Kay died, I was lying in bed reading, with Leif the cat curled up beside me. The children were asleep in their rooms. Suddenly Leif woke up, rose to her feet and stared into the shadows of the open bedroom door. Her back arched and her fur stood up. She let out a hiss, leapt to the floor and disappeared under the bed. I was so startled I couldn't move. "Is someone there?" I said. No answer. But in my head I heard a voice, "Oh, there are those pillows I gave her."

Bunny, Jacques and I went back to Mom's, stayed up all night, Bunny and Jacques made speeches about Dad's treatment of us. We talked about Mom, her affair with Dad's training analyst during the war, Dad's seventeen-year affair with a woman named Jacqueline.

We agreed, that although Mom had been a smoker and drinker and had had high blood pressure, we had not had a premonition of her death. At the same time, we felt that she had willed it, or at least, had not resisted it.

On Saturday, Bunny, Jacques, Marc and I drove to the funeral home in Westwood in L.A. Mom had prepaid for everything. I stood by her for ten minutes. She lay on a cart with wheels. She was waxed, her hair done, mouth drawn down in an uncharacteristic way, hands folded under the sheet. Low piped music.

She was cremated from 10:30 to four and while we waited at the cemetery, we sought out Marilyn Monroe's plaque. Then we picked up a metal box within a cardboard box, wrapped in brown paper, for me to take back to New Mexico.

Jim,
Listen, I don't think it's a good idea to scatter your Mom's ashes down the hill. Everyone will be tracking her in all over the floor. I have an idea. Why don't we bury them at the base of one of the juniper trees and let her go back into something loving? And when Bunny and Mary come they can sit under the tree if they want. I think that's what I'd like for myself.

I carried the urn in a brightly colored tote bag on the plane. Back in Arroyo Hondo, Phaedra, Alexander, Sara Kay and I buried her ashes high on the hillside above the house, beneath two piñon trees and an outcrop of rock.

Journal
My mother's death has affected me in ways I have trouble grasping. She died March 12th. I spent ten days there, two weeks back home, then four weeks in Carpinteria with Phaedra and the kids settling the estate. All that time, I felt fairly positive but at the end of the stay there, I grew moody and angry. It barely registered with me when Saigon surrendered to the Viet Cong and the war came to an end.

Back home, I lost my initiative. Nothing made any sense. I saw her face, not her living face but the thin, haunted gray face of her dying.

I can barely write about her death. I am occupying

myself with practical things: the theater, Los Niños preschool, the estate, and now, plastering the outside of the new rooms. I have a powerful sense that life is meaningless. Despite the activity, I have no energy. I want to sleep all the time.

A week later: Only now am I getting my bearings, entering a phase of self-awareness. I have changed, am changing. I am not who I think I am (and never was?).
What effect will her death have on my writing? It is certain that it was connected to her. Was I trying to live her dream of being a writer? Will I let it go, or is it fully ingrained in me?

In the spring we decided to put up a swing for the children. We bought dozens of feet of hemp rope, some chain to weave into the top and make it secure. Jim sawed an old board and created a swing seat. Then we went down to our favorite spot by the river where a cottonwood branch arches over the bank. The trick was to get the rope over the branch about thirty feet up. We made a noose in the chain end. To the other end we tied some string and a stone to the string. Jim heaved the stone over the branch, hauled the rope over, pulled it down through the noose and then tightened it up on the branch.

The swing was a big hit, right from the start. Alone, the kids could twirl around on it in circles. When we sat them on it and pushed, they swung out over the river. It wasn't long before the neighborhood children discovered it, too.

Our big goal was indoor plumbing. We had inherited some money from my mother but didn't have enough to drill a proper well. Instead, we decided to do what Gary had done next door. We hired a local to dig a hole with his backhoe, fourteen feet deep down in the bank of the little river, and dropped an aluminum culvert into it. We covered the well with plywood and slowly the culvert filled up with about eight feet of clear water. Pipes were laid into a trench to the house. The water was not clean enough to drink, but available to wash with and water the plants.

We pored through catalogues and ordered a five-and-a-half foot apple-green bathtub that I was able to lie down in. There was a shower fixture so we could take real showers. We also ordered an apple-green sink and toilet to match, and installed a hot water heater in the bathroom closet. It was a happy sight to see Sara or Alexander wallowing in bubbles, playing with rubber ducks.

I was pulling on my jeans one summer morning, having trouble closing the zipper. My belly seemed to be bulging out more than usual. Then it dawned on me. I lay down on the bed, pressed my belly and felt the tell-tale lump, a little stow-away already tucked in place for the voyage. I sat straight up. Oh my god!

I scrambled to the kitchen and told Jim. He looked at me from the omelet and fried potatoes he was cooking at the stove. "What? You're kidding!"

"No," I said, close to a whisper. "I can feel it. I haven't had my period in a couple of months. But I thought that was

because I was nursing." Apparently the foam I was using had failed. I had also tried an IUD, but it had to be removed when it started migrating up into my uterus.

Jim set down the spatula and took me by the shoulders. "Don't panic. It might not be true. Let's get you to a doctor."

After he had examined me, I stumbled out of Knudson's office. It was raining. I sat in the driver's seat and bawled like a child, tears and snot running down my face. Trapped. There was no easy way out. I was already ten weeks along. Sara was just a little over a year old. I was still hauling her around on my hip, washing diapers. In six months I wouldn't be able to lift her up anymore. This new life would take me over. And Jim working so hard at the theater. When I ran into George at the market and told him, he said "You're doing it again." As if it was illegal.

Beyond the thought of another year of washing diapers, trying to take care of two babies at once, I was aware of the population boom. It was okay to replace yourself. We'd both done that.

"What do you want to do?" Dr. Knudson had asked me in a solemn tone as I sat on the edge of the table.

My immediate response was, "Get rid of it."

How could I say "it"? Something in me turned against this little stowaway.

"Think of it as weeding," Dr. Knudson said. "That's what you have to do when plants grow too close together." He paused and let that sink in. "If you're going to do it, you have to do it soon. Wait even another week and it will be too late."

"I have to talk to Jim," I said, woebegone.

He looked at his schedule. "The only day I have open for

a D&C is August 24th."

"No. That's my birthday."

He looked at me. "I'm sorry. But that's the only day available."

How could I possibly have an abortion on my birthday? What kind of gratitude was that for being born?

When I got home, I cried in Jim's arms and he did his best to comfort me, saying it was up to me. He also pointed out the expenses of a third child, food, clothes, doctors, and maybe college.

I knew he was right. But when I threw the I Ching to gain some perspective, I got a different story. The I Ching was always right and I never went against its advice. I got "Pushing Upward. A vertical ascent from obscurity and lowliness to power and influence. Fear not."

Nevertheless, on the day of my thirty-third birthday, I found myself being wheeled down a corridor into the operating room. Part of me wanted to scream. No! No!" Throw off the sheet and flee. But I quelled that impulse. And regretted it for the rest of my life.

Phaedra's abortion aroused my sense of responsibility. I realized that our kids would want to go to college someday. I took on extra work at the theater, became the janitor on Saturdays and Sundays, in between the matinee and evening show and after the last show, for seven dollars a cleaning. I pushed the carpet sweeper and mopped the bathrooms. Too impatient to put on gloves, I plucked the perfumed cakes out of the men's urinals and replaced them with fresh ones. The paper towel dispenser made me nuts. It required a tiny key to open and load with flat brown towels that had to be stacked just so or they didn't come out right. When I loaded them, they came out either in clumps or didn't come out at all.

I took pride in being a projectionist and janitor. I enjoyed smelling the oil from the projectors on my fingers. I was earning a living and supporting the dark-haired beauty and sweet-loving angels at home. Who was going to do these things if not me?

Harvey came to town for a week and a half. He and I practiced reading poetry in the casita, each nervous and giggly, then read together at the Plaza Theater Bar at two in the afternoon, to a crowd of twenty people. The reaction was subdued. Phaedra and John Nichols read the next night to about the same number.

One afternoon Harvey came by the house and eyed the Indian stuff he had left. He took a vase and a rug, not noticing that one was missing. One day when George and I were trying to get the tractor started, we opened the fuel line and the tractor burst into flames. I ran into the house, grabbed one of the Navajo rugs off the floor, and smothered the fire with it.

I tried to give Harvey back what he wanted but it was hard to do delicately. He mentioned again buying the property back, paying for the improvements. I wondered, did he see me?

The two of us went to La Cocina to dinner, then walked around the plaza, went up to the theater bar and ran into Kelly McMillan and her friend Donna, drank five bottles of champagne with Joe Becker, Michael McLaughlin, Bill Hardy, Bob Draper and Mary someone. We thought we were witty, saying what celebrities we each looked like: Ann was Faye Dunaway in Chinatown, Harvey was the reservoir; I was Jack Nicolson's nose. Then I said that Harvey was Susan Sontag on cortisone and I thought that was the funniest thing I had ever said in my life. He and Kelly danced and got off on it; Donna and I danced, she grinding her pelvis into me, kissing me. I drew back, saying I didn't want that. Besides her young son was crying in the corner.

    I held up the rocket firework her son had brought and Ann lit it. I let it burn. Everyone scrambled out of the way. I pulled the fuse from the rocket. Champagne bottles popped. Miguel Ortiz started to have a meltdown about his estranged wife and we hustled him outside. Indians were fighting with belts and chains. Teeth knocked out, blood everywhere. Big fat guys, with fat women watching.

Early in 1976, I began volunteering at the public library at the Harwood Foundation. My mother had been a volunteer there in the late 40s and early 50s and this was a way for me to be with her. I would go to the library around three, prepare new books for the shelves or do other simple tasks, then lock up around five-thirty. The staff had given me my own key and I roamed the stacks after everyone else had left. Then I would go to the projection booth, eat a sandwich, and show the evening movies.

    My job was getting tedious. I felt that I had been going from the cave of the projection booth to the cave of the lobby and back again my whole life. I was at the point when, in the past, I would have quit, but there was no question of quitting now; we were in debt and we had those monthly mortgage payments, as small as they were. I looked into teaching – I had a life-time credential from the state of California to teach in secondary schools – but New Mexico said I would have to go back to college and get a New Mexican certificate. I applied for a job as a social worker worker for the State of New Mexico but didn't get it because I am not on "the State register", a waiting list which I couldn't get on because I didn't have the necessary degree.

Dear Harvey,
My father is coming to visit in the last week in October. No doubt it will be quietly strained. In theory he likes the children but they get on his nerves. He doesn't approve of me and I too get on his nerves. After a day I become strident. Phaedra then becomes sweeter and the two of them go off to galleries to look at art. In other words a jolly time will be had by all. Care to join us? You can knead in some humor, beat with six broken jokes, fold in some gloom, blend and heat and flee claiming duties elsewhere, the best kind.

Alexander just showed up, with rain-smudged announcement about School Photography Day. He is in his room bawling because the bicycle light he salvaged from the Super Sugar Crisp box is not where he left it and Sara Kay is bawling in sympathy. I wonder what they would do if I started bawling. I am sitting here in my nightshirt spilling coffee down my front and singing the dirty dishes blues. Our latest joke, Phaedra's and mine, is – let's move to New York and get out of this rat race. But no: My Duty Lies Here, in the best Protestant sense, to be the Grown-Up.

I've been writing poetry but am thoroughly discouraged. My poems sound like translations from some Eastern European country – who was it who said translations of poetry leave out the poetry? I have to believe there is an audience, even an audience of one. I've been taking more time for myself and it feels good. Phaedra and I had a talk. We got off on the wrong track. I admitted that I have been feeling resentful taking Sara and cleaning house and etc. We found time (a wonderful euphemism) to go to bed together (another). And now I think we are back on track.

Next day. I am calmer. Have I told you, Mom's estate was larger than we had imagined. She left us – Bunny, Mary and me – her house in Carpinteria, which we sold for $90,000. We each get $3,800 now, then $183 a month for ten years.

Journal.
Big news and little news. Jimmy Carter has been elected president and NBC filmed George, Phaedra and me about the communes. The crew was three guys – director, sound and camera. The director asked us to describe life in the communes which is funny since I for one never lived in one, although Phaedra and George did. It played on a Saturday night and we went to George's for dinner and

watched it there. The irony is – and I said this loud and clear on camera but they cut that part – the hippie scene is over. Almost all the communes are gone. Only New Buffalo hangs on but it is a refuge now for the lost; there is no vision for a new way of life, just an avoidance of the American dream. I should talk. And Lama is still going, spiritual as ever although the founders have left – it's run by committee I think.

The whole counter-culture movement has died down and everyone is turning to something else, religion or back to school or real jobs, but it had a tremendous influence on northern New Mexico, which ceased being a backwater and was on the cutting edge of new social ideas. At least that's how hippies saw themselves. The ideas weren't viable in the end for they rested on idealistic notions of human nature that turned out to be naïve. But what a ride. The truth is, northern New Mexico influenced the hippies more than the other way around. The Indian and Hispanic people taught them about how to survive the winter, how to scavenge the hills for firewood, how to delay planting until the lilacs bloomed, how to avoid the census for either instinctual or good reasons; about hunting deer and elk, repairing old cars, eating peyote and raising a family. The empty land and vast sky taught them about solitude and humility and death. Or maybe I am projecting; it's me who has learned about these things from living here.

If I were asked to summarize the hippie invasion of Taos, I would say they were far from home and ignorant as dust-balls. The first wave, in the mid to late 60s, tended to be educated and idealistic, more into dope than alcohol.

They shared their dope because paying for it was just not cool. Housewives, gurus, poets, trust-babies, they were young Americans torn loose from their roots and looking for authenticity by living a lifestyle based on anarchist principles.

The next wave, in the early 70s, were less educated, bringing a mindless anti-intellectualism to the movement, and using as much alcohol as drugs. It was this steady stream of drop-outs, draft-dodgers, mushroom-eaters and boozers that so alarmed locals.

The final wave, which gave the coup de grâce to the movement, were mostly society's dregs who were more or less criminal and mentally ill.

I had a different take on the hippies. I made friends in the counter-culture. To this day I recognize the values and ideals we shared as true, even if we couldn't live up to them: caring for Mother Earth and for each other, living in voluntary simplicity and making healthy choices even unto the seventh generation. Some of our values were absorbed into the mainstream such as recycling, organic food and goods and the idea that "what goes around comes around". Other cultures, such as Taos Pueblo, also honored the sacredness of life, the need for clean air and water and the interconnectedness of all living creatures. Maybe the communal experiment didn't work, but we tried. When the women and children abandoned the communes and the men were just hanging around cleaning their guns and smoking dope, we knew "the Age of Aquarius" was over.

What did the counter-culture bring to the table that sur-

vived the movement itself? *As Arthur Koestler says in Insight and Outlook, if you go out into the desert and come back with a vision, your hope is that your vision will be incorporated into the mainstream, and society will make a paradigm leap forward.* That's exactly what happened. Not just because of the counter-culture, but also because it coincided with a timely exploration of space travel. When the Whole Earth Catalogue featured on its cover a newly released NASA image of the earth from space, it became one of the most widely circulated photographs in the world: a stunning blue and white planet floating serenely in space. The astronauts who took this photo looked back on planet earth and felt awed and protective of our fragile home. This iconic image evoked in humans around the globe a sense of shared destiny.

Jim's sister Marianna, Glenda and I – and most of the hippies we knew–not including Roget and Elaine, who were not hippies, nor Harvey who was an environmentalist and poet – but most of the hippies we knew were waiting for the apocalypse. Our version of it was a gumbo of the Biblical four horsemen and earthquakes in diverse places; Edgar Cayce with the eruption of Mt. Etna and California falling into the ocean and the "Day of Reconciliation" in the Hopi Prophesies when opposites were reconciled and "No white man's hand will be on the red man's rein ever again."

It was obvious–to us anyway – that our greedy, poisonous consumer society was not sustainable with a population that we saw triple in our lifetime, a wobbly economy, chemical spills, toxic waste dumps and unstable nuclear waste. We were hoping that the whole thing would come down gently in a world-wide economic collapse that would STOP the rape of Mother Earth sans an all-out nuclear war and subsequent nu-

clear winter.

In our naiveté we imagined a metaphorical village, a circle of grass huts where we lived together in harmony, sharing food, goods and tools, where the children ran back and forth between us and everything belonged to everyone. We never envisioned in our worst nightmares an apocalypse of world-wide climate change, the thawing of the polar ice caps, rising seas, ferocious storms, fire and drought and the sixth mass extinction. We believed the angels were on our side, that we could fight and win, that reason and love would prevail. When the collapse was over we would crawl out from under the rubble, pick up a shovel and start again.

Dear Bunny,
I am awake, not by choice. Sara Kay came padding into our room this morning dragging her "panket," thumb thrust in her mouth. She stood beside the bed regarding us silently, blond hairs stuck in the corners of her eyes. Phaedra let her into the bed of course. Not to be outdone, Zander stood at the foot of the bed with wide serious eyes. "Mom," he said, "there's a big spider in the bathtub." Phaedra and I surrendered and got up.

But I am not complaining. I love them madly and love the time we spend together. We play "rocket," which consists of Zander running towards me and between my legs. I catch him and hold him and he counts, "One, two three, fire!" which is my signal to launch him into the air, flip him over and land him, giggling, between my feet. Then it is Sara's turn. She waddles towards me. I catch her. She counts, "Two ... six . . . four, fire!" Then she too is up in the air, and lands safely between my feet.

    While I was cleaning the ditch, Sara toddled up and sat in an anthill. The ants swarmed her and she screamed. She has a swollen eye and face, rash on chest and back. Trouble comes in waves. No rain in a long time. Three cottonwoods died, two apricots, and one of the new trees.

Sara Kay

Jim and I have started writing down the startling things Sara says. "Monsters are not real. All monsters are not real. People are real. Cats are real. Birds are real. All birds are real. Furniture is real. Walls are real."

Me: "What about noses?"
"Noses are real. But King Kong is not real."
Pause.
"Mom, are snakes monsters?"

She opens the door and says, "Birds are coming." After she has let them in, she slams the door. "No, we don't want elephants."

After seeing "The Iron Claw" she goes around growling with her claws up. She is also a great giant killer. She says she has killed "many" but not "the cute giant that has no teeth."

In imitation of Alexander she counts on her fingers and can count up to nine even though it's all on the same hand.

Observing Daddy swimming in the Rio Grande, she says, "You take off your shirt, put on your pants and you swim!" Long pause. Wrinkling of the nose. "I wouldn't do that."

Sara asks me: "Is duck-duck an animal?"
"Yes."
"Are you an animal?"
Pause. "Yes."
"What kind of animal are you?"
"I'm a person."

She laughs as if that is the funniest thing she has ever heard.

"No, you're my mommy!"

Another day she toddles up to me and hugs my knees. "I love you."
"How do you know?"
"Because I feel it."
"Where do you feel it?"
She rubs her belly. "Inside."
"Where inside?"

"All over!"
I told Jim, *"That's the nicest thing anybody has ever said to me."*

I'm standing in the hall listening to Sara having hysterics because Phaedra asks her to take a large rock out of our bed. Sara hugs it and gets stubborn the way she does.

"Put it on the floor," Phaedra suggests.

"It will get dirty."

"Well, put it on the trunk."

"It will be in a mess."

"How about the window sill? Then it can watch the stars."

"Rocks got no eyes."

She is stroking the rock. Finally Phaedra says, "Do you love that rock?"

"Yes."

"Does that rock have a name?"

"Name is Judy Rock."

Dear Bunny,

It's a glorious summer and we've been going down to the Rio Grande by the John Dunn bridge and walking up the east bank of the river to "our spot." The river runs past, green and slow but with a powerful current. We are protected by a sandbar which has formed a pool of shallow water where the kids can play without being swept away. There is also a sense of safety because the high cliffs loom over us.

We often have the river to ourselves, or see an occasional fly fisherman or someone in a kayak. All 1900 miles of the Rio Grande and we secure for ourselves about fifty yards. Zander bobs around on his goose tube; Sara wades; Phaedra floats down the river. We play shark, with me floating up to the kids and nipping their ankles. We build sand castles. There's a juniper tree that provides shade but we spend most of the time in the water or on the sand, messing around without a care in the world.

The water is cold even in mid-summer because the snows are still melting in the mountains, so we can stand it only for a while, then lie in the sun. It's idyllic, and I can't imagine being happier. When great summer clouds rise above the Sangre de Cristo mountains and shut out the sun, we head for home. Sometimes we stop at Lucy's Take Out taco stand and have chicken tacos and cold Cokes and beer. It's just a trailer, with torn, dirty car seats in front to sit on, and tabs from beer cans strung together as decoration. Chickens root around in the dust, sometimes on top of the table. Celso is usually drunk and Lucy serene. She cooks, he serves. Our tacos come with green olives with pimentos. And something undefinably delicious. Maybe love. We stuff ourselves, head home and conk out.

Isn't there a passage somewhere that says we don't know when we're happy until later? But I know when I'm lying in the shallow water with the kids clinging to my back, that these are the happiest days of my life.

There is a dark side to the river however. Almost every year it takes a few people. This year it was a fourteen-year-old boy. He was playing in the water and it took him away. He had never learned to swim. Many Taoseños don't know how to swim. The public pool just opened a few years ago. Search and Rescue found the boy's body two miles downstream.

We both hated it when the children got sick. Sara had a croupy cough that grew worse over the day. Concerned, I called Mike Kaufman and asked him what to do. He said that if she could get through the night without coughing, she would probably be okay, but if she started to cough again in the morning her throat could close up and we should rush her to the ER. Jim and I set a vaporizer inside her crib and Sara and I got in. He stapled a large sheet of plastic over the crib to keep the moisture in. After he left, I sat up with my back braced against the crib bars. Sara crawled over to me, draped herself across my stomach and fell asleep. I sat there all night long without moving, afraid to wake her. Up to that point in my life, I had no idea I was capable of such endurance. Sara was such a snuggly child who enjoyed being held. I guess I didn't get enough snuggling myself when I was a girl, because I loved to hold her, carry her around. It made me feel complete. When Sara woke at dawn, the croupy cough was gone.

I had a sudden urge to go back to work, to at least earn my own groceries. With two children and a mortgage, we needed more money. I took on a part-time job, twenty hours a week doing medical typing for Taos Medical Group. Jim took care of Sara, but he found it too exhausting to babysit for her and then put in a whole evening at the theater. So we left Sara in nursery school with a lady who seemed to know what she was doing. As I walked out the door, Sara began to scream. I stood for several minutes with my back against the door, gritting my teeth. Why was I putting our daughter through the same trauma I experienced when my mother went off to work as a filing clerk at Kelloggs? Two days of this, Sara screaming inside, "No! No! Mommee! Mommeee!"

When I came back to pick her up that second day, she was resting on her mat. She didn't greet me, but lay staring into space, sucking her thumb. "She's been like that for a couple of hours," the lady said. I leaned down and picked her up, whispered into her hair, "Come on baby, we're going home."

We never went back. When I informed Michael Kaufman that I had to quit because of Sara, he suggested I borrow the office typewriter and transcribe the tapes at home. I was amazed and grateful.

I didn't have the car the day Michael came home with the typewriter, so I walked over to his house to pick it up in Alexander's red wagon. With Alexander pushing from behind, I hauled that expensive electric typewriter up the hill to our house. I installed the typewriter on my blue desk under the window in the back room. Every couple of days Michael brought home tapes of patient visits and handed them off to me. I typed medical transcripts for him and the other doctors for $2.50 an hour. I often parked Sara in her rocker beside my desk and rocked her with one foot while I typed.

Our income gradually rose. We upgraded our used cars; we started buying clothes instead of wearing what I made; we fretted that we were becoming bourgeois.

Norman was the only grandparent our children had. There was always tension between him and Jim, but he kept showing up. He and Jim usually had at least one fight. But with every visit it came sooner until at last they had the fight in the car on the way home from the airport, and after that, the rest of the visit went smoothly.

I confronted Norman once myself, told him straight out: "Jim doesn't feel loved by you."

"Oh, that's nonsense," he said, waving me away. "Of course he was loved."

I'm sure my criticism stymied him. He had no idea what I was talking about. Yes, he was sensual, loved the sun, his meals, his routine, his life, but he wasn't physical with us. Like my mother, his hugs were brief and formal. He wouldn't pick up a kid, caress her, or smooth her hair. He might end up with egg on his shirt. In spite of his sensuality, he seemed to live mostly in his head. He was true to the idea he had of himself: a Freudian psychoanalyst, he was a handsome, well-respected and successful man. And the outside world seemed to agree. None of which made me like him any less. I had no expectations.

In the early days Norman stayed with us in the spare room in back of the house. He wore a tweed overcoat and a bolo tie with a silver Navajo stone, and sometimes a tooled western belt with a huge turquoise and silver buckle. The one he said he was going to leave Jim when he died. He also wore too much cologne. Inside his vintage leather suitcase he stashed a silver flask. I'm not sure how often Norman took a nip or if he had it "just in case." I never saw him tipsy.

Like Jim, Norman said he didn't want to accumulate any more things. He was still wearing clothes he bought fifteen years ago. Also like Jim, he was not fussy about what he ate. He bought us a rib roast, which I didn't know how to cook. I just stuck it in the oven and it came out okay, served it with wild asparagus and mashed potatoes. For dessert I made a big *apple pie with walnuts and raisins, which we devoured with melting scoops of vanilla ice cream. Yum!*

"Aren't you worried you'll get fat?" I joked when Norman asked for a second helping of pie.

"Oh, I might gain a pound or two, but I'll take it off in the pool when I get home."

When we went to town he brought presents at Tio Vivo for the children and had them wrapped, with lollipops taped to the colorful boxes. Did he love his grandkids? Love us? All I know is, he kept showing up. And I felt grateful. Maybe that was love.

Whaley offered to contract my work out to me, making me self-employed rather than an employee. I would make more money. I would be projectionist, maintenance man, janitor, assistant manager, and game-arcade person, and I could hire others to do whatever portions of the work I didn't want to do myself. Phaedra and I had a long talk about our values and concluded again that time was more important to us than money. Bravo for us. I think Whaley was trying to find a way to keep me.

I was, in effect, freezing our income at an employee's level, and if inflation continued, we would have to stop expanding our "needs" and start cutting back on them. I was willing; Phaedra, in her heart, was willing too, but it was harder for her. She said she didn't want the children going to school in ill-fitting second-hand clothes the way she had.

It was true, as Phaedra said, that I had a horror of success. I had contrived to live on the margin of the economy for so long that I was reluctant to move into it. Yet we were becoming more bourgeois each year.

There was a whole other factor. With both kids at school, I didn't see them during the day and I worked at night. I determined that I would have to leave the theater and get a day job.

Jim made up games and stories, like the raindrop stories that usually began with a raindrop who was afraid to leap off a cloud and splash down to earth, and an M and M that was worried about melting. We read to the children constantly, Little Bear stories, the Golden Books, The Little Engine that Could *and fairy tales. "A fairy went a-marketing/ she bought a silver bird . . ." Mother Goose rhymes.* The Velveteen Rabbit, Katie and the Big Snow. Smashing Cars. *Later we moved on to* Paddle to the Sea *and then Tintin and his bizarre adventures.*

We built kites and flew them off the roof. When Lego came in, we bought Alexander many sets. I loved to sit on the rug and play Lego with him, building things that had never been discovered. Nobody knew what they were.

Jim says when he grows up he wants to be a mushroom. Or, like Faulkner, a vulture. Alexander says, "You know what my best wish is? I wish I could talk to the animals and understand what they're saying. I wish I could be part of nature. Maybe if I try to be nicer to my sister, God will let me."

After an evening of playing really bad chess, dealing with a broken boiler, trying to repair a faulty projector, I lay in our cherished bathtub overwhelmed by existential clichés:

the futility of life, the horror of old age and the inevitability of death. I would be thirty-seven in October – still youngish but definitely halfway. I felt that I had accomplished nothing in life. I'd written four mediocre novels, a handful of essays and stories, a pile of poems that had inspired no one. I wondered if my inconsequential life was one of choice or just a result of my being an incompetent loser. I thought I had deliberately chosen to live this way, on the fringe of society, out of a disdain for the American dream, but now it occurred to me that maybe I just wasn't bright enough to hold a real job or have a career.

Alone in the house one day, in the midst of laundry and cleaning, listening idly to the phonograph, the words that caught my attention were: "I don't know where we went wrong/ but the feeling's gone and I just can't get it back."

It struck me to the heart. Even more painful was the burning ache between my thighs. I walked barefoot through the back room, plunked myself down on the step and wept in frustration. How long had it been since Jim and I had made love? Weeks? Months? We were both exhausted all the time, straining to keep up. To be there for the children. Was he bored with me? Maybe I wasn't attractive anymore. Why didn't he come up behind me, touch my hair, kiss my neck? Take my hand. Hug me? Why couldn't I overcome my shyness and initiate it? Why did we never spend time together, just the two of us? Whatever became of "just the two of us"?

I began to wonder if he had another woman. Nah . . . he didn't have time for another woman. I loved the man and our children and our life. I wanted the gardening, the dishes, the games, the PTO, the work. Baking rafts of cookies, making costumes for the kids. All of it. But I couldn't understand what had gone wrong. Why this distance between us?

Nobody told me that marriages run through cycles, sometimes up, sometimes down. That's why you have loyalty and commitment. I didn't understand that you have to give up your idea of self, give up your ego and grow.

Nobody told me there would be days of feeling empty and sorry for myself. My writing wasn't going anywhere. I needed nurturing. Friendship. Adult conversations about things that mattered.

I joined a women's group with Stephanie Sonora. Eight women met in an art gallery in town, sat on pillows on the wooden floor and talked about our lives. We committed to keeping journals, to meeting once a month to share our thoughts and dilemmas. Stephanie's question for all of us was: "What keeps us from getting down to our art?"

She was about ten years older than the rest of us, a Jewish princess, and well-read. She could talk about anything: culture, racism, art, politics, history. I came away from these meetings feeling excited. It was empowering to discuss women's issues, women's rights. To feel myself part of something larger than my nuclear family.

Of course none of this would have had much meaning if I had no family core to love and protect.

Tally Richards, who owned the gallery where we met, was also in the group. And Soge Track from Taos Pueblo. Anita Rodriguez came to our first meeting. She had once been known as the town beauty, with her heart-shaped face, glossy brown hair and graceful hands. She was trying to make a living as an enjaradora, plastering and building fireplaces. She said she was "in a rage" for years, trying to work with macho men. "Women think they're neurotic," she said. I laughed. "We are." "No, we're not. It's society that makes us crazy." She bit her bottom lip. "You may think you can do whatever you want. You may even think (turning to me) that you can be a liberated woman. But you can't. Society won't let you."

She went on about how she couldn't get jobs even though her work was just as good, if not better than a man's "because they see I have tits."

She mentioned her previous husband. "I can't stand marriage. You want to go off into your room to write a poem, but he's out there in the kitchen kicking things and swearing, 'Can't even get a god damn sandwich around here!' Men!" she says. "I guess I hate 'em." A low chuckle. "I like them in bed, though."

Dear Harvey,
In San Francisco with Phaedra and the kids. We've seen a lot of Deirdre (who is now Pema). Evelyn and Ewar and I went to the Broadway House to see two comics, Terry McGovern and Martin Mull. Pema and I took a walk and talked about her new life. She is very calm, aloof, in that Buddhist way, both worldly and above the world. With her hair chopped close to her head, she looks much older, shorter and plainer. She explained that she was finished studying with Lama Chime and was studying with Chögyam Trungpa in Boulder. She's already taken the bodhisattva vow to seek enlightenment and help others do the same; now she is thinking about taking the full ordination as a nun. She explained all this to me in that serious

little-girl-acting-like-an-adult voice that she gets when she is, well . . . acting. But she isn't. She's serious about this and was meant for it all along. Says me, who is glad to be out of it.

Little flashes of anger appear – they are scary. I see how furious she still is. She told me that for a year she fantasied burning the Hondo house down, hurting Alexander, killing me. After saying that, she laughed as if to say, how silly of me. Sometimes I think that her entire Buddhist career is simply to show me that she can do without me. I know that is my egoism talking – you'd have to be here, at the moment when she turns to me with a sneer and refers to "one of your women," as if I had had two dozen. At the same time she idealizes Phaedra and says she is so courageous and clear and free.

The Deirdre I loved wanted out of her privileged upper-class situation – wanted life, more life, and she got it with me. But life included conflict, pain, loss. She thought life was a solution but it wasn't. It turns out she wanted a solution to life, not life itself.

I asked her to explain Buddhism to me but she didn't fall into that trap, not even a little bit. She probably knows my feelings about it from the days I stood in the middle of the living room in Mexico and ranted against Buddhism and other things I didn't understand. Not that my opinion has changed that much. Buddhism's dismissal of the senses and renunciation of all one is attached to is foreign to me. To the extent that spirituality conflicts with life, I reject it. As for treating all people the same – Pema says this is one of her vows. I wonder if this includes me.

And here is news: I want to be married. We're talking about it. It's the same impulse I had with Deirdre, to get married, feel secure, have that settled. Also, Social Services says I can't adopt Zander unless we are married. I want us to be a family forever, not in some hazy counter-culture way but in some permanent way. I think I feel Phaedra is slipping away. She goes out a lot, to a writer's group and a women's group and to political events, and it is as if she just wants to get away.

So, we've decided to get married. I resisted for so long because things were going well and why rock the boat? But I suppose this is the next logical step. And the children will be more secure. Not that they aren't. Mother will be jubilant. Dad not so much. He won't have any excuse to criticize me and cut me off from Mother. Do I sound bitter? A little. We've decided on a June wedding. It's too bad Kay isn't still alive. I wonder if she'd be pleased? She liked Deirdre and remained loyal to her. I must have seemed like a renegade Jim picked up in some commune. But guess what? It turns out this Phaedra person really loves her son, wants to make babies with him. And she's a writer.

Journal
I am volunteering six to eight hours a week at the Harwood library and have given myself an interesting assignment, to make a list of books that the library should have.

Zander is five and three quarters, growing harder, less a child, more independent. Sara two and three quarters, more communicative, affectionate, still fiery. We are very much a family. Phaedra and I share the chores; she does most of the cooking and I do most of the dishes. I stand at the sink after dinner and shout along with Linda Ronstadt like a drunk. It's my favorite time of day, being with the family while fantasizing about Linda – with her dark hair, peasant blouse and exotic upbringing she is a pop version of Phaedra. I feel good about our plan to get married. It's a good step. My impulse is to keep it a secret but then think that would be silly.

Dear Harvey,
I've been meaning to write for weeks but I've been so busy. And I like being busy. I know that is heresy. But we change.
 The big news is, Phaedra and I got married on June 14th. I slept late and when I got up, the day was already hot and Phaedra had already hemmed her wedding dress and was ironing my shirt.
 "It's not every bride who gets to iron the groom's shirt before the wedding," she said.
 "Thank you."
 "And thank you for making the bed this morning."
 "I haven't made it in a couple of weeks," I said.
 "I know."
 "Well one reason is you're usually in it when I get up."
 We put off getting dressed, afraid we would get our clothes dirty. As it was, we left at the last moment. We threw little Sara into the car – she was perverse as usual and announced that she didn't want to go. Then, halfway out the driveway, she began wailing for her doll Cindy, so

Phaedra dashed back and got the doll and her doll clothes. None of us wanted Cindy to miss the wedding.

It was a perfect day. Hot and sunny. We stopped by the Lilac Shop for flowers, carnations. While Jim was paying for them, I slipped out. From the car I had glimpsed some wildflowers along the ditch. Trying not to get runs in my stockings, I picked yellow roses, lavender sweet peas and some yarrow to mix with the carnations. The bouquet was gorgeous. The whole car smelled of roses.

Jim and I were both very nervous. This felt like a huge life-changing decision. We picked up John Nichols and Stephanie Sonora at his house and drove over together. I had invited Stephanie to be my "best woman" and John said, "I'd like to come too." The more, the merrier. John was looking relaxed and boyish in a clean white shirt open at the collar and dark slacks, his wild locks dancing in the wind. Stephanie was gorgeous in a black and white designer gown she had worn to some prestigious party in Denver. I was wearing a shimmering dress of watered silk that I had made myself.

We went to the small adobe house of Emma Vigil, the county probate judge. When we had asked her to marry us, she suggested we do it at her place – it would be nicer. Our three witnesses were already there: our friends George Robinson, John Nichols, the author of *The Milagro Beanfield War*; and his partner Stephanie Sonora.

We had a choice between the short ceremony (fifteen dollars) or the long (twenty). We chose the long.

We all went into the yard. I was very nervous and I

could tell that Phaedra was too, but there was no going back now. I looked at Alexander, six years old, handsome in his white shirt and long pants, and Sara, in a dress for once instead of the overalls she usually wore.

Emma Vigil put on purple robes. Another women and what appeared to be two retarded boys stood off to the side, watching. On the table was a huge embossed Spanish translation of the Bible but she conducted the ceremony in English. She pronounced troth truth and mingle mangle, but we understood well enough. There was the part about giving and receiving without reservation. Phaedra told me later that was her favorite part. I liked the part about sacrifice, how in perfect love one will sacrifice joyfully.

In the middle of the ceremony, a flock of sheep wandered into the yard. I thought they were going to walk right through us but they stopped and stared. Sara was sitting in the dirt and lifted her dress up. We discovered that in our hurry to get out of the house, we hadn't put any underwear on her.

Thus we were married. I kissed Phaedra; she was so beautiful in her dress. Then kisses and hugs all around. I held out my arms to George, who stiffened, but we hugged. I could smell his shaving lotion.

We went inside to sign the papers. When John signed, he said: "When I get the Nobel Prize, you can sell this."

"Right," Phaedra said, "this was all just a ruse to get your signature."

"When we get the Nobel Prize," he corrected, glancing at both of us.

Mrs. Vigil lit candles and placed them on the table, a nice touch. She had baked a cake and served sangria. We were all pleasantly surprised and we ate and toasted. Then we went to John's for champagne and the rest is a blur.

We drove back to John's house and drank champagne. John kept refilling my glass and I got so swacked I was slurring my words. Speaking about our vows, John muttered, "Sacrifice. Huh! They're not going to put all those locusts on me and tell me it's joy." We fell into an earnest discussion of male-female conflicts, who takes care of the children, who works where and when. John said, "It seems much harder for women to get their act together because of their confusion about their roles." He said that when he and his first wife Ruby were together he took care of the kids while she was going to school, while she was working as a waitress, while she was going to Cuba to pick sugar cane. He said, "It's too much to expect me to take care of the kids and earn the money too."

Stephanie sipped from the rim of her glass and looked at me with steady green-gray eyes. Her hair was almost all gray, but her face had the natural beauty of an old tree. She said, "I know hundreds of women painters who, once they got the man or had the children, that was the end of their careers. The only women who made it were the ones who wouldn't have children or who gave them away — to their ex-husbands usually. These women are working in cramped quarters while the man has the enormous room."

The subject changed to sex and touching. Stephanie said, "Italians and Mexicans are much more physical and able to listen."

John objected, of course. Jim said, "The touching is why I

like contact sports."

John took another gulp of champagne. "Contact sports are really mean and sadistic." (When he was in high school, he lost some teeth playing hockey.)

I announced in a drunken revelation that I felt I could love both men and women, even feel a sexual attraction for other men, but not fall into bed with them.

In a pout, John said, "No one ever comes on to me. I don't know why."

Stephanie sat back and surveyed him. "It's because you have a wall around yourself, because you're a writer."

We fell to discussing a woman we all knew who embraces everyone. John and Jim agreed they were confused about her intentions and didn't like being "handled." Stephanie said, "I love to embrace. I love everyone."

I said in a silly formal way, "I like to reserve my embraces for people I'm actually fond of. Loving everyone is loving no one."

Stephanie frowned. "Hmm. Maybe I should start shutting down some."

Dear Harvey,
You ask a good, the logical question. Why did we get married after five years and two kids? On one level, it is to "regularize" the situation. I tried to adopt Alexander last year and social services said no. Or rather, they said yes, I could adopt him but that Phaedra would have to give up her rights to him. I said, "That's crazy, I live with his mother; we have a common law marriage." But they wouldn't budge and said that if we were legally married I

could adopt him. So now we are and I am going to.

Journal

Back to reality. It was nice to come home to my own cozy bed and be with a man familiar to me. It's enough of a jolt getting married without going through all those physical changes, too.

Jim bounced out of bed this morning and went off to work early. I spent the day sewing what I was going to wear to Denver on our "honeymoon" next week. I took the kids in to see the movie ballet "Romeo and Juliet" with Fonteyn and Nureyev. Beautiful! Jim was happy to see us all, but was very busy in the projection booth. When one of the previews snapped and unwound in shiny coils on the floor, the kids and I stayed out of his way.

After things calmed down, Jim whispered in my ear, "Do you feel any different?"

I smiled. "It hasn't sunk in yet. You?"

He gave me a sheepish grin and hugged me. "Yes. I feel more secure. It also reaffirms my determination to stick it out."

That's good to know! It feels good to have our affection renewed. I don't have to cringe when I cash a check or when we sign a hotel register. Or eye every cop in the rearview mirror. We're as legit as anyone.

Jim has been wondering about my journal, how can I reconcile the private aspect of it with the idea of reading it aloud to the group or maybe even publishing it, as Stephanie suggests. I said I would never publish it without his approval. But the value of sharing personal experience transcends the issue of privacy. It's important for women to communicate, not only with each other but with the world. The effort could be something really significant. I want to contribute to that.

Typed medical tapes and got ready for our trip. Jim says, "I've got to be careful with you keeping those journals, knowing you're going to be reading it to every female in town." Not that I do. Poor Jim. He's going to get tired of trying to live up to his image of himself. He certainly is helpful these days. He made the beds this morning. I said I'd be sure to write that in my journal. The feminists would be happy.

After dinner Jim went out to play chess. I whipped out some material and tried to figure out how to cut two yards of shirt out of a yard and three quarters. This is a shirt I intended to give Jim for a wedding present to wear to Denver. It took about an hour, but I did it while I also bathed and fed the kids.

After nearly four years of non-communication, on their 40th anniversary, I sent Mother a birthday present and a Mother's Day card announcing that Jim and I had gotten married. My brother said about Dad, "You may even have him speaking to you again."

Jim's father called to congratulate us in the saddest voice I ever heard because we didn't invite him to the wedding. I couldn't respond to such self-pity. It seemed childish. Jim wasn't home, so I just went on in as pleasant a tone as I could, thanked him for calling, blithe and cordial.

Journal

I worked till noon, fed the kids and then drove them in to story hour at the Harwood with Dr. Rob Hawley, a cardiologist. The children fought in the back seat till I had to pull the car over and threaten to tan their hides. I use my voice as a weapon, scream instead of hit, calculating my pitch, sounding to myself nasty and mean as any bitch in the alley. I hate it, but I don't know what else to do. If I spanked them they would scream in the car all the way to town. I kept thinking, Why can't this be a pleasant afternoon that I devote to my children? Because they're tired and I'm in a hurry. When am I going to slow down?

I have to remember something Jim said. "We don't have to be perfect parents. All we have to do is love them."

Alexander did enjoy the stories and so did I. The "old storyteller," as he called himself, wore a straw hat and sat with us on the floor. Sara was restless and we almost left early. Zander asked to go again. He is just the right age for storytelling.

Jim was looking cool and collected behind the desk as a volunteer at the library. He checked out my book for me and tried to change my card from Greenwood to Levy. I wouldn't let him. He doesn't understand. Levy is for the kids and the legal stuff. Greenwood is my nom de plume, my soul name. The identity I retain by choice.

Journal
We heard about the forest fire in Bandelier National Monument out towards Los Alamos. I went out and sniffed the air. I could smell smoke. The mountains to the west are already obscured and now the sun. We can barely see our own mountains. Yesterday while I was typing there was a sudden violent gust of wind that blew the windows open and the curtain out the window and down the hill. The power went off for a second. Jim says that it probably came from the fire exploding. It is very bad. I keep thinking of the deer running for their lives and all the lesser creatures being cremated alive, the forest all blackened.

Felt rather ill on the way to Stephanie's party last evening. I had taken a nap and slept for hours and hours. I was really tired. I wonder why? My night life is catching up with me. The kids are wiped out, too. Stephanie said she doesn't believe in the commercialization of art, but she is in a gallery. She has no job, no money, and a son to support. I said I wanted my stories to sell, but realized that I was afraid to be ruined by success, swept away by ego. Jim would like to be recognized "post humorously." He swears he would rather be himself than Picasso who died without a will and caused one suicide and untold agony over the distribution of his estate.

Keeping a journal on a daily basis is beginning to feel like just one more time-consuming obligation. On the other hand, it is the only writing I'm doing these days. I also feel that on a spiritual level it keeps me aware of all the internals of my closest relationships and the importance of working on these.

Journal
I am a junkie who succumbs to his daily hit of doubt and angst, a junkie who can't break the addiction of writing, quits, then starts up again and thinks he can control his habit. The kids are not used to me nodding off on them.

If I could write as I play basketball, with joy and confidence, then I would be on to something. With basketball, I enjoy pushing the game to its limit, crowding the opponent into mistakes, dominating the other team. I know my strengths and weaknesses and maximize one while minimizing the other. Now that is how I should write.

None of the images fit me: insouciant amateur, old pro, junkie, athlete. When I said I was giving up writing, everyone shrugged, didn't even bother to say that I often say that.

I imagine myself an alchemist who works in secret, a Jacob Boehme, the shoemaker who was a visionary, and who then produces a blazing book. The secrecy, appearing less than I am, is important. This scenario works well in the early stages. I cackle and stir and think Wait till Harvey and Phaedra read this, wait till the world sees this, and I am revealed as the Poet (at least) or, my favorite, the Mystic Hermit. Where the strategy fails is at the other end, after I have worked up enough courage to send something out and the world's response is . . .

And what does Linda Ronstadt know about all this? "You're no good, you're no good, baby, you're no good."

Dear Jim,
I really like it when you agonize over writing. I suppose this could be some new form of literature: The Agony and the Angst by Jim Levy. Welcome to the throngs of the rejected. I'm now getting back stories that were initially accepted, and poems no one ever read. I hate it when they fold it in three and stuff it in a long envelope because I have to type it all over. Will I give up? Can I give up? Stay tuned.
    Love you, fellow writer.
    Phaedra
PS Wanna make gingerbread houses in the garden?

Journal
I'm taking my cue from M. Esther Harding's The Way of All Women. She says, "There is, moreover, a great tendency to let things slide and not to make an issue of slight misunderstand-

ings."

This reminds me of a conversation Jim and I had the other day. We were talking about beautiful women. He said he thought I was beautiful, but it was often hard for him to perceive it because I was so much a part of him. If he was in a bad mood, irritated or tired, he wasn't thinking of my beauty the way he would a strange woman on the street. That's true for me, too. Most often I see his beauty in the evening when he's lying in bed, relaxed, reading.

I was struck by the part where Harding wrote that when a woman finds that she can no longer look him frankly in the eyes, her true feelings have begun to stir. Jim said of a couple we knew, the girl bragged, "At least now we fight." Jim shook his head. "As if that was a good thing. I don't think it is. It's very upsetting to the children."

Yes, violent, destructive quarrels are upsetting, but just as destructive is a relationship where the hostility is silent, where two people cut each other off.

Jim and I never fought for what? – the first four years? Not that there wasn't an unspoken undercurrent of resentment from time to time, but it never emerged. Our first verbal disagreement came at his mother's yard sale shortly after she died. Auctioning off the furniture, etc. And all the emotional pressure and physical exhaustion. I had collected a modest list of things we needed for the house, pot holders, a door mat, cups and saucers, flower pots, her sewing machine. We had hired a guy to drive a truck to Taos with a couple of desks Jim wanted. There was plenty of room. But when I brought up what I thought would be useful he said, "We don't have room for all that stuff." I blew in one angry sentence. Then ran out into the driveway for ten minutes, trying to calm down because I didn't want to say anything destructive. I've often thought that when all the doubts and negative feelings hit you, it's better to let it blow over than risk making it actual by voicing it. But basically, repression is not a solution because it comes up again later.

When we talked about it that evening, Jim said he felt threatened by all that stuff, by owning things. I conceded and left behind the sewing machine, potting soil, dishes and other things, but we did take the desks.

Harding says, "The routine of their lives leaves little opportunity for attending with sufficient concentration to the emotional side of their relationship. The intensity of love or the urgency of disagreement requires time if it is to be assimilated. Many married people find it easier to repress both under the mask which they habitually wear before the family."

All this is leading up to the idea of making my journal open to Jim to read if he wants to. That may take some courage, but I feel that I have more to lose by repressing my feelings than by revealing them.

Before I get into all the negative stuff, I do want to say that I feel this marriage is appropriate, that we are in some deep way balancing each other and good for each other. I like and appreciate Jim, his communicative side especially. I feel that he is basically mature and steadfast and honest and there is everything to be gained from being as open as possible with each other.

Journal
One night Phaedra and I blew a fuse. I became furious at the course of events but when I tried to say what those events were, all that came out was that I had to do the

dishes too often. Even I know it must be something deeper. It certainly has to do with my mother's death, and with writing. Or not writing. During one of our night-talks, she said that if I give up writing my life has no meaning. I don't like to think that this is true, but it is probably true. And it's true for her too.

Phaedra is right. I must begin to write again. She said I used to be – what was her word? – elated. She didn't have to say what I have become.

Journal
Yesterday I went into town to do the shopping. It was raining and when I got home around two, the driveway was running with water. Trying to back the car in, I got stuck in the mud. I wondered why Jim didn't hear me and come out. I went in and found him in bed reading a story to Alexander. He didn't get up. I brought in all the groceries by myself and put them away.

When I told him I got the car stuck, he patted my arm, "Well, dear, I think it would be a good lesson for you to get it out yourself." I should have laughed and jumped in with them and left it. But no, I got that "unloved" feeling thinking, Well now that he has me, he thinks he can treat me any way he wants and I'll stick around. Maybe his true feelings will emerge and he will be callous and unloving. Then I began to feel he didn't like me anymore. All this mixed with self-pity.

Later when we were in the kitchen I burst out, "You don't like me anymore!" He pinched my arm and tried to make me laugh with a bad joke. I pulled out of it before our guests arrived. When they left, he hugged me and thanked me for making a good meal and I felt better. I really don't know what has been going on inside of him, but I realize that often my guesses are off. I think right now it has something to do with having lost his mother, because he keeps bringing her into the conversation. He says she is the one person he has total love for without ambivalence. That except for Alexander and Sara, the rest of us he loves with ambivalent emotions. That means me. Is it true of everyone? I'll have to think about it.

After seeing the Woody Guthrie movie, I brought up the subject of gambling to Jim. "What for?" he asked. To make a lot of money? Then what? So I can agonize over writing all day? I don't want to do that. What I'm into now is the development of my soul. Self-discipline, life discipline."

That's okay for him, and I admire him for saying it, but what about me? It's been scratch and save and sew and patch, make and make do all my life. Maybe I'm ready for something new. But seeing how our fortunes are linked, it's going to be tricky leaving Jim poor while getting rich writing profound truth, balancing my ego and maintaining self-discipline.

Journal
I am haunted by people in my past: Deirdre, Evelyn and Edward, my mother . . . thinking of Deirdre and how I longed for her when she was married to David, only to flee her eight years later. I try to stay in touch with her and the two kids, but their lives are carrying them away. Part of me feels abandoned by my abandoned wife and children, which is stupid, I know. I am absent from their lives, rooted in Phaedra and our two children. And when I am honest with myself, I see the beginning of the end here too,

Phaedra distant and committed to her women's group and writing group, me longing to get out of Arroyo Hondo and see the world.

So, since the death of his mother, the man who gave up his wife and two stepchildren and is twice empty, has gone down into the dark of his pain and does not know why or where he is. It feels it's the end of the line knowing it's a point on the line and wishing it were over and done with and secretly believing he will be given another chance.

Journal
Jim took the kids down to the Rio Grande to swim. I wanted to go too, but I'd made my choice. I wanted more to go to the writer's group. I find it very stimulating to get out and see and talk to people, although it could be very distracting after a while.

There are eight women, most of whom were in Natalie Goldberg's first writing group. We meet at each other's houses, light candles, drink tea, sit in a circle and write together, then read what we've written without commenting..

That night, we got onto the topic of old age, a subject that we agreed most American women haven't come to terms with. We wrote and read. Towards the end we were writing each other's thoughts. Eerie. This happens. It seemed natural at the time. Cecile read her poem about Manhattan and New Mexico. We listened to Dylan Thomas read, "Go not gentle into that good night." Leah talked about menopause. We agreed to each buy a book, read it and pass it around so we can all have some common ground for discussion. The next meeting will be at our house in two weeks. My assignment for them was to write about the severing of a close relationship. This should be interesting. It's going to be ironic if I'm so busy running around to this and that for intellectual stimulation that I don't have time to write. The only writing I've done in the past two weeks is in my journal.

I was late picking up Jim. He was angry. I felt embarrassed and defensive and apologized. He said, "I wouldn't be so angry, but you don't even say you're sorry." I burst out, "I said I was sorry twice. I'm not going to keep saying it all night." I fell back a step. "I don't know what you feel about anything anymore."

He looked at me. "Don't say such a thing. It isn't true. What? About you?"

"Yes, me."

What I really meant was I didn't understand why he had been so snappy for so many days. He apologized for being so grouchy, but didn't answer me. It's like fixing a leaky roof. You don't want to when it's raining, and when it's sunny, forget it. Still, I'd like to know what he's been feeling.

This morning when I woke up at eleven, Jim smiled and offered me coffee and said he didn't realize I'd been so wiped out. "When I'm that tired I moan and groan, but you don't, so I can't tell." Anyway, he's very pleasant and normal again. I stayed home and pottered around all day. In the evening we took the kids to the drive-in, a big annual event. It was "Winnie the Pooh." Jim laughed and laughed.

Zander fell asleep right after dinner and I read to Sara. I closed my eyes for a moment and heard myself reading from a dream story. Sara woke me, "Not a wolf, a chicken!" Then Zander woke up, so I read to him, too. Jim came home and wanted dinner. He was worn out from a strenuous day, wired and unable to sleep. We fell asleep late and got up early.

I'm so tired. I feel a compulsion to activity, a restlessness that won't let me rest even though I'm worn out. There's so much to do and not enough time.

Spent all day typing medical tapes while Jim supervised the kids and did three big loads of laundry and hung them out. He dug holes for my peonies. There's nothing down there but rock. I'll have to fill them up with topsoil. He says our apple trees are dying because there's no soil.

After dinner Jim went to work and I made a bow and arrows for Alexander. He was bitten by a red ant and got hysterical. It was in his shoe! Both kids seem very tired, probably from Mom's hectic social life. I'm trying to get things back to normal.

We went down to the swing and found a garter snake impaled on one of the ropes, high up on the rope where the kids couldn't reach it. I felt chilled. And very sorry for the snake.

Met with Stephanie at her gallery. We had a long, somber discussion about censorship in the journals and what direction we want them to take. Stephanie wants it to be more than "true confessions," a wider consciousness and broader perspective. She says the women she has talked to about the group are "explosively enthusiastic."

When I got home Jim and I had a long discussion about censorship of the journals. He said he's such a private person, he wouldn't want to reveal any of himself to "complete strangers." I explained that the journals weren't meant to be a massive bowel movement to "get it out," but a controlled art form.

I'm reading *Revelations: Diaries of Women.* For Anais Nin her diary became a place where she could let her real self have its day. A place where she could let her demons out. I'm not advocating that our diaries should be just to let the demons out, but we should be flexible enough to let them out when it furthers our purpose.

Jim came staggering home from basketball and wanted to make love. Both too tired. Jim was up three hours last night. He and Zander took a dawn walk around the apple tree. Later we went down to the Rio Grande with our inner tubes. Sara narrated each stage of the journey. She wanted to walk, not be carried. As we threaded our way along the path under the cliffs she said, "Oh, this is a far walk. This is a hard time." She loved climbing over the rocks. "I'm a strong grill!" She waded into the quiet pool off the sandbar: "Brrrr. I'm so cold! I'm so naked. My body feels good."

While Jim and I were preoccupied, she waded into the deep spot up to her chin. She didn't cry but let out an "Ahhh!" and tried to reach the rock. Jim pulled her out in a hurry. We took turns keeping an eye on the them both after that. Zander "boated" around in the inner tube singing, "Oh, I love the inner tube, inner tube, inner tube!" He enjoyed sliding his feet along the soft muddy bottom. Holding my hands Sara swirled me around and around in the water saying, "Now you're there. Now I'm here." Then she sang "Ring around the rosy" and we both fell down in the water.

In the evening Cecile, Leah and Silvana came to our house. I read two horrible versions of the severance of my relationship with my father. Nobody vomited or fainted. They gave me a lot of good feedback. Cecil said she thought I hadn't transcended, that it wasn't a story but didn't seem genuine as a letter either. I had to agree. She wanted something concrete. When we wrote, I wrote the story of Dad and the pet mouse that self-destructed. They said it was "powerful." None of them had done the assignment. I had them write for twenty minutes and they each came up with something, but there was no interest in revising. They just want to write in the Allen Ginsberg mode, "First thought, best thought." Leah read some poetry she brought and Cecile read some short pieces. It was a pleasant evening.

Journal
Sat down with Jim this morning and talked over our financial situation for the next six months. We have some big expenses coming up so Jim will not be depositing seventy-five dollars a month into savings anymore. We talked about ways we could cut back, limit ourselves.

Back to my medical typing. Poor Jim was having a terrible time building the bathroom cabinets. He came in and shoved a sandwich at me. Apologized for lunch, the cabinets, "Everything!" The lunch was fine. The cabinet door is remarkable. It fits, opens and shuts and seems sturdy even though all the boards are on a slant. How did he do it? It's like an optical illusion. Then he came in to tell me that he had inadvertently stuck his fingers in the saw and ticked the blade. I begged him not to cut his finger off because he was so tired of carpentry. He said he just wanted some attention. Love. I *think that was it. God!*

At bedtime I tried to kick Apollo off the bed. "Go on. Out! I'm tired and I don't feel like putting up with you tonight." Jim said it's a good thing the house isn't bugged. We had a good laugh.

The events of this summer have been so hectic and ominous I cannot begin to sort them out. I was driving to work around four thirty and a man waved me over on the Hondo hill. He said a car had gone over the edge and he had gone to Celso's bar to call for an ambulance. He left for town and I went down through the brush; the car was upside down. A teenage boy was lying on his back on top of a large bush, his eyes open, his legs and arms splayed out as if he had been crucified. Another boy was trapped in the car calling for help. The ambulance arrived and the EMTs extracted the boy from the car and carried him and the other boy to the ambulance. I went to the theater to start the show; then called the hospital. The boy on the bush was dead. The other one had sustained a head injury and they hadn't been able to save him either.

Dear Jim,
Last night I sat in Cohn's café and listened to you admit that you had read my journal before I gave you permission. I heard this with a feeling of foreboding and woke this morning with the feeling that the first small rent has been made in the fabric of our love, in the bond of trust and friendship between us that I have always valued so much. I feel this is too big an issue to skirt or suppress because it touches the very foundations of our marriage.

It was not simply that in a moment of weakness or anger but because you felt "indifferent" that you performed a deliberate violation of my mental privacy, because the journal happened to be on your bed in your way. I feel a little foolish when I think how proudly I bragged to the ladies in the diary group that my husband would never do that because he was a poet and he understood the mental need for privacy.

I want to go back now to the beginning of our relationship as we lay in front of the fireplace on the living room floor talking about marriage wondering how relationships could ever work. You felt so relieved that I did not try to possess you, to invade your mental space. I said I prized these things myself and would not deliberately deprive someone else of them. We agreed, at least I think we agreed, that this would be a necessary element in any future relationship, that only relationships in which two people could grow, both together and apart, would remain vital and valid. We spoke of the dangers inherent in clinging to the other person in fear because he might grow away in a different direction. I believe we agreed to take that risk rather than creating an A-frame relationship in which neither can stand alone.

Now you perceive I am growing in a direction which may lead me away from you. "What will come out of this? Will she become a career woman? A lesbian? Go live in another country?" Of course the instinctual thing to do is to try to pull me back. You need my reassurance. But my original bond, alliance, allegiance, is with you, to you, and for you. If you give me the freedom to grow within this framework of our marriage, friendship and understanding, I will always, gladly come home.

Love, Phaedra

Ewar has come to spend a month with us. Next year probably less, and less and less. He is only sixteen but already six foot three. Sara ran away when he first said hi to her, but after her nap, she gave him a welcome smile. In the car Alexander nestled up to him and Ewar and his friend Hoski patiently read several books. Zander loves the big boys, loves having bigger brothers, is fascinated with all they do.

Journal
A tremendous day. My adoption of Zander has been approved by the Court. I can apply for a new birth certificate with my name on it as his father. Phaedra and I agree that we'll wait until he is about ten years old and then we will tell him about it.

    Planted nine more trees in the orchard. Spent two days cutting willows off the ditch, digging holes for new fruit trees. Zander and I spent hours together in the ditch, cutting willows, he rattling on, me tense and not listening. Best when we sat to rest on the bank and watched clouds drifting.

    Phaedra spent the afternoon at someone's house in lower Hondo and didn't come home for dinner. I fed the kids and was worried. She came home around ten and said they had been smoking dope and she lost track of the time.

Jim is down in the orchard irrigating. He's been miserable since he slammed his finger in a door. The nail is turning black and blue. His finger is so swollen, it might be broken. He was in so much pain night before last he took Ewar's old pain pills. Still in pain last night, but he did manage to get some sleep. He woke up once while I was reading, looked me straight in the eye and said, "I'm all confused." "About what?" He looked blank. "I don't know." And fell back to sleep. He didn't remember anything about it the next day. Is he really confused? He doesn't seem to be. He seems very sure of himself. A psychologist would say, "See, that proves it!"

Journal
Phaedra and the kids were in town and I sat on the bed reading Dahlberg's *Because I Was Flesh* about his boyhood in Kansas City, living with his lady-barber mother and no father. It was a blustery, rainy day and the wind blew the curtains into the room and then sucked them out again. Dahlberg never knew his father. He had a photo of him and sought him in the photo and in a rocking chair and in the rug of the sour apartment where he lived with his mother; but there was no father. It was October 6, my 37th birthday and I sat in bed with my knees drawn up and thought about my father, his odor and his ring: father, a word, a nothing, an emptiness and an unfathomable pain: feeling and father, and time running out for us.

The way the air lifts the curtains and holds them for a moment, then pulls them into the afternoon, is not a thing words convey very well. When I tried, I realized that if the place of father was empty, for Dahlberg and for me, I would fill that space in Alexander and Sara. If my father didn't recognize my anguish, then I would not let him know my happiness.

Dear Roget,
The director of the Harwood Foundation has resigned and I've applied for the position. If I get it, I will have fulfilled my father's forgotten hope that someday I might amount to something. And me also – I too thought I might someday amount to something, a great writer, and that now seems like something far in the past.

Dear Bunny
Big news. I have a chance of getting the Harwood job. The last two directors have been certified librarians from out of state and it hasn't worked out. I asked the Taos mayor, Larry Santistevan, to write the university of New Mexico, which owns and manages the property, to recommend a local for the job, namely me. Harvey also sent a good letter to the committee that is doing the hiring.

    One reason I have decided to leave the theater, besides being tired of the routine, is that Zander is gone from 7:45 in the morning to 3:45, just about the time I have to leave for work. Right now I don't see him at all because Star Wars is playing for three weeks and the first show starts at 4:30. I miss him and he misses me.

Dear Harvey,
I am still waiting to hear from UNM. I want this to happen. I know I can do it. The future of the Harwood is like a complex puzzle that must be worked out. The picture that emerges will be mine if I'm capable and energetic.

    Thank you again for the good letter to the university. It's hard to wait and nerve wracking because Whaley hasn't scheduled me to work at the theater past Dec. 15th. I may end up without a job!

If I do get it, I'll have to give up writing. I don't know if I can. I hatch plans to write from five to eight a few mornings a week, and from eight to eleven a few nights a week and hope that suffices. Saturdays will be for the kids and Sundays for rest. I worry for my family. Phaedra is off to her groups and now I may be off into the "real" world. As a family we are incredibly tight but the marriage has suffered. I thought – a thought deeply ingrained in me – that Phaedra would experience my love for the children as an extension of my love for her. I think I assumed this to be true of all mothers. But I wonder if she feels that my love for them diminishes her in some way, that it subtracts from my love of her? And her reaction is not to challenge me on it but to assert her independence. Which looks – and feels – like fleeing.

Dear Roget,
The University of New Mexico has hired me as executive director of the Harwood Foundation. I will make $9,027 a year minus withholding; they withhold my testes so I'll be a good boy. It's not much more than I am making now at the theater but I'm not in it for the money. I'm in it for the female librarians. Evelyn send me a note congratulating me and saying now I am "somebody."

I was driving home from town, coming down the curve into Arroyo Hondo, and I saw smoke, the flicker of a grass fire, and a lone woman stomping it out. I pulled over and jumped out to help. She was a small woman with short, dark hair, wearing a white blouse, black skirt and heels. Together we stomped out the flames.

She turned to me. "It was small, but in this dry weather, you can't let it go. It could spread fast." She coughed a couple of times and adjusted her glasses, and stuck out her hand. "I'm Fabi Teeter."

I introduced myself and we had a brief conversation. She is married to an Anglo and she works for Legal Aid in Taos. When I told her I lived in upper Hondo, she asked if I knew about Taos Ski Valley, their plans to build a bigger sewage treatment plant so they could expand. Would I be willing to take a petition around against the proposed new plant.

"I think it would be better if someone Spanish did it," I said.

She pushed up her glasses and eyed me. "I don't think it would make any difference."

Journal

Of the three Harwood buildings, only the library is functioning. The museum holds Taos Society paintings but few people ever visit it. The east wing and Alcalde building stand empty. There are no longer any concerts or plays in the auditorium.

This is about to change. The Harwood got a federal grant for $350,000 to renovate the unused buildings and the contractor is in the midst of doing that, but without a plan for how to use the rooms. So it is up to me to plan. We are going to make the south rooms into a spacious children's library, the upstairs rooms into rental apartments, and the east wing a caretaker's apartment. Two storage rooms are filled with books, which we will sell at a series of book sales and open the rooms up as special collection rooms. The library itself is intact, but stale; it hasn't been vitalized in decades and is used almost entirely by Anglos.

I did as Fabi Teeter asked, took petitions around the village, knocking on doors for two miles down the road through upper and lower Hondo. I met many of our neighbors, ranchers, businessmen, housewives, farmers, talked to them about the river, how important it was to protect it. "Who knows? Someday we might have to go down to the river again."

So far, so good. It took a couple of hours. Everyone I talked to signed. The last house I went to was the only one where I met any resistance. Ida Martinez, a graceful, white-haired grandmother, gave me a short lecture that ended with, "I was here first." She had raised eight children in Arroyo Hondo and insisted, rightly so, on el respeto, respect. In the end, she said she would sign because I had bothered to bring the petition to her door. Then she smiled and asked if I had children. We walked out together and she peered through the back window. Alexander and Sara had fallen asleep in a tangle of coloring books and crayons, their mouths smeared with ice cream. "So sweet," she said.

I smiled. "They are the reason I'm doing this. I want them to have clean water, clean air."

Journal
This job is trickier than I imagined. I've had to go to the legislature in Santa Fe to try to raise funds. UNM doesn't

want to keep the Harwood, but can't get rid of it because Lucy Harwood transferred it to the university "in perpetuity." The senator from Taos hates the representative from Taos and they will not talk to each other, so they give me messages and I run back and forth. After a full day of this, I came into the parking lot and needed some aspirin for my splitting head. I couldn't get the top off and threw it on the ground and stomped on it, shattering the bottle. I picked up some pills and swallowed them. But in the end, the house and senate agreed and funded the Harwood with an additional $75,000 which is going to allow me to hire more staff. I'll hire a children's library and assistant, a part-time curator, and a caretaker.

On the home front, Phaedra has gorgeous red and yellow tulips growing by the side of the house. She talks to birds or whistles to them and they whistle back. The rest of the time, she neglects the house in favor of her groups, poetry group, journaling group, a group to save the Rio Hondo and another to fight nuclear weapons and power plants. It is as if, now that I have a respectable job, she needs to prove something to herself or to me.

Journal
"I want to lay aside the idea that my job is easy," he says. "It takes a lot out of me. I come home so exhausted I can hardly stand up."

He is right. I have been letting the housekeeping slip. "Would you rather I was an ordinary house frau?" A pause. "Of course you would."

He doesn't deny it. "I suppose you're sick of this scene," he says in a hard tone.

"No, I'm not. I love my home. My family is the most important thing I'm doing."

"My home, my family? I thought it was our home, our family."

He is picky about what words we use.

He gives me a skeptical look. "But it's not enough."

I take a deep breath. Sigh. "No, there isn't enough mental stimulation. I need that too."

He settles back, props himself up on a pillow. "I get that from my job. Plus a new sense of security, being able to support you and the children and to plan for the future."

"You mean you weren't happy before? It was all a lie?"

"Well, that's a bit strong. Let's just say I had trouble expressing my feelings, so I gritted my teeth and carried on."

I touch his arm. "You used to ask me didn't I want some time to myself? And I'd say, 'Oh, no,' even though I did. I martyred myself. But now I feel more confident, that I deserve the opportunity to develop myself."

He gives me a wary look and tugs at the sheet. "Deserve? This is a new note."

"It's true we have to make sacrifices. At first I did it out of guilt, because I felt worthless. Now I try to do it out of love."

I ask what he wants in terms of housekeeping.

He frowns. "Emptying the garbage. Dishes once a day and sweeping the kitchen floor."

I agree to that and don't mention that yesterday I vacuumed the living room and mopped the bathroom. But I asked him to leave the dishes till tomorrow.

Journal
I've become very involved with the Hondo school, heading up the Parent-Teacher organization. I got a grant for $27,000 to build a playground where there was only dirt and rocks. We put out a call to the village to help us, but practically no one showed up and I had to ask the maintenance department of the Taos School District to assemble the equipment. Phaedra and I painted the lines on the basketball court.

I tried to get Celso Gonzales transferred from the Hondo school. The superintendent told me that he would be transferred to the Jr. High. Instead, he was named Head Teacher. I wrote the school board protesting, then appeared before them in executive session with the second grade teacher. We testified to Gonzales smacking the children on the head and the inappropriateness of naming him head teacher. They came out and "reaffirmed the appointment."

Journal
I have become more and more involved in politics. Fabi and I and others have formed the Committee to Save the Rio Hondo, to fight the expansion of the water treatment plant at the Ski Valley. I am the secretary. It is a paradox, for you would think that we would want a larger, more modern plant that would clean up the river, but we know that if they build such a plant, they will use it to build more houses and hotels and restaurants which will soon be polluting the river again.

I go to Celso's little market a couple of days a week to buy the Albuquerque Journal and read the state and national news. I'm active in the fight to stop the Waste Isolation Pilot

Plant, which everyone calls WIPP, where the feds plan to bury tons of radioactive waste. As if that isn't enough, I participate in Sane Freeze, the national organization that is fighting to reduce nuclear power plants and weapons. The Three Mile Island facility almost melted down and scared the shit out of me and everyone else. Jim and I have agreed to give up Hershey bars, which are made close by the plant. Ruth and Arty Sharfin, card carrying communists who run the China Shop selling things from China, organized a protest and about fifty of us marched around the plaza chanting "Two four six eight; we don't want to radiate." The children marched with us. I made a placard for Alexander to carry, a drawing of the planet earth with the words, "We are in this together."

And I still go on with my poetry, journal and Rio Hondo groups. Two nights ago I went to the poetry group and Jim stayed with the children for the second night in a row. He didn't want me to go, but I went. He called two hours later while I was sitting in the quiet circle of women, writing. He was almost hysterical with feelings of being abandoned. A call for help. I thought it would be nicer to stay put and avoid that drama. But it's not fair. I can't ignore it. I wanted to defend my right to go out, but I excused myself and left.

I OM-ed all the way home, prayed for clarity, not to be sucked into the vortex of his bitter emotions. Having pushed him over the edge, it would be my job to try to bring him up out of the abyss. If he was writing again he wouldn't care so much. If he could fill his own empty places, I wouldn't be required to do it. Maybe we could go back to a state of innocence we once had when we were first together, sparking each other, dedicating our lives to art and beauty, to inspiration. I know we can never recapture it completely, but we can rearrange our *lives around values that have meaning for both of us.*

Jim's voice on the phone sounded like the end of our relationship, our home, our life together. Everything was at stake: the children, our little adobe with the blue window frames. I told myself not to be defensive because that only leads to tears and trembling, being a little girl, confused, attacking back. Besides, he has this way of demolishing me with his logic. We would never get to the heart of the problem that way. I must be reassuring, say something positive. Tell him I love him. Yes. Turn the conversation back to his feelings and needs. I must not be coldly analytical, but warm and human. Then maybe we can come through this together.

When I got home Jim was asleep. I thought, Good. I won't have to go through with it. I crawled into bed and opened my book. He rolled over, looked at me with those deep eyes. "I'm sorry. I'm sorry I called."

I hugged him. "I love you. You're a good man. I'm glad you called. I want to know if you're having such awful feelings. I wouldn't have gone out if I had known you'd be so upset."

"Did you tell the ladies why you had to leave?" he asks.

"Of course not. My first loyalty is to you." When I hear myself say these words I realize it is deeply true.

I say, "Even if your job goes well and you and I are happy, is it enough to meet your needs? To fulfill you without your writing?"

There! That word. A long silence. Then he launches into the worn script about how he has no talent, that I shouldn't have pushed him to publish, typed out his manuscripts and sent them off, only to have them rejected. I should have let him continue at his own pace. Encouraged him to write with as little ego as possible and not show it to anyone.

"I've read some of your recent poetry," I say. "It's stunning."

He sits up, sets his coffee cup on the bedside table. Astonished. "You're saying this to me?"

I smile. "Yes."

He spits out his words. "My writing is neurotic and self-indulgent."

"But it can be creative."

He tosses the covers aside, jumps up and begins to pace. "I can't write without destroying the family. All artists are selfish and destructive to their families."

I lift my palms. "What about me?"

He turns, laughs. "What have you done?"

"The story I'm working on."

He brushes it aside like a wasp. "I can't stand the artist imagining he is above the common man. I accept the humiliation. I'm channeling all my strength into one activity. Family."

After fifteen minutes he flops down on the side of the bed, hands between his knees. "I can't."

Now I'm up and pacing. "If you believe you can't, you can't."

Suddenly he turns to me, a light in his eyes.

"Okay. I'll do it."

Zander, Sara and I drove to town and did the laundry. Phaedra was at a party at Anita Rodriquez's. I left the children at the movies. Then we went to Juan Romero's for his son Chris's graduation reception. His wife, daughter, three sons, cousins, nieces, nephews, brother, grandson a four pound baby now up to 39 pounds, all of us jammed into a long trailer. Juan teased me for not speaking Spanish.

I had a long talk with Carmen Medina and her husband Gil, who repairs large equipment at the Moly Mine. I talked to their daughter Angie, a college student in physics and chemistry and biology who told a story of being in a restaurant in Denver with her parents and waiting an hour to be served. She asked her father for two dimes and called the Better Business Bureau.

Zander and Sara stayed pretty close to me. On the way home Zander said Juan is nice because his name is the same as wand.

Sara asked me to look in her ear and there is a big light in there and can I see the thinking? She says before she was born she was a seed.

Journal
I can rise to a great challenge or sacrifice. It's the daily struggles I have trouble with. I offer to give Jim back the L room. He decides he'll be okay with a corner in the living room. I agree to that. He asks for half the bedroom. I say sure, and find myself weeping, "I'd do anything to have you go back to your writing. I've always believed in you as a writer. It's half the reason I fell in love with you."

"Whew!" he says with a red-faced grin. He's on a roll. Let's cut back our lifestyle, give up the insurance, the vacation, a second car.

I agree to all that so that we can live as artists in "voluntary simplicity."

"Yes," I say, "that would be better."

"*Like acupuncture,*" he laughs. "*Stick it in a little more.*"

But in the aftermath, it's not enough for me to capitulate and make sacrifices. He has to agree to a few things, too. Put the records back, hang up his clothes, make his own bed. Keep the kitchen counter clear.

He has volunteered to get up two mornings a week to send Alexander off to school, and fold the laundry when he drags it out of the laundromat dryer so I won't have to iron. I hate ironing.

We need to get our commitments down on paper. I explain again that I was just taking off one day to recoup when he freaked out.

"You mean we could have avoided all this?"

"Not really. Something has to change."

Journal

I contemplate the passing of these events which have been and will be repeated endlessly by me, by everyone, in one weather or another. The world has turned right wing again, with Margaret Thatcher in England and Reagan here. What matters? Only caring. My life is now based on responsibility, to my job, to the children, to Phaedra. I am afraid I will fail – them, myself. I am superstitious. If I do not do the small things, I will lose the big things.

We sometimes go for walks up on top of the mesa. Our strip of land extends all the way to the Forest Service fence and has a great view of the mountains. Jim throws up his hands. "A great view, but what can we do with it? No water. No road. It's not even good for grazing."

I fantasize that someday one of the children might build up there.

One day a man comes by, knocking at our door, looking to buy land on top of the mesa. His name is Phil De Caro, a lawyer from California who is retiring. He is short, with a shrewd, rugged face. No water? He'll drill a well. No road? He'll build one. On the way out he gets his car stuck in our driveway. We have to go out and help him push his car out of the mud.

Journal
Phil De Caro and his wife Gale Gatto offered us $2000 an acre for 80 acres. We countered with $3,000 and explained that we would restrict development to eight single family dwellings. They accepted, and just like that, all our vows of poverty went out the window. We said we didn't need much of a down payment, $15,000 would be fine. From there, however, things have broken down. Although Harvey has been great about granting an easement, the Kaufman's are opposing the deal and then stipulating a variety of stringent restrictions. I doubt that this is going to happen.

DeCaro and Gatto offered what would now seem like a ridiculously low amount per acre for the portion of our land on top of the mesa. But to us, it was an unexpected windfall. "We'll be rich!" Jim said. "We can buy a decent car. We will have more time to write."

I was ambivalent. De Caro wants neighbors and also to make money by selling off plots. We have restricted them to eight. The sale, for a total of $240,000, would provide steady income over the next twenty years. Jim could quit his job and write. De Caro brought in a dowser by the name of Joe Graves, a dark-skinned man with carved cheeks and a turkey feather in his leather hat. He walked the top of the mesa. Where his willow stick pointed down, he said to dig. The drilling went on and on. I didn't know whether to pray they struck water or pray that they wouldn't. I had a nightmare about a subdivision growing on the hillside behind the house, noisy cars and trucks ruining our privacy forever. The deal was, if they hit water De Caro would pay for the well. If not, we would pay for half the drilling and the deal was off. We waited in suspense. They struck water about a thousand feet down. Not much, but enough.

Our neighbors had spotted the drilling rig. Suddenly, all up and down the valley, people were talking about how the Levys had sold out for a housing development. The Levys! who were fighting to save the Rio Hondo. Who were supposed to be environmentalists. We found ourselves at a public meeting at the school house where accusations were fired at us by the same people we thought were our friends. Jim stood up and explained that it wasn't a housing development. It would be only eight parcels on eighty acres, with restrictions on constructions. The roar subsided to a low growl and receded at our heels with suspicious mutterings.

What followed was weeks of wrangling with our neighbors about how the land would be used. I stayed out of it, partly because I had no standing. My name was not on the title.

Jim and I discussed if we should move to town if the land sold. We could rent the Hondo house and put the kids in better

schools in Taos. I asked Jim if we could please not leave Hondo for at least a year, and he agreed.
Journal
Carl Rakosi was a poet who quit writing in 1939 to live his life. He began again in 1965, twenty-six years later. Of course he had been a success the first time round.

A cartoon: a man in a vegetable bin, saying to a shopper "Every once in a while I have to be a vegetable."

The sale of the land has lightened my load. Although I dislike health clubs, I've joined a spa and am working out with weights. I listen to Dallas football games on the radio and the news: there is something called HIV and MTV and PCs. I've become an average guy.

I stayed home from work today and Phaedra and I made love and exercised and talked. Nice without the kids. I weigh 217 and that is muscle turning to fat. I give myself eighteen weeks to lose twenty-seven pounds, 1½ a week. Despite my size, I see myself as small, hidden and clever. If I am an instrument of revenge, who am I revenging? My mother? My self, who is my mother?

After lunch Bridget the dog and I walked to the Hondo school. The smell of cow manure, sheep manure, warm fragrant air, the sound of the lead sheep's bell – I felt alive for a moment. At the school I judged the Halloween costumes and lay in the coffin as Frankenstein in the spook house. I signed up to do it again tomorrow and have agreed to be Santa Clause at Christmas. Phaedra says she'll make the Santa suit and beard.

Stepping Up

When we received the down payment for the eighty acres, we took a shopping trip to Albuquerque to buy a new car. Well, not exactly new. The Subaru had been used as a demo and had some miles on it, for which we received a discount. But there we were, in the first "new" car we had ever owned. The family wagon. We made the rounds of the malls where everyone got to buy something they really wanted. For Zander it was a dirt bike; for Sara a girl's bike; for me wine glasses and an umbrella. For both of us, a king-sized mattress. We poked at each other with ironic humor, faintly queasy with guilt for having betrayed some unspoken vow to stay poor and happy.

Journal
Alexander started soccer practice today. I drove him to town and a friend came back with him and spent the night. Sara as usual has no friend. She is almost always with us or alone. I went into her room and she was drawing and playing "Lonely for my love," a Disneyland record about Rapunzel, on her tiny plastic phonograph. "Here in my room, I'm so alone, no one to hold in my arms – I can't go on without you – I am so lonely, I'm lonely – I'm lonely – I'm lonely for my love." I held her on my lap and rocked her and then began to sing the words. She joined in. I asked her if she was lonely. No, she said brightly. She showed me her big black spider ring on her hand. I pretended to be scared. "Don't be afraid," she said. "He's my friend."

She does seem lonely at times but incapable of making, or keeping, friends. She's become vivacious, tells jokes, sings songs and chants cheers. She doesn't have bangs now, her hair falls over her eye like Tatum O'Neal's. Gary

Walker calls her a character, and says that she is, despite being distinct and somewhat odd, feminine.

"Daddy, know what?"

"No, what?"

"Oh, nothing."

She picks up songs and cheers quickly just like Phaedra and spends hours singing them. She can count to 100 by ones and tens, does some addition and subtraction, knows her alphabet but doesn't read at all. I taught her the alphabet years ago and then didn't follow through.

Sara

My sister Lyn called from California to tell me that Mother was in the hospital, about to undergo exploratory surgery that she might not survive. She was down to ninety-seven pounds and very weak. They thought she might have cancer. I panicked. No way I could get out there before the surgery. I called her and we talked briefly on the phone, with the unspoken understanding that this might be our last conversation.

"Good-bye, sweetheart," she said.

I couldn't bear it. I hung up, dropped my head on my arms and wept like a baby.

Mother survived. I flew out the next day, spent time with my sister, stayed with Dad in the tiny trailer in the redwoods near Santa Cruz, and anchored myself to Mother's bedside in the hospital. She and I had long talks about family conflicts that we should have discussed years ago. In the chaos of uncertainty, my father opened up to me, made his apologies about things he had done or not done when we were small. In the shadow of Mother's death, I was able to forgive him and let go of my bitterness over our hardscrabble childhood.

By the end of the week, Mother's doctor sent her home with a diagnosis of pancreatic cancer. Dad was relieved to have her back, but I wanted the hard truth and pinned down her doctor. We stood in the hallway of the hospital in the waning afternoon sunlight. He said in solemn tones, "She does not have long."

My heart quivered and shrank. I couldn't bear it. My beautiful mother.

I flew home and a week later drove back with the whole family in what Mother called "your new blue Subaru." Mother hadn't seen Sara since she was a baby or Alexander since our first visit when he was a year old. Tom flew out from Michigan. It was the first time the our family had been together as a family since Mother, Dad and Tommy fled to Hawaii in 1961, leaving Lyn and me in Detroit to fend for ourselves.

Jim had never met my parents. We spent the afternoon together in their trailer park in the redwoods, sitting outside in folding chairs. Mother wore one of her shirtwaist dresses and braced herself in the chair. Her face looked gray and gaunt, but she smiled and took it all in. Jim said how beautiful my mother was, even so sick. "She has classic lines. You get your beauty from her." He was careful not to confront Dad about any of the things I had told him. Dad and Tom and I sat outside while Dad fed the jays and squirrels.

Mother put on a good face, but she was fading before our eyes. I walked alone in the redwoods and wept in secret. A week later we said our good-byes and the Levy contingency drove back to New Mexico. Mother died at home a month later.

I regretted that I hadn't made more trips to see her, that I had let Dad push me away. I couldn't believe she was gone.

Because Reagan is threatening to close the Economic Development Program I rush to get a grant of $150,000 to renovate the Alcalde building. As before, the program is designed to give employment to minorities, and since the contractor's crew will be 85% Hispanic and Indian, we got the grant. I had applied for it two years ago and now the amount won't cover everything but better something than nothing. With this, the renovation of the complex will be complete.

Funding has increased dramatically, mainly from the New Mexico legislature but also from the Town and County, and because we have made a consistent effort of outreach by radio and newspaper, the Harwood is now a full community center. People from all three cultures use the library. The children's library is a huge success, with many children and their parents using it. We've started storytelling on Saturdays and Reading is Fundamental book giveaways once a quarter. The auditorium is being used for concerts and plays, and we've expanded the display area in the museum.

At the same time, I have served nineteen months on the Citizen Advisory Committee that the Forest Service set up to advise them on the expansion of the Ski Valley sewage treatment plant. We finally pushed through a limit of 4800 skiers a day, reduced the new plant to 80,000 gallons. Phaedra and the Committee to Save the Rio Hondo were the hammer, suing the Forest Service and the sanitation district.

The Levys in Mexico

Jim is restless. He took us to the beach at San Blas in Mexico for ten days, and now he says he is ready to move to town. I am too, although I am dreading it. It will be best for the children. All the blondies have left the Hondo school to car pool to gentler situations in town. Our children are the last Anglo kids in the Hondo elementary. Zander is picked on at school and his so-called friends come over and steal his toys. Sara doesn't like her teacher and has trouble making friends. She is droopy when she slouches out the door in the morning and often in tears when she comes home. She complained so often about a stomach ache that I took her to see a pediatrician. He said she was developing an ulcer.

    Although I know it is time for a change, it is with a sense of disbelief that I find myself rolling up the rugs, taking down pictures, packing boxes. When I was a child my family moved on the average of once a year and I have never felt I belonged anywhere until I came to live in this quiet valley at the foot of the mountains. The land that has enfolded us in its dusky arms, the bright stars we look up to for reassurance, the steady mountain peaks resonating through all four of us. Our days in Hondo have been, for both Jim and me, the happiest days of our lives.

I am scared of the changes I have brought about. Phaedra and I built a nest which has been good, an island of love. Now I, restless and bored, am jeopardizing it. The house and land have been for us the center of the universe and the rock of our existence. I am afraid that in selling part of the land, I am inviting in the world, a road, traffic, houses, people, and eventually the flux of the world which will sweep us away to darkness and death.

Yet I am glad. The money will enable us to start a new phase of our lives. For me personally, leisure to live, write, love. Why not live? Why not live, and love, and create?

Epilogue

After selling eighty acres and moving into town, we bought a house in Taos, took Alexander and Sara to Europe for five months to roam through Spain, Sicily, Italy, Switzerland, France, England and Scotland on a tight budget, eating in our rooms in cheap pensiones. Because we wanted better high schools and colleges than New Mexico could offer, we moved to Chapel Hill, North Carolina where Jim got a job and Phaedra studied writing at Duke. Jim lost an eye to a retinal detachment which caused a great strain on our marriage. The climate didn't suit us and we moved to Boulder, Colorado, and continued to work.

Most of our friends left Taos. Roget and Elaine moved to Zuni and lived there the rest of their lives. Harvey divorced his first wife, married Alicia so that she could stay in the States, but divorced her and married three more times and now lives with a partner in southern France. He has published five books of poetry and memoirs. Evelyn took a trip around the world by herself and has lived ever since in San Francisco working for nonprofit organizations. Ewar worked in a hot tub spa as maintenance man, then decided to go to college, then law school and is a partner in his own maritime law firm.

Pema received the full bikshuni orientation in the Chinese lineage of Buddhism in Hong Kong, became the first director of Gampo Abbey in Nova Scotia, and went on to publish many best-selling books about her approach to life.

Ken, Alexander's birth father, moved away and we never heard from him again. Alexander attended North Carolina State in computer engineering, joined a group seeking spiritual enlightenment, traveled to Vietnam and started a company selling greeting cards. He works as a videography in the Bay Area. Sara majored in psychology at the University of Colorado and has worked at Whole Foods market since 2003. She runs a Whole Foods market in Littleton, Colorado and is married and has three stepchildren.

As for us, after twenty years our marriage ran aground and we both needed room to grow. We were separated for two years and then got divorced. Phaedra moved back to the house in Arroyo Hondo and worked five years at the Taos News as a journalist and compositor. Jim continued to work at the Boulder Housing Authority. Although we saw each other at family events with the children, we both had a variety of romantic affairs and each had one serious relationship. When those didn't work out, we realized that we had never stopped loving each other and after eleven years apart, resumed our life in Arroyo Hondo. That was sixteen years ago. Phaedra works as a freelance videographer and writer, Jim has retired from nonprofit work, and we finally got down to publishing some of our books.

Pema, Jim and Phaedra

www.ingramcontent.com/pod-product-compliance
Lightning Source LLC
Chambersburg PA
CBHW051747040426
42446CB00007B/255